Adopted

From the Natural to the Spiritual

Monica Blackman

authorHOUSE®

AuthorHouse™
1663 Liberty Drive
Bloomington, IN 47403
www.authorhouse.com
Phone: 1 (800) 839-8640

Published by AuthorHouse 05/29/2020

ISBN: 978-1-7283-4406-5 (sc)
ISBN: 978-1-7283-4405-8 (e)

Print information available on the last page.

Scripture quotations marked NIV are taken from the Holy Bible, New International Version®. NIV®. Copyright © 1973, 1978, 1984 by International Bible Society. Used by permission of Zondervan. All rights reserved. [Biblica]

Scripture taken from The Holy Bible, King James Version. Public Domain

Editors:
Stacia Browne
Professor Dr. Elizabeth Watson
Elizabeth Hardwick

This book is printed on acid-free paper.

Dedication

A dopted is dedicated to my children; Stephen Roger, Lisa Monique, Sacha David and my grandson Bryce Austin.

It is my fervent prayer that having read Adopted, they will have a better understanding of the journey their mother and grandmother has trod. May they find joy in discovering that all things work together for the good of those who love the Lord and are called to His purpose.

Acknowledgements

I must thank God first and foremost for His love, mercy and grace which helped me to conquer giants so I have been able to transition to a fruitful life.

Several people have been integral to my journey: some for the short term whereas others have been there for the long haul. Documenting the complexity of my journey has given me a chance to publicly acknowledge the unwavering support from some of those people who made a huge difference in so many significant ways. A special thank you:-

To Venetia and Russell for your parental guidance in my early childhood.

To Antoinette (Nettie) and Stanley for giving me life.

To my children and grandson who I cherish so much. Thank you for your love, the joy and happiness that you continue to bring to my life everyday. I am proud of you.

To my siblings, Ulit, Hopeton, Danny, Dawn and Fredericka (Shirley). You have helped immeasurably by putting key pieces of the puzzle in place as you individually opened different doors to an old, yet new world.

To Doreen and Hyacinth, the nannies who offered the love, guidance, attention and support my children needed. Your presence in our lives was invaluable as it enabled me to invest in my career and allowed me space to provide for my children in ways that would have been extremely difficult otherwise.

To my friends Yvette and Joan for recording fond reminiscences of our friendship. Friendships survive when you can love, value, support and push past the differences and deficiencies in each other's lives.

To my church family and prayer partners world-wide; words cannot express the depth of my gratitude.

A special mention to Michelle Edwards, the later Roseanne Whittaker, Stacia Browne, Carl Moore, Alison Jordan, Marguerite Moe, Elizabeth Hardwick, Jean Sommersall, the late Professor Dr. Elizabeth Watson, Roberta Springer-Proverbs and Elsie Blackett.

To all of you, I say a resounding thank you for holding my hand as I have walked this road through the rain and the sunshine, so I wouldn't let go.

Foreword

Adopted is a story of my life presented in six chapters. The first four chapters represent the main spaces of my life's journey as it meandered through the Caribbean island of Jamaica, New York City, Ottawa, Canada and Barbados also in the Caribbean. Chapter five represents my spiritual journey – the fulfilment of my life's purpose while chapter six showcases the return to my roots.

Never in my wildest dreams could I have imagined that I would have the courage to take all the masks off and expose my life experiences in such a public way. To be able to document the story of a child who was easily intimidated, who felt inadequate most of her life and that she didn't fit into most conversations, is indeed a miracle. I have had many struggles, but the time has come to give a voice to that inner self, find peace and comfort in knowing that God was always in charge and that's all I needed to do: just let go and let God.

This narrative of my life is not just about where I lived, but what influenced my successes or failures. I have grown from being a child born of very humble beginnings and plagued by a host of insecurities, to realizing as an adult that I was designed by God to be exactly who I am. This has happened despite what others might have thought or said about me. I now revel in a life where each day is rich and full.

From being **Adopted** as a child **in the natural** in a rural town on a small island in the Caribbean and transitioning, to being **Adopted in the spiritual** by my Heavenly Father who has re-established all aspects of my life, is the ultimate.

There are themes throughout the story of coping with migration, change, broken relationships, transition, but in hindsight, it was faith in God and His providence that rescued me from becoming a victim for life.

There will be a few surprises in store for many reading these pages who are not aware of the winding road I have travelled of love, happiness, abandonment, rejection, abuse and confusion. I have lived, I have laughed, I have loved, I have cried, I have lost, I have felt depressed but by the grace of God I have survived and thrived. I have discovered that with God all things are truly possible because His love and grace have set me free. It is this freedom that allows me to make better choices, to triumph over obstacles that confront me and not give way to the spirit of fear – hence I am able to share these intimate stories.

As a young woman, my mother constantly reminded me of a passage of scripture from Psalm 91: (KJV)

He that dwelleth in the secret place of the most High
shall abide under the shadow of the Almighty.

Over the years, I have read this verse many times, but it only came alive to me in it's fullest meaning during my adulthood. It's never too late to learn some meaningful lessons and I am also reminded that if you train up a child the way he should go, while he may stray, he will not depart from the basic Godly principles.

I pray that this catalogue of events will give you hope. If God could bring me from various ominous situations to propel me into a Kingdom lifestyle, then you too can and will rise from the ashes of doubt and despair. As an overcomer, I can state categorically that there is one thing I know for sure, I wouldn't change my life for anything and as for me and my house, we will serve the Lord.

Monica Blackman (Peggy McDonald)

The Journey

Chapter 1   Jamaica 1

Chapter 2   New York 52

Chapter 3   Canada 129

Chapter 4   Barbados 154

Chapter 5   The spiritual side of life 220

Chapter 6   Returning to my roots 236

Epilogue 241

Biography of the author 251

Chapter One

Jamaica

*In the beginning was the Word and the Word was
with God and the Word was God -John.1:1
God foreknew me - Romans 8:29, so nothing about
my life came as a surprise to Him.*

I t all started in Jamaica. For all Jamaicans, the land of our birth is
much more than the air-brushed touristic postcards of crystal-clear
aquamarine seas, never-ending white beaches and spectacular sunsets.
For us, the island's fauna, flora, culture, history and people are complex,
intertwined and crucial to what makes us who we truly are. I begin my
story by introducing you to the Jamaica that served as the backdrop to the
early years of my life.

Jamaica, the third-largest Caribbean island, has a lush topography of
mountains, rainforests and reef-lined beaches. Within its landscape you

will find nestled, clusters of British-Colonial, tropical and contemporary buildings, all designed to withstand heat, earthquakes, humidity and hurricanes. The island is divided into 13 parishes with Kingston our capital city.

The rich history of my homeland can be traced right back to the Arawaks, also known as Tanios, who are believed to have been the original inhabitants of Jamaica. History suggests that the Arawaks, originally from South America, came to Jamaica approximately 2500 years ago. The Arawaks, the original settlers named the island Xaymaca, which in English means - the land of wood and water. In 1494, Christopher Columbus was the first European to set foot on the island. In 1655, the Spaniards would battle unsuccessfully against the English who would go on to take possession of the island as part of their "spoils of war". The English cultivated the fertile land with a variety of crops that they traded with the "motherland". Eventually and for many years after, sugar-cane would become the principal crop and economic mainstay of the island.

Sugar-cane cultivation, with its conversion into much sought after sugar and its by-products - rum and molasses – are labor-intensive activities. To provide the volume of labor needed to cultivate and process sugar-cane, many thousands of enslaved Africans were brought to Jamaica to work on the sugar estates. The granting of their emancipation in 1863 left the planters bereft of this steady source of cheap forced labor and to fill this void, indentured servants from India and China were brought to the island to supplement the existing Negro workforce. Initially, racial boundaries may have been strictly observed, however, over time inter-racial coupling occurred, resulting in a 'rainbow' of mixed-race offspring.

Jamaica's richness is diverse and unique, not only in terms of its natural resources but also the profound talent and artistry of its people! This island was the home of iconic world-renowned reggae artist Bob Marley whose music is the root of many modern music genres; the famous rounded peaks of the Blue Mountains, known for producing some of the world's finest coffee; her ability to produce world-class, successful athletes like Merlene Ottey, Arthur Wint, Herb McKenley, Patrick Ewing and most recently and notably Usain Bolt. The landscape offered an abundance of magnificent white sandy beaches for sunbathing, deep-sea fishing, diving, snorkeling and sailing. The island has been the pioneer for Caribbean cultural identity with extensive renditions and displays of music, art, and dance featuring stalwarts such as the Jamaican scholar, Rex Nettleford and comedians, Louise Bennett, Ranny Williams, and more recently Oliver. Music for dancing exploded with Millie Small singing "My boy Lollipop" and more recently reggae dancehall music featuring Buju Banton. The island has also captured the world's attention with the exposure of beauty queens who secured titles like Miss World and Miss Universe. Jamaica stands proudly as a treasure and tower of strength in the heart of the Caribbean Sea.

When the sugar-cane industry became less profitable, tourism became the main economic activity and the primary source of foreign investment/income. The magnificent white, sandy beaches were increasingly sought after by international film producers who began using the island's diverse landscape as a backdrop to movies such as Dr. No starring Sean Connery as James Bond and The Harder They Come, featuring the multi-talented reggae personality, Jimmy Cliff. By the 1960's, the island was one of the most developed of the Caribbean islands. Jamaica's natural beauty and proximity to the American mainland made it attractive to many well-known international celebrities and the frequency of their visits, helped Jamaica become a very popular tourist destination.

Just as the island grew in popularity internationally, so was the unfortunate and shameful legacy of colonialism, that is the use of race and skin color as a means of determining one's social status, which became disturbingly apparent. The privileges of respect and deference accorded to the white plantocracy (overseers/planters) especially by workers on the estate, were recognizably superior to that given to affluent black people. These overseers were employed by the Jamaican government to manage the sugar plantations, and their families resided in the largest house on the estate. Their homes were staffed by locals who served in all of the domestic needs, which would have included – but not limited to – housekeeping, cooking, child care, gardening, maintenance and any general chore required for the smooth running of the household. The overseers boasted of having the most luxurious vehicles in the community, underscoring the fact that they were deemed more privileged than most, including the better-educated, black professionals who worked in the same parishes.

Something quite insidious had penetrated our post-Slavery society. Blacks, no matter how well educated or what important positions they held, were always considered inferior to their white counterparts. "Blackness" was then further "calibrated" on how dark one was, and so arose a social spectrum that coincided with shades of black. The color of one's skin reared its ugly head in every sphere of life and became the base of all kinds of stigmas. Perception being, the lighter your skin, the better your chances of being recognized, given certain jobs, gaining promotions or even finding a husband. This social ranking based on color extended well into the post-colonial era and it is sad, of course, that there are still traces of it today in 21st century Jamaica.

I learned very early that men, on the whole, were perceived as the dominant sex and they were also given considerable liberty in spreading their wings, not to mention their bodies across as many lives as they could. They had neither care nor consideration for any consequential "fruit" that may have resulted from their carnal escapades. As some men fed their sexual appetites with wild abandon it resulted in many families and individuals suffering great loss and pain. Promiscuity was an acceptable norm, especially among some of the itinerant salesmen who travelled from parish to parish; some were married men whose wives were oblivious to their husband's antics and then there were "single" men who were already involved in multiple relationships, even with women who lived next door to each other! It didn't appear to matter whether the women were single or married, as some of these men were seemingly not governed by any rules. These practices were rampant and encroached on the lives of the innocent and the needy.

Fostering romantic heterosexual relationships was no different from it is today. For women who were not well educated, whether single or married, they depended on men for their survival emotionally and financially. This was even more so in the case of unmarried mothers. From the days of slavery women had to make the decisions concerning their households as the men went to work on the plantations so even though the women looked to the men in their lives to find fulfilment, alas there were many 'empty' promises. They were just aspiring to a better future and they entrusted their bodies and emotions recklessly and to reckless men. Most of these women, particularly the young girls, were naïve, without any frame of reference on how to navigate male/female relations. They were dreamers with very low self-esteem and few role models to help discover what constituted a better life. They had big hopes and dreams, that those relationships would have been the pathway to their nirvana.

❦

Paul Island, the little village where I was born is located in Westmoreland on the south-western coast of Jamaica. As a child, this village was densely populated with generations of descendants of enslaved Africans and indentured laborers from India and China. They were all hard working people determined to make this country their new home. Their roles in the district were somewhat different as will be explained later on.

The social services consisted of a Postal Office to which everyone had to visit as there was no delivery service and a Primary School. Then, there was a general store or a little shop that was situated below the residence of its owners and it was there that one could buy some basic supplies. The village thrived on agriculture and although villagers maintained a very humble lifestyle, they were very happy and our little community was subjected to little or no crime.

The little village market had a varied selection of meats bought directly from the butcher who allowed them to get their choice cuts of beef, pork, lamb and mutton (goat meat). Close by were fields planted with various ground provisions, which were harvested by local farmers. Customers were allowed to hand-pick the produce they desired themselves or if they preferred, they went to the big market which bustled every Saturday morning. All fresh produce was washed, the vendors constantly replenished their trays and spent hours haggling for sales. Each vendor tried to offer a better deal than the other to get your business, some becoming visibly annoyed if you ignored their offer. Some ladies shopping came out with their beautifully woven straw baskets to collect their purchases and obviously looking for the best deals.

Primary schools in these communities, were usually quite small, but very well organized. These schools provided not only academic opportunities but most had large grounds/pastures with well-manicured playing fields where children could play and enjoy various forms of sports and games. Each schoolyard had huge overhead water tanks to supply running water for the facility, as there was no publicly funded water supply.

Close to villages, were rice paddies that were harvested mostly by the Indians who resided in nearby districts and the sugar-cane fields were harvested mostly by the blacks. The crops were healthy and well maintained so that physical investment provided steady employment and income for all villagers. The distribution of labor was clear: Indians planted; Negroes reaped. Everything was done manually, unlike today when sugar-cane and other crops are mechanically harvested. Once the sugar-cane was reaped, one could see topped sugar-cane stuffed onto the back of large lorries being taken to the factory to be converted to molasses, brown sugar and rum.

As is common in most small villages, everyone knew everyone's business so all activities and events were scrutinized and dissected thoroughly. Of course, everyone gossiped and shared their opinions freely about the lives and events in other people's lives. There was no escaping.

Transportation between the village and the nearest town was infrequent as there was no organized, public bus service. There were however a few private bus companies that offered ad hoc services between the town nearest to the village and the capital of the parish, Savanna-la-Mar. Other modes of transportation for the villagers were bicycles, little scooters, hitching a ride with someone who had a vehicle or even a donkey cart. Quite often, donkey carts could be seen struggling under the weight of the large number of supplies needed for the days and weeks ahead.

Weekends were always a hive of social activity for the young people of all ages in my sleepy village, as they would have their little gatherings, playing games like jacks, cards, jump rope, snakes and ladders, rounders, hide and seek, hopscotch, hula hoop and climbing trees. There were a few privileged children who had badminton nets installed in their gardens and who quite often could be seen trespassing on the neighbour's property to retrieve the shuttlecock. Most all of the daytime activities for the children were outdoors and those included helping to tend to any farm animals the family owned. There seemed to be so much joy emanating from these kids are they scampered around with no care as to what the future may look like as long as they were having fun and could look forward with great excitement to the next day. Unfortunately, not all households shared that joy and laughter, as activities behind some closed doors and drawn curtains were not publicly exposed. There must have been murmuring and whispering throughout the village when secrets began leaking and filtering into the welcome ears of those who loved to "carry the latest news".

While inter-racial marriages were not the norm back then, village weddings were rather grand affairs and guests were invited from all the races. On weekends, one often observed someone carrying a layered cake, balanced on his or her head and covered with a lily-white net cover. The rich wedding cake was made from dried fruits (raisins, currant, peel and cherries), which had been soaking in rum and wine for several months. Standard ingredients for wedding cakes included a cornucopia of spices and sweets, molasses, cloves, vanilla, cinnamon, nutmeg, brown sugar, allspice and other spices. Several small cakes of different sizes were baked and stacked to create as many tiers as the couple requested. Encasing the wedding cakes were thick layers of hard icing and topped with a traditional figurine of a bride and groom. It was easy to become intoxicated from the mere smell of the rich alcoholic content of these cakes and as kids, we giggled at the idea of getting a sniff.

After carefully manoeuvring the rugged terrain, the cake-bearer would place the cake proudly on a table at the site of the reception. Homemade tents were made of sturdy bamboo poles and covered with coconut branches to shield the food from the intensity of the sun. The carefully guarded cake remained covered until the official start of festivities. Once the marriage ceremony was concluded, everyone gathered for the reception where traditional specialty dishes such as curried goat served with white rice; a soup called mannish water (made from the intestines of the male goat which was and still is considered a delicacy today) and several other dishes which were expected to be part of the wedding feast. These ceremonies often lasted late into the night and usually ended with someone who had become completely incoherent, having to be taken home after imbibing a little too much rum.

The closest town to my village had a much larger population and therefore boasted of having more services. There was a primary school, a large open market with a butcher's shop, a movie theatre, a hardware store, a police station, a gas station, and a variety of shops. Also, there was a drugstore (chemist), a cobbler and several houses of worship. The Anglican Church was the most prestigious as it was the established church of the state. There were funny stories of the some of the demands of the chemist, familiarly referred to as Dispenser. He would be asked by customers to sell them potions like, "oil of send me way" and "oil of bring me back". These potions were supposedly to affect relationship partners to either leave or stay. Of course he obliged these trusting, gullible individuals by whipping up a concoction of strong, scented oils and made the sales.

There would be a convergence of two divergent women, who would create my origin. This thread of polar opposites on the social spectrum would become the theme of this life story as it meandered. It would be central to the story, Adopted. One woman was Antoinette, who was affectionately known as "Nettie" and the other was Venetia, who was referred to as, "Miss Mac", Vin or Mom. The mere difference in how they were hailed represented differences and distance in social standing. In addition to coming from completely opposite ends of society, the difference will become more obvious as my story unfolds.

Nettie was born in Westmoreland and is fondly remembered as a petite, black woman, with a winning smile and fragile nature. She was also a tender, loving, caring, giving and trusting person. Although tiny in frame and quiet, she was also rather feisty, definitely displaying that sassy Jamaican personality. She was always willing and quick to forgive those who trespassed against her. Nettie attended primary school and later worked on her grandfather's farm. She was athletic and had a fondness for music and singing and for some time, she worked in a factory that made guava jelly.

It is said that some of Nettie's character traits may have worked against her for years like her inability to discern the intention of her suitors. Nettie's personality along with the absence of a protector/mentor made her very vulnerable to being exploited by capricious men. So, quite often when the odds seemed stacked against her, she made very poor decisions in the hope of stabilizing her lifestyle. Often, her decisions ended with more heartache but Nettie believed that her faith and salvation were the things that lasted forever, and as such, she never lost her ability or desire to pray.

At a very young age, she bore her first son Hopeton, whom she eventually suggested that he live with relatives at the other end of the village. Before long, Nettie was swept off her feet by a rather charismatic, half-Chinese man named Stanley who had very fine features and was easily able to coax the ladies into a relationship. During their time together, Nettie's charismatic paramour made serious-sounding promises of a better life. But, as was the norm in situations such as these, he did not live up to his promises or Nettie's expectations. During the period of their relationship, Nettie would become pregnant, twice in two years, producing two girls.

Nettie gave birth to her first daughter Peggy, but by then she was at a crossroad and plunged into despair about herself and her child's future. She had no other family members to whom she could turn for support as they were already looking after her first child. Nettie recognized that the challenges of looking after and caring for a family were quite onerous and her hope that the father of her two girls would be the answer to her prayers for a more stable lifestyle were quickly dashed. During this period of hardship, the principal of the local primary school became enchanted with Peggy and suggested to Nettie she was willing to care for this child if she would allow her to live with her and her husband. This was intended to be a temporary arrangement and it also seemed to be an immediate answer to Nettie's prayers, so she agreed to the arrangement. She shared later in life that in her heart, she felt it would allow her to get back on her feet, so after some deliberation, plans were put in place and soon the life of the three-year-old was about to change forever. Nettie's younger daughter, affectionately known as Shirley, was allowed to live with her biological father, Stanley (same father as Peggy).

It took several years and minimum communication between Nettie and the principal, Venetia, before it became necessary to formalize a legal agreement concerning the young child. Peggy was now fast approaching high school age and proper documentation would have been required to satisfy the requirements of the educational system. After further consultation with Nettie and with mutual consent, just before the tender age of 10, Nettie's first daughter was officially / legally adopted by Venetia and her husband, Russell. Nettie, however, may not have fully understood the finality of the situation at the time, but she seized the opportunity to get the help she desperately needed and so as painful as it must have been, this was now permanent. The unbearable pain and guilt that a mother must feel handing over a child to a stranger must be one of the hardest acts to endure. Conversely, for the child discovering she was given up for adoption, what does that feel like? By now Nettie had moved from the parish and relocated to Kingston, where she settled into another long-term relationship. Her family continued to grow, producing five more children. The cycle continued for Nettie, as she had entered another tumultuous relationship and her hopes and dreams were dashed on the discovery that while this relationship allowed her to give birth to wonderful children, the love, passion and desires she longed for, once more eluded her.

In researching this book, I have been told that over the years as Nettie aged, she never lost touch with her reality or those life-truths that make us real people. She was a star in her own right, rising from knowing and being true to herself, no matter the circumstances of her life. She never encroached on people with power, money or connections, but was honest and humble; always giving away whatever she could. She never pretended nor sought opportunities to look better than those around her, but instead reached out to help as many as she could. She took everything and everyone in her stride: rich, poor, deserving, undeserving, vagabond, saint – she valued everyone, without compromising what was good and true.

Although she was not a "Bible-beating" Christian, Nettie's life reflected a chapter and verse of her faith that could only have been grounded in God. It appeared that God was the source of such strength in the face of adversity and the shocks that her difficult life dealt her. Although she suffered deprivations and many betrayals, Nettie felt neither deprived nor bitter. She showed a down-to-earth sensitivity that was part of the care and genuine friendship she gave, never losing her sense of humor. At one point, when faced with a medical issue, Nettie appeared to have given up and all those around her thought for sure the end was near. She, however, continued to fight the good fight for many years until the time came to say goodbye. Nettie lived at the mercy of a very cruel man who fathered her other five children, but thankfully circumstances changed and she was able to leave that household to a more peaceful lifestyle and re-establish a relationship with all her children. God granted her peace in the end.

The other woman who played a central role in the story was Venetia who grew up in the parish of St. Catherine, which is located in the middle of Jamaica. Her nuclear family consisted of a mother, father and two brothers but she was the apple of her father's eye. Venetia was constantly celebrated by her dad and often catered to as if she was royalty. She challenged everyone intellectually, was very argumentative and determined at an early age to be successful in life. Intuitively, Venetia knew that education would be her road to success so on completing her primary education, she continued her studies at the Shortwood Teachers' Training College in Kingston. Towards the end of her training, she met a Public Health Inspector named Russell and within months of courtship, they were married. They established their home in the parish of Westmoreland where she had accepted the position of Principal of the Primary School in Paul Island. Venetia and her husband never had any children of their own and one may wonder if that was a disappointment to her. In those days, women who didn't bare children of their own were secretly ridiculed as being barren and that stigma often left them feeling deficient and a failure. This may well have contributed to the burning ambition that she had in other areas of her life and her fierce push to be recognized as someone who was accomplished and important.

As Principal, Venetia was entitled to occupy the Head Teacher's house (referred to as the cottage) located across the street from the school. This proved to have advantages and disadvantages because they never really left work. The Principal's cottage was a very sturdy, large wooden house with a wrap-around veranda that provided a good view of the expansive area, including the periphery of the school compound.

Venetia's demeanor and the conflicts that developed with her husband were likened by many, to the well-documented clashes between the Campbell and McDonald clans in Scotland. She was the Campbell and he was McDonald. Venetia was 5'8" tall and towered over her husband who stood at 5'6". Image was an important factor for her and so to enhance her flawless, dark skin which showed no signs of aging, she exercised a daily facial routine consisting of a combination of glycerine and rose water as her an astringent. She was always impeccably dressed and took great care in her beauty and health regimen.

Russell held a senior position in the community through the Ministry of Health and was very well respected by everyone. He spent several months in Illinois in the U.S.A. furthering his exposure to developments in his field before returning to the island to pursue new job opportunities. He was comfortable in his position and did not have the aspiration to advance academically or socially as his wife did. He was content to enjoy the people within his sphere of influence, he did not need to be recognized, he had a terrific sense of humor, was soft and gentle and he was loved by many. He was incapable of managing his relationship with a wife who was much stronger, more ambitious; more driven to succeed which, to some degree may have been intimidating to him. He gradually developed a love for alcohol and the camaraderie of the friends he made in the rum shops who appreciated his mild manner. They validated him as a person and he did not show any form of superiority or discrimination towards the friends he had. He flirted with women such as the maids who were often referred to by Venetia as "commoners". Clearly, this was not behavior that was met with approval by his wife who held a certain social standing in the community and strove to achieve a higher position in the society.

The girls were able to connect the dots as the shrieking screams of anger and despair got louder when all "hell broke loose" for days after one of his nights out. This demonstration of emotion however did not impede Russell's desire to repeat the process the following weekend to enjoy the time spent "shooting the breeze" with his buddies at the bar. That was an audience with whom he now developed some simpatico and celebrated a couple hours of irresponsible behaviour with no explanation necessary. Unfortunately, it seemed that the ranting from Venetia fuelled his desire to continue that reckless lifestyle and he seemed to have become impervious to the expected reaction on his return. This was the one area of his life he obviously felt she could not control and he needed to demonstrate that he had choices and although not good ones, they were his to make.

There were many stories over the years but I believe that because Russell was either unwilling or incapable of contributing more to the marriage relationship, with time, it disintegrated. He never talked about the breakdown much and Venetia never stopped sharing her side of the story and her disappointment about their marriage. They were not the right match, to begin with, and as she became more successful in her career and got more recognition, he felt less adequate and perhaps emasculated by her increasingly strong, domineering posture.

I lived away from home for many years and was not aware of the intensity of the stress surrounding their progressively failing marriage. The tension became very pronounced when I returned for the holidays and each one would calculate how much time Ulit and I spent with them. We never could have imagined that there would be such jealousy and the fierce attempts to gain our attention and affection. My dad had not invested his income wisely and consequently, he struggled financially to maintain a reasonable lifestyle in his latter days. In hindsight, one can see that his wife envisioned that those days were fast approaching and had feared they would both be destitute if she had not made the financial decisions she did. As a result of her good business acumen and sound investments, she had to give Russell a financial settlement after their divorce. Through it all, his gentle manner was a perfect foil for Venetia's turbulent personality and he always maintained a calming effect on the children with whom he helped create a family.

In many ways my life as a little girl in this household was good and I became quite enamored with my neighbors who were some of the first generations of Indians to come to live in Jamaica. With limited resources, these Indians built and lived in mud huts, designed exclusively for the comfort and security of their families. They were very hospitable, frequently welcoming neighbors into their homes and taught me the art of eating with my fingers, as was their cultural practice. The staple of their meals was the rice they had harvested from their paddies which was served with a stew made from seasoned, spicy curried split peas, called dahl. I loved those meals and it became common practice for me to cross the fence to invite myself for lunch. With time, I learned how to hold the rice between my thumb and the other four fingers and squeeze a portion together to keep it in place. The key was to dip the rice ball into the dahl and slurp it with great gusto, just like my hosts. The customary way of eating with knives and forks, was alien to these families in those days and I can't remember being told to wash my hands or face before those meals, but that didn't matter, I just knew I wanted more.

Growing up in a district that had a large Indian community meant we were exposed to a lot of their cultural traditions. One that stands out was the annual festival called Hosay. For a child unfamiliar with this tradition it was the scariest experience to witness. Teams built enormous floats that were decorated with yards and yards of colored paper, fabric, beads and masks made out of papier-mâché. The men, who were very small in stature, wore giant size costumes with their heavy masks that completely hid their faces and added massive head-gear that seemed to be pressing towards the stars. They marched to the beat of rhythmic drums and other hand-made instruments throughout the streets, traveling for miles. There was lots of chanting along the way as they stomped the ground with such intensity, following the strategically selected route to the sea. They completed their ritual by tossing the floats as an "offering" into the ocean, presumably gifts to the gods of the sea. Many children within hearing distance hid at the sheer terror of the images that were conjured in their minds; images that lingered for a while, long after the ceremony ended. There was no visible improvement in the quality of life for these people after those rituals were completed. They seemed to live in abject poverty and squalor but they continued to observe their traditions, following the religious calendar without being deterred. They lived in faith and hope while creating a safe and loving environment for their families.

With no postal delivery in the village, when I became old enough to ride a bicycle, to gain pocket money, my first job was to collect the mail from the local post office. I loved to ride as it gave me a great sense of adventure and freedom to be out of the house and an opportunity to show off my skills by avoiding the numerous potholes on the very bumpy road. One day, two boys challenged me to a race. Never one to shy away from a challenge, I persuaded one of my friends, Priscilla to climb onto the back wheel of my bike and off we went. Well, five minutes into the race, my bike hit a stone; my friend and I went flying up and over an embankment, crashing into a fence. The bike was mangled and I tore the skin over my right eyebrow causing a steady stream of blood to rush down my face. I was not as concerned about the pain I was experiencing on account of the 'crash' but more about how I would explain this accident to my parents! I immediately hustled off to the woman in charge of the post office who very kindly cleaned and bandaged my wound. This bought me enough time to develop a plausible story - I hit a stone and fell off the bike - neglecting to give them the full story. Had I told the full story there would have been a good chance I would not have been able to sit, lie or rest on the lower part of my body for a while. My body managed to escape the lashes of a leather belt that would have inflicted real pain.

Week after week I observed the Indian and Negro women carrying baskets loaded with ground provisions that had been harvested from their plots to the local markets to help support their families. To support heavy baskets, the women took large pieces of fabric, rolled them very tightly into a round flat knot called a kotta, which they placed on their heads to cushion the baskets placed there. Once placed firmly in position, the kottas became the base for the balancing act to follow and no hands were needed to support the baskets. The women had to walk several miles to the nearest market with their kotta-balanced baskets. These women's feet were cracked, bruised and calloused, but they were on a mission to secure much-needed income for their families and rarely complained. Life was hard for these women but they were resilient and strong enough to endure under the pressure. I was learning at a young age, the strength, character, determination and commitment necessary for a woman to get the job done. The women shouted to everyone along the way and folks would return their greetings with equal enthusiasm. The ladies had great posture but that back-breaking exercise was considered to be just another day of work.

Throughout my youth, I talked about and yearned for an older brother. I had no idea why this was such a deep desire of mine and had no idea that my wish would be granted one day as the mysteries of my life's journey unfolded.

I was about six years old when a little girl who was about four years old at the time was invited to the house and before long she was introduced as the newest member of the family. Her name was Ulit, a scrawny child, with long straight, black hair. She was very timid, scared in fact when she arrived and had a hard time settling into her new surroundings as her mother had recently died. It was Russell who was responsible for this new addition to the family. He told the story that one afternoon he saw an Indian man sitting in a bar with a little girl sitting on his lap. Russell was so concerned when he saw them, especially considering the location. Due to his compassionate nature, he engaged the man in conversation to determine what was going on. The man told him of his recent loss and how desperate he was for help with his little girl. Without too much thought Russell offered to help and the distraught father accepted the offer from Russell and his wife to care for his child. During the conversation, the father had shared that he had no idea how he would be able to care for a little girl without a woman's help and he also had another child to support.

The gentleman was relieved and convinced that his precious little bundle was now in good hands and he could get back to the business of working to earn a livelihood for himself and his son. It would take Ulit quite a while to become adjusted to the family. It did not help her anxiety as she knew that her dad lived nearby - within walking distance to be exact. She was too young to understand the working of a clock but within days, she had figured out when it was time for her father to pass our house on his way home from work. There was no other route he could take so this was it. She learned that she could cleverly hide behind a vine that grew on the large veranda of our house; just around the time that her father was due to pass the house after work. The poor man on each occasion would try to hide from her, hustling along, desperate to avoid eye contact with his daughter. Little did he know that Ulit was vigilant in spying. On her first sighting, she cried out in her tender, child-like way, "Papa!" This was the heart-wrenching cry of a child so desperate for the familiar smell and warmth, of her father's embrace. Her father, shocked at being discovered quickly picked up speed, pumping the pedals on that bicycle, clanking lunch box on the side, hustling away doing his very best to keep his distance. It was a vain attempt on his part to separate himself emotionally from his determined child who insisted on forcing a connection with her sole remaining biological parent. One can only imagine how painful that must have been for both parent and child especially due to the proximity of the homes.

One evening, after the housekeeper had bathed and dressed us for the evening, she asked us to sit in a certain location in the house, which we dutifully did. It was a routine exercise so there was nothing unusual about it. On this occasion, the housekeeper who lived on the property went to prepare herself for the evening not knowing that the little miss decided to make a dramatic move and run away to her father's house. I cannot imagine the expression on his face when he opened his front door to see his little girl, all clean, dressed, and ready for bed standing there in the doorway. He must have been consumed with fear and confusion at that moment as he grappled with the situation, but it was too late to return her to the house so he allowed her to spend the night. How determined was this little four-year-old to go back to a home she was familiar with? She was so fiercely determined to be in the presence and comfort of her father's arms. Her plan was short-lived however, as the first thing the next morning, she was returned to her new place of residence. Both families must have realized at that moment that this episode would have had a profound impact on this little girl and that more than ever she needed to cuddled and feel loved. Little did her dad know the fate that awaited little Ulit after he walked away. The little miss received a few firm lashes on her buttocks as punishment to warn her that running away was not an option and an act that she vowed never to repeat.

As part of Ulit's assimilation into the family, she got a special "makeover". Her very long, flowing, straight black hair was cut, shampooed and brushed. It was such a beautiful sight that I stood in awe of her image. As she seemed so sad and very shy, to make her feel welcomed, I offered her my only doll, Betty, to hug and be comforted. Betty was made of straw and almost as big as Ulit was. Well, without skipping a beat, the young lady proceeded to dismantle Betty, head first. My beheaded doll was now rags, tossed to the floor and leaving me in floods of tears. You can well imagine the anguish that caused! Ulit was unfortunately denied the pleasure of enjoying other playthings until she understood the consequences of her action.

For a long time, I was very jealous of my new sister because she was considered the "better looking" child. Each time visitors came to our home, they all remarked on how beautiful Ulit was, especially mentioning her long, dark, flowing hair and smooth olive skin. Everyone without exception found her attractive and there was no focus on me during these visits. Russell also made disparaging comments about my appearance making constant references to my skinny ankles and my pug nose, which, according to him, were all supposed to have been said in jest. Additionally, onlookers often told me that I had the same slanted, sleepy eyes and flat derriere, typical of the Chinese race. Throughout my teenage years, I was not able to understand the label and there were neither hints nor clues to help me clarify what was being communicated. I remained clueless for many years until linkages emerged later in life but I was always very attracted to that race. My father's negative comments concerning my physical features would only serve to deepen my insecurity and subsequent low self-esteem.

So obvious was the shame and pain of how I viewed myself that when I became an adult and it was fashionable to have cosmetic surgery, one of the first things I considered doing was to having my nose straightened. There was nothing I could do about my ankles – unfortunately – so that was a done deal. I loved the gentle spirit of my dad, but he had no idea the pain he caused me for years with his obsessive focus on my looks. My physical features would influence my choice of clothing for many years and once I was in a position to create my style choices, I only wore form-fitting, tailor-made, long pants and if on some rare occasion, I wore a dress, it would be maxi-style as long as it covered those ankles.

Ulit and I lived away from each other for most of our lives but we always shared a bond as sisters and became even closer when we were mature enough to reflect on our personal experiences as children. We were quite different in many ways. I was the strong, bold one, using every opportunity to get my way, taking chances, oftentimes paying the price, and being punished for my misdeeds. Ulit thought I was very daring and in later years recalled many of the risky activities that I dared to engage in. Because she loved her big sister, Ulit would happily tag along in the mischief that I was getting into, sometimes getting the lashes instead of me. It all seemed so unfair to her, but she admired my spunk to defy the odds, regardless of the consequences. As Ulit grew into adulthood, she developed a special bond with Russell primarily because of his even temperament, was the gentler parent, the more compassionate and life with him was easier until the dramatic change in his personality during his final days. She was faithful to continue to care for him throughout.

Ulit shared with me that she had decided at an early age, not to go against the grain of the household and to accept things whether she liked them or not. She didn't challenge orders like I did and wouldn't object to things offered to her even if she hated them. She decided very early that her life would be a whole lot easier if she did not express her true feelings. This became a character trait she adopted and continued into exhibited throughout her adult life. She felt fear and a sense of unworthiness in sharing her true feelings and passively accepted things as a given, even if that meant being uncomfortable in her relationships. Ulit became increasingly fearful of Venetia and shared an incident when her school shoes were damaged that she was afraid to report it because she was worried that it would been seen as a complaint and a cost. She felt she was not entitled to have the best of anything and so she didn't raise an alarm about anything, including her damaged shoes. For many years she assumed I was the privileged biological child and she was the adopted "outside" child. It seemed obvious in her childlike mind that I had negroid hair and I looked more like our parents. She watched as I had my hair washed and the struggle it was to untangle the knots with large brittle combs that kept exploding. There was no such thing as detangling shampoos and conditioners back then, so I had to endure the pulling and the tugging for at least an hour. There was no magic quick fix, you just had to grin and bear the pain. There was no empathy either just intermittent sighs from the housekeeper, who had been given the task of combing through this mop of tangled hair.

My godparents Sammy and Ethlyn owned a beach house in Negril, a small township in the most western parish of the island. Our families spent many weekends and holidays at this beach house when we lived in Paul Island and Grange Hill. Negril's fame is its lily-white, seven-mile-long sandy beach which presents an unobstructed vista that stretches forever. This vast expanse, lined with sea grape and coconut trees, provided shelter for sea bathers from the intense blazing sun and its potent UV rays that penetrated even the shaded areas. It was and still is a breath-taking sight.

To be awakened in the early morning by the ocean lapping against the seashore and with the gentle, tropical breezes drifting wantonly through the trees, was magical for us, even as children. We laughed, frolicked a lot, and ate the ripe sea grapes from trees, which surrounded the property like umbrellas. The sea grapes were a little tart but no one cared, we just kept eating. There was a sense of freedom that life was good and in those moments we had no concern about our future. We just lived and enjoyed life at that moment.

We watched little crabs as they scampered down into their little burrows when they sensed our presence was near. Even these tiny creatures had a sense of danger and hid in their secret places. There were lilies in the little ponds nearby with tiny, lilac flowers strewn atop their leaves. Frogs hopped purposefully from leaf to leaf making their way to their next adventure. Birds chirped early in the mornings as they went searching for food while the roosters from the neighbors nearby would begin to crow at the crack of dawn announcing it was time to rise and shine.

The aquamarine sea water was crystal clear - allowing us to see the bottom of the sea for miles out. Along the seashore, we gazed at seashells of varying sizes as they tumbled to the shore with each motion of the waves. We collected a lot of seashells in those days so that at our leisure we could compare the shapes, colors and sizes and marvel at the uniqueness of each one. No two were alike. Just as God created each one of us to be unique with different fingerprints, so did He also create the seashells. We placed the shells in jars to take home as a reminder of each visit to this very peaceful, divine location, uniquely created by God. A creation no man could have conceptualized or directed. The Bible says that God knows the number of grains of sand on the seashore and He is the one who says to the ocean, this far and no further even at high tide. This, in my mind and heart, is the unprecedented design concept by a wondrous Creator.

There was no electricity in Negril, but we had running water in the taps throughout the property and we were told that the best time of the day to shower was early in the afternoon as the sun would have heated the water slightly. For light at night, all rooms were candlelit and there were also lanterns, with wicks that were trimmed daily for maximum effect and filled with kerosene oil. Our meals were cooked on a stove fuelled by coal, similar to today's barbecue grills. We ate heartily as kids, indulging in as many of the tropical fruits as we desired and drank coconut water directly from the shell of the coconut. It was common practice to have the "coconut man" the vendors are known, prepare the coconut for us. He would cut the top and pry an opening which we placed to our lips and carefully drank the refreshing liquid. It didn't matter that some of the juice ran down our cheeks, onto our garments, because during the moment we were enjoying a refreshing drink and that was all part of the experience. Once we drank all the liquid, the "coconut man" would split open the coconut so we could use a spoon made from the husk to remove the delicious and nutritious jelly that was nestled inside. If the coconut was young, the jelly would be very soft while the older coconut was firmer and one could enjoy it with a little dark brown sugar sprinkled on top.

There are no words to describe the ambiance that came with the sunsets; the kaleidoscope of colors reflecting on the water. When one looked out to sea the horizon appeared to be a convergence of the sky and sea. It was then and still is impossible to explain the magnificent beauty of Negril. Those sunsets were breath-taking and majestic as the colors changed gradually with each passing moment. We often watched the sun disappear behind the clouds, as the sky got darker and darker. Negril was such a serene place for us to visit as a family, and we would sit for hours and watch the waves move in their undulating manner along the seashore. One could look for miles along the coastline, as the lights slowly dimmed at various intervals, when people in their homes, were finally settling in for a good night's sleep.

There were times when the peace and serenity of Negril would be broken with shouts from the adults, who played bridge well into the night, in various locations in the house. While the games were in full swing one could hear words like "no trump, raise, lead, bid", as they challenged each other along with their partners to win each game. As children, we were too young to understand the intricacies of the game but we were happy to occupy ourselves in other areas of the house.

We found real joy in playing with and dressing dolls with the outfits made by mother's dressmaker, or paper dolls with cut-out clothing and accessories. Can you imagine having dolls that were wearing "designer" clothes in those days as well as home-made toys? Life seemed so civilized, uncomplicated, and non-competitive back then. My creative side was starting to kick in as I developed an interest in making bedside mats from scraps of fabric from the dressmaker and creating pencil sketches of trees on a sheets of drawing paper.

At the end of our idyll and many hours of bridge games later, we returned to our respective homes to prepare for the next phase, back to school and back to work. Over the years, Negril has become busier as a community featuring significant changes with the introduction of all-inclusive hotels, bed-and-breakfast establishments, hedonistic resorts, and beach bars. Negril has enjoyed worldwide recognition for many years and managed to remain consistent with its offer of hotel rooms, restaurants and entertainment.

❧

During my early days at the Primary school in Paul Island, I was very attached to Venetia but I felt even as a little girl, that the punishment she meted out to Ulit and myself was unjust considering we were just little girls exploring the world around us. There was always the need in Venetia's mind to constantly correct or even chastise her children if they mispronounced a word or used a word incorrectly. Other topics for her derisive comments included the fact that she felt we not well versed enough in any subject; or that our grades were never good enough. We were always compared to other children who more often than not lived in much more "civil" households than we did. A very firm hand, almost military in style, ruled our household. Perhaps Venetia felt that a firm hand was one way of ensuring that her daughters grew up to become "proper" cultured, young ladies who practiced sophisticated social graces such as etiquette, manners, fashion and deportment.

In my childish naivety, I had no idea my parents would be watching the schoolyard as closely as they did. They monitored my after-school activities as I would learn one day, much to my dismay! I had been told not to associate with a specific group of rowdy girls. I couldn't imagine what was wrong with the group and why my parents were so adamant and imposed such strict rules concerning them. I was known to be strong-willed and stubborn (as the locals would say, "she own way"). On the day in question, I noticed the girls with whom I was strictly forbidden to associate with, so I grabbed the opportunity and joined in the fun for only a few minutes before it was time to go home. What I hadn't realized was that Russell was on "security duty" and could see my antics from our veranda. There were no pleasantries when I arrived home; instead, I was met with the very sharp end of his tongue. I had never seen my dad that angry as he was always the reserved, even-tempered parent but he found his weapon of choice, the back end of a long-handled hairbrush to issue the punishment. After a few gentle taps on the buttocks, I apologized and vowed not to repeat the offense. I was spared on this occasion because

Venetia, on the other hand, would have used a long, leather strap - the one that she kept rolled in her desk drawer. When we committed a "crime" and saw our mother heading towards her writing desk, we would brace ourselves for the corporal punishment that was coming. We would start to cry and beg for mercy before the tornado hit, but most times our pleas fell on deaf ears. Those lashes would hurt for several days. The reminder was there each time we tried to sit.

I believed I was a good girl in those days as I didn't get into too much mischief or so I convinced myself, but even good girls tell little fibs to get out of trouble. One day I was caught sneaking out of the pantry having just indulged in a handful or two or three, who was counting, of salted peanuts, snacks reserved for guests who came to play bridge. I thought I would leave just enough in the tin thinking no one would notice. This covert act didn't work as I almost had a head-on collision with my dad as I tried a stealth move and I tiptoed away from the scene of the crime. We were both shocked at the chance encounter. Recovering first, dad immediately asked, "Were you eating the peanuts?" I looked him squarely in the eyes and said that it was Ulit who had rummaged through the can. What I didn't realize was that the evidence was all over my mouth as the salt granules had created a pattern around my lips. There was an abundance of lashes, not only for what was considered stealing but also for lying about my misconduct . . . oh, the mischievous happenings of a child. Ulit stood at a safe distance hoping she was not wrongfully accused again and included in the petty larceny.

After a few years, Venetia finally transferred to a larger school, located in Grange Hill. Our family settled very quickly into our new accommodation and other than the change in locations many things remained the same. Mealtimes were special in our house. The dining table was always beautifully laid with freshly starched tablecloths and matching cloth napkins placed in sterling silver napkin rings. Fresh flowers from the garden adorned the table and each serving dish had the appropriate serving utensil carefully placed beside it. There was always an ample supply of food to include left-overs for the following day. The housekeeper who served was provided with uniforms comprising aprons and little cloth tiara. The adults of the household would be addressed as "Sir" and "Ma'am" or Mr. Mac and Miss Mac while Ulit and I were addressed as Miss Peggy and Miss Darling as she was called then. Before each meal, we gave God thanks for His bounty and these prayers were scripted so there was no need to find the right words to say. Venetia's home had all the trappings of an aristocratic residence.

There were many breakfast choices like a variety of hot cereals, made from grated green bananas, cornmeal or oats, cooked in cows' milk that was delivered in large containers by a designated farmer from the area. These healthy cereals were topped with slices of ripe bananas from the garden, freshly ground cinnamon, and nutmeg. There was always a variety of hand-picked, fresh fruit available so fruit salads were always served with each meal. There were heartier dishes from time to time: calf's liver fried in onions and served with green bananas; ackee and salt fish served with fried plantain and dumplings; fried fish, bammy (flat bread made from cassava) and so many other traditional dishes that we all enjoyed.

There was another tradition surrounding the meals on the weekends. On Saturdays, lunch was a variety of soups like beef, red beans, fish or cow heel. A staple of all soups was the inclusion of a combination of ground provisions from the garden or nearby market. These could include yams, dasheen, eddoes, breadfruit and of course little Jamaican style dumplings called spinners. The soups were well seasoned with fresh herbs from the garden and for extra flavor an uncut scotch bonnet pepper was added. That was considered the first course for the Saturday lunch. The second course consisted of a stir-fried dish of highly-seasoned minced beef with white rice, steamed vegetables, and as a side dish, some of the starchy ground provisions (from the soup). Families ate heartily on weekends, however, after such a feast, everyone needed to take an afternoon siesta.

On Sundays, the table was always set with fine china from our parents' wedding collection. Sunday lunch consisted of the usual three courses starting with fruit, usually a grapefruit cut in half with a cherry on top, an entrée with two types of meat, starches and vegetables. The third course was a homemade treat and it was recommended that you always leave a little room for dessert. We were responsible enough to do chores so Ulit and I did the cleaning up after the meals, which allowed us to have the last little crumbs from the dessert tray, while our parents took their afternoon nap. Ulit was and still is an excellent cook and enjoyed spending time on Sundays engaging in that activity. On the other hand, I hated the kitchen and volunteered for other chores, but I did enjoy going back to sneak another spoonful of the delicious rice 'n peas cooked with coconut milk or a slice of cornmeal pone with the soft jelly-like topping that our mom made so well.

From an early age, education, proper manners and developing proper, social graces were inculcated as the hallmarks and values of our home. We had to speak well, dress well, be polite, respectful to our elders at all times, and ambitious. Unfortunately, my self-consciousness about my flat nose and small ankles caused insecurities while my father's constant reminders and comments by others about my appearance did not help. My thoughts were: I wasn't as good-looking as others, and nor was I as intelligent. In my mind, I just didn't measure up. I didn't have hair that was long or straight flowing down my back which was the preferred style. I was in fact that 'nappy hair' girl whose combs would break weekly as I attempted to detangle sections of my Negro hair. I was considered rebellious and often challenged the *status quo* even at a young age, so I took advantage of the first opportunity I had to use a hot comb to "straighten" my hair.

At Grange Hill, I spent countless hours absorbing the music I heard at home. Songs by musical icons like Nat King Cole, Mahalia Jackson, Louis Armstrong (Satchmo), Paul Robeson, Andy Williams, and other well-known singers of the time were frequently played. Many of these songs were infectious. Once I learned them, I would sing lustily at the top of my lungs not caring if the neighbors heard me or were disturbed as I imitated these singers as well as I could. For me, one of the advantages of living in the country was the vast amount of space between houses. I can only presume that the comments were, "she a- sing again". For a while, I had the desire to become a professional singer so it was not unusual for me to keep singing around the house with the hope that one day my talent and passion for singing would be recognized by my parents at least. When I did get the nerve to ask to be enrolled in a class to pursue that dream, the idea was immediately dismissed without any discussion at all.

While carrying out my daily chores, I sang songs like "Singing in the Rain" and "Go Down Moses" or my theme song, "You'll Never Walk Alone" which began:

When you walk through a storm, hold your head up high and don't be afraid of the dark. At the end of the storm is a golden sky and the sweet silver song of a lark. Walk on through the wind, walk on through the rain though your dreams be tossed and blown. Walk on, walk on with hope in your heart and you'll never walk alone...

To this day, the words of this Rogers and Hammerstein hit song are poignant reminders of that period of my life. At eight, nine, even ten years old, this song captured the hope I had about many things. Hope to be heard, hope to be validated, hope to achieve.

One of my passions was and still is to rearrange furniture, much to the horror of my mother. I took great care of my space (bedroom) and moved the furniture as often as I could. Everything had to be in perfect order; it had become an obsession; however, I was allowed to exhibit that passion in my little corner only. Designing interesting floral arrangements, dusting and cleaning were some of my pleasurable activities as it allowed me to establish structure and to create functional, comfortable spaces. I felt the need for things to be picture-perfect all the time. While carrying out these chores, I discovered a hidden talent and that was - I could repair small household items at a very young age. This caught everyone by surprise considering there was no training or any role model who I could have learned this from. I would repair and replace small things every opportunity I got to enhance the existing décor. A wonderfully unique gift I embraced.

One Christmas, Venetia thought it was a good idea to attach the cards that had arrived from the UK, US, and Africa to a cord stretched across one wall in the living room. I thought it was the most ridiculous thing I had ever seen. So, I decided to pull the cord and create my design with the cards in the form of a Christmas tree on the wall. On arriving home, Venetia was furious, to say the least, when saw how this daring child decided without consultation to rearrange her design. "How dare you move my things around? This is my house and I will do as I please," she declared vociferously and demanded that I return everything to her original pattern. This early experience signaled to me that something was amiss but I was a pragmatist and knew that one day I would have my place to decorate in my style. I knew that I had a flair for interior decorating which would be validated some 40 years later when Venetia visited my home and announced: "You should have studied interior decorating!" I thought, "Really?!"

I was quite fashion conscious, so from an early age, I determined to get rid of the dresses with bows neatly tied at the back. When I had saved enough of my pocket money, I bought some green cotton fabric and I asked my best friend's mother to make a new more fashionable outfit. The design had a fitted bodice with a skirt shaped into what was referred to as box-pleats. Ulit and I were due to go to a concert at the school one night and I decided that I would wear my new dress. I was a teenager now and I couldn't imagine not dressing in a more mature and "fitting" way. So, the clandestine moment came as I arrived at my friend's home, changed into my new outfit and off we went. We both had a great time at the concert but Ulit was worried about how our mother would react to seeing me in the dress she had not purchased for me.

As the fearless one, I was determined to deal with each issue as they unfolded. When Venetia picked us up at the event, one could feel the tension in the air and the car. We drove in silence, dropped off our friends at their respective homes before heading to ours. The moment we pulled into the garage, questions were hurled in my direction about this mysterious dress. I honestly explained how I saved my pocket money, made the purchase, and who made the garment. While my truthfulness was admirable, often, the consequences were very painful. Venetia ordered me to take the dress off and give it to her immediately. Her next action was most shocking. She promptly took the dress outside, grabbed her scissors, and cut it into shreds before putting a flame to the pieces! It was such a severe action that it left us all stunned and wondering what were we supposed to learn from that very dramatic exercise. If the funds had been stolen or had I had lied about it then Venetia's action, though extreme, may have been justified. But none of that had happened. The confiscation and destruction were mystifying.

Something changed while the family was at Grange Hill and I began to realize that the love and tenderness I had hoped for and expected from my family was non-existent; it was truly a dysfunctional family. I felt shortchanged and muzzled. I couldn't express myself as I wished to develop my creativity in the home. Children were only allowed to speak when spoken to otherwise they were considered insolent and disrespectful. How does a child come to grips with those feelings/restrictions? The spirit of control affected and nullified the creative tendencies of both Ulit and myself. As the more vocal one, I would make requests, even though I was aware that nothing would change. I tried to have a voice regardless of the consequences. Our mother's strict demands and unbending rules about so many things seemed excessive to us. The verbal slaps in condescending tones that were regularly issued, obliterated any sense we might have had that we were truly cared for and loved.

As I grew older and my thoughts matured, I would experience sensations of mental isolation from the family that I was a part of. I felt that no one paid any attention to my concerns regarding what I wanted to do with my life even though I would occasionally drop hints about my interests including creating opportunities to help underprivileged children. No one seemed interested - after all, I was just a child. What did I know about the future? How could I know what was best for me? My emotions were consumed with these what-ifs and maybes. The few young people in my circle appeared more grounded and responsive to their parents and I never heard them complain. I found myself continually questioning who I was and what I aspired to become. I was constantly reminding myself that I was born to do special things and impact lives in a meaningful way, but I was not allowed to articulate those feelings or initiate or invite any adult to participate in any such conversation. I was just one of those dreamers who had big dreams. That was just how life was back then.

My insecurities escalated over the years and there was very little anyone could say to allay my fears that beauty was only skin-deep, which I had heard often enough. To me, it was not visible in the reflection that looked back at me in my mirror. Even though I repeated that interpretation to myself often enough, this nappy-headed little girl knew that deep down inside, there was something bigger, better, and special about her and physical beauty was not it. You see in my household, I always felt that I lived at the end of a correction point. Even at a tender age, I recognized that no matter what I said, how I looked, or how I performed a task, I always came under harsh scrutiny. It was never enough. It was never good enough. Was this how love was supposed to be expressed? There was never any conversation that I can remember that included the words, "I love you", "forgive me for being so hard on you, but…". We just never had that level of interaction.

Ulit and I always felt as though we were expected to frequently show gratitude for the 'opportunity' we were given, to live in the lifestyle to which we had become accustomed. As a consequence, we felt obliged to adhere to the draconian rules of the household. We lived in fear a lot of the time and quietly grumbled among ourselves, always ensuring that the walls didn't have ears so we were never overheard.

Reflecting on our lives, Mom was extremely influential and accepted as a powerful force within the community but she was oftentimes intimidating to those in her midst. I suspect she was well aware of this. She commanded a great deal of respect, which was unusual for a black woman of that era. Her determination to forge ahead and become one of the best in the business caused her to set very high standards for her students, insisting on hard work and sacrifice. She was relentless in her quest to succeed. Over the years several of her students went on to achieve tremendous success and always credited her for instilling a good work/study ethic in them.

Unlike Dad, Mom was ambitious, a high achiever, more socially aware and she also wanted to maintain an important status in the community. She was educated, politically active but never ran for an office in the government. She fought hard for women's rights, was proud of her race, not very popular, heavily criticized for being too stern, too demanding, too proper, and always being too politically correct.

She was always engaged in her community and the value she held for people of color. I can remember an occasion that was unique when a young, very beautiful, black girl wanted to enter the local beauty pageant but she didn't have the confidence to participate. My mother was determined that this young lady was an eligible candidate for the competition and made it her mission to ensure that the young lady was included. In the end, the young lady was not crowned the winner but the fact that she was allowed to participate was a pivotal moment for the naysayers who said it couldn't happen. The underlying message was that young, black women could and should valorize their skin color and learn to fight for opportunities that would establish them as equal partners in every facet of society.

Some of the popular, public events held in the parish every year were called garden parties. These were always well attended and especially fun as the children got together; ate junk food like hotdogs and cotton candy and visited Madame X who was a fortune-teller. Madame X sat in front of a dark curtain with her crystal ball and for a few pennies would tell you what was in store for you in the years to come. As children, we were fascinated with Madame X and walked away in awe of her ability to tell us about ourselves. This activity started a curiosity in me about mediums having the ability to tell you what was going on in your life and giving a false sense of knowing what the future had in store. It opened a door for me to believe that other than God there were people on this earth who also had a prophetic gift and could help guide your future.

The racial mix in my parish included the Chinese who started to arrive in Jamaica from Mainland China from as early as the late 1800s. By the 1930s, families from both the Chinese and Syrian émigrés settled in Grange Hill. They were very astute business people and before long, they occupied a good stretch of land and developed an infrastructure, which would eventually become the merchandise hub for all the nearby villages. For several years, they did not marry outside of their race and so the success of their businesses and the wealth they generated, remained within their close-knit communities. They owned the supermarket, hardware store, movie theatre, haberdashery, clothing store, variety shop, shoe store, and gas station. Integration with Negroes and Indians was superficial because even though their children were educated in the same schools they did not mix socially. Interestingly, despite their financial power, neither the Chinese nor the Syrians became involved in partisan politics. In those days they remained publicly silent about issues that affected their communities but one could hear them speaking in their native tongue to keep their views and concerns within their ethnic groups. It was fascinating to watch how they supported each other. They needed to look after their people and this was often manifested in the way they invested in helping each other to start a new business.

I can't remember any conversation about xenophobia back then, as everyone seemed accepting of the cultural mix and respectful to each other. I became particularly attracted to the Chinese residents in the town. I observed how methodically they went about their business: they opened their stores fairly early in the morning until late at night and they taught their children from a very young age to assist in their shops. These acts were paramount to their community's success and longevity but in the meantime, I envied the access those children had to all the stuff that was behind the counters. The children of the Chinese in the community never invited the other local children to their homes nor were they interested in visiting the homes of other children. There were so many within their community that there was no shortage of playmates. I was unaware even then that something from my past may have triggered this unexplained interest.

Over the years, Venetia's firm belief that education was the road to success, and her desire for upward social mobility remained unshaken. During our formative years, she accepted a scholarship to study at an Ivy League school, New York University, in NYC for four years. While there, Venetia was accepted as a member of the prestigious Alpha Delta Kappa Sorority which, most likely, she would have considered being a major achievement on the road to achieving her desire for acceptance. On the completion of her studies, Venetia was offered a scholarship to enroll in a teacher-training course in a very remote area of Liberia, West Africa. Her sojourn to this African country caused Venetia to have a greater appreciation for her own country, her lifestyle at home, and in Jamaica's educational system.

While in Liberia she had to travel 30 miles to the nearest church, which, as you can well imagine, was not very often. She had to learn to eat food that was different from that to which her palate was accustomed and adjust to living without what she would have considered, at home, to be the bare essentials. In those days there were no telephones in homes, no internet or cellphones so there were long intervals between our communication with her. I can't remember if I missed my mom in those days, as the relationship with our dad was so much more liberal. He was so loved and respected by so many. Unfortunately for him, his personality and lack of ambition meant he did not think about or plan for the future. Things would just happen when they happened.

While our mum was abroad, we were well cared for by our dad and nanny. On one of her visits home for a well-deserved break from her studies, Ulit recalls we traveled the five and a half-hour drive from our rural town to the airport to meet her. Initially, there was much excitement that mom was coming home, I believe mostly for the gifts she would likely bring. All that excitement came to a screeching halt when the reality set in on seeing her disembark the aircraft. Suddenly, I began to cry. Later, Ulit would recall how confused she had become by the mixed emotions associated with the occasion. I couldn't fathom what caused my joy to so quickly disappear and become replaced by floods of tears. This rapid change in my emotions scared my little sister seeing her strong, boisterous sister reduced to this fragile state. After many years of soul searching both of us realized that we had enjoyed many months of bliss, with no harsh punishment and that this was about to end. We were both afraid of the wrath of Venetia could rain down on anyone, at any time.

While Venetia was stern and had a forbidding countenance, there was a softer side to her and she easily extended a charitable hand helping less fortunate children. She constantly gave away school clothes, books, and meals to children who didn't live with us. However, many times some of those same kids felt that what was expected in return was unreasonable and so, they fled the scene without looking back or even saying thank you. She assisted not only those in her neighborhood but also members of her extended family. Venetia was an educator and so the perception was she would concentrate on helping the females in her extended family to qualify for places in some of the best schools. From time-to-time, some of them were invited to stay for a while with us but their stay was usually curtailed by the military rules we abided by at home. Things were often so dire that once they left Venetia's home, they usually convinced themselves that they were better off not communicating with her for several years. We, on the other hand, who were permanent residents of the household, had no choice but to stay. Ulit and I would often overhear the mumblings and grumblings of those who came to visit, but as children, we could not participate in those conversations.

Onlookers must have seen and surmised that Venetia's daughters lived in a very harsh environment and felt sorry for us as expressed by a friend later in life. They just couldn't imagine what life was like daily and would have heard stories from other people. The chant would have been, "Miss Mac not easy you know" or "She is a force to be reckoned with".

Even at a young age, I was uncomfortable with the use of the word "maid" to describe the household help, and more often than not they were referred to a "helpers". The gardeners and helpers who worked for Venetia were afraid of her as well, as she wouldn't hesitate to unleash her fiery words of discontent in a derogatory manner in an instant. People would leave her presence feeling either unworthy of their existence or if they were someone of the upper echelon of society, they felt inspired and important. Venetia's signature stance was her very superior attitude and mien. It caused great pain and completely alienated her from those she cherished, as well as those few who may have genuinely cherished her.

Because of her sharp tongue, Venetia's kind and generous spirit oftentimes went unrecognized. She had a brilliant mind but unfortunately, she had no concept of what bridling one's tongue meant and lacked tack when communicating with people whom she considered not to be her academic equal. It never occurred to her that she was insulting anyone. She treated them as though they were simply stupid. Humility was not a word in Venetia's vocabulary or part of her lifestyle. With her very sharp mind, it was Venetia's mission to educate those in her presence while establishing a paradigm shift in established social relations. She demanded that she was recognized for her academic ability and she was not going be ostracized or marginalized because of her dark skin. It is a tragedy that someone who was so talented and offered so much to so many ended up living her final days in total isolation - even by her close family members.

Sundays were the only days when we all went to church, except Dad. There were very strict rules about punctuality and we were punished for being late. There was always the threat that if the car was in motion and you were not in it, you were expected to find your way there, regardless. Neither Ulit nor I wanted to find out what the consequences of being late were, so we always got ready on time. Our hearts were always filled with trepidation when Mum drove up the very steep incline to park on the church compound. At our young ages, we were not confident about our mother's driving skills, so it was always a relief when we would finally arrive safe and sound at our destination and park.

At the Anglican church in Grange Hill that we attended, the white overseer from the Frome Sugar Estate and his family were entitled to occupy one pew towards the front of the church. The explanation we were given was that they were being recognized for their generous financial contribution to the church's upkeep and so no one else dared to occupy those "reserved" seats. If the family was absent from church any Sunday even for weeks at a time, the pew remained empty and the congregants were very respectful of the situation and dutifully kept the space vacant.

When the contract for the British appointed overseer came to an end, he and his family returned to his homeland. As the pew became vacant, it didn't take long before Venetia's self-confidence, ably buttressed by her position of Principal, led her to believe that she had earned the right to occupy those seats in the church which were associated with social position and community standing. Immediately after the overseer departed, Venetia advised the cleric of her intentions and even he could not have argued with her. Our family took up occupancy of those exalted pews, thereby visibly advancing her standing in the community. One cannot be sure if there was any further discussion on the matter or if she just decided to "possess" and "own" that space! The significance of this became clearer much later in life as the impact of colonial legacy, the structure of the Diocese of the Anglican church and facts associated with racism vs. classism continue to be a strongly debated issue.

From that moment on, each Sunday, Venetia positioned her family in the front row of the church as she had dutifully offered her little envelope with her pledge to assist with the maintenance of the church as well as the needs of the priest and his family.

There were several uncomfortable moments for us as children, when on a few days we happened to be late for church, we would have to march up to the designated pew to be seated. During that period my rebellious streak emerged, so if we were late, I would quietly slip into one of the pews towards the back of the church so I didn't have to be noticed as a latecomer. That, you can imagine, was unacceptable and did not sit well with the powers that be! We were often embarrassed when Venetia who was tone-deaf, lustily sang her favorite hymns even though we all knew she couldn't carry a tune, but that didn't deter her from praising God as best she knew how.

Venetia was always immaculately dressed for church. She had her seamstress, as they were called in those days, custom-made the majority of her clothes. She was a trendsetter in her time and her garments always fitted her perfectly. For church outings, she wore hats that were embellished with various trimmings such as feathers, roses, buttons, bows, and ribbons of all colors and which were designed to coordinate with the colors of her outfits. She always took great pride in how she looked and always wanted to be well-groomed regardless.

She coordinated her outfits with a collection of filigree earrings, matching necklaces, and dainty little handbags including gloves for those special occasions. Some of her more fashionable handbags were intricately decorated with beads or tapestry. Her hair was straightened with a hot, iron comb and curled with an equally hot curling iron that had been heated on an open flame on the stove. Quite often Venetia liked to wear her hair pushed back with a tiny little hairpiece creating a chignon bun towards the nape of her head, a conservative style that created a very sophisticated look. She was way ahead of her time concerning fashion and style. Her philosophy was that one should always look and be at their best, regardless of your setting.

As I grew older, I was compelled to adapt to Christian principles and church participation so that they became an integral part of my weekly routine. As a result, I became a junior member of the church choir and tried to assimilate in my life the routine established by the much older women who felt a sense of obligation to "serve the Lord". They were in fact, happy to have anyone join to increase the numbers and add to the importance of the ministry. It is not clear if my decision to join was voluntary or following the ruling of a parent. Children were required to do as they were told. I grabbed this opportunity however to share my passion for singing, get out of the house for another occasion, and to interact with some friends and other parents in the community. None of the members of the choir had pursued any form of vocal training so the women struggled to determine if they should be singing alto or soprano parts. They couldn't harmonize so it was often ghastly to sit through rehearsals. No one openly complained, though, as it would have been offensive to identify someone singing off-key. The choir wore long robes with long sleeves and matching little pill-box hats and the colors changed according to the season on the church's calendar. The order of service was set and handed down from the Church of England considered to be monolithic and all Episcopalian churches around the world would recite the same prayers Sunday after Sunday. At this church so often, people left a service feeling uninspired and I am sure unchanged. Their day-to-day lives showed no evidence that they were any different having gone to church and so even at that young, tender age, I questioned the validity of this exercise as I had observed it from one year to the next and the next.

The dynamics among the choir members were interesting. One expected that as churchgoers, a certain standard of behavior would apply. However, it didn't take me long to realize that all was not "peaches and cream". Some members came to church not speaking to each other and left the church still without speaking, despite having just partaken of communion from the same silver chalice. Some of the church members lived very promiscuous lives, committing adultery, having one-night stands, etc., but none of that seemed to matter. There was no accountability, no discipline or counseling - even within those who sang in the choir. Younger members of the choir would overhear sordid stories of traveling salesmen coming to town and that the revolving door that was alive and well with some women. The behavior of some of those folks was quite an eye-opener, especially for someone who had lived until that time such a sheltered life.

The hymns sung during the Lenten season were especially touching and had the same effect year after year, particularly those sung on Good Friday. I can remember singing songs about the Crucifixion and the thought of Jesus dying in such a horrific manner on the cross, would cause tears to cascade down my little cheeks. Even though I didn't have a full understanding of my emotions, these were poignant moments to sing songs that Jesus loved me and He died that I might live. What did that mean to a young child? There was an awakening to be sure that was taking place within me and it was real.

Venetia was very involved in the national political agenda. There were constant political debates in our home as everyone in the household campaigned for the candidates affiliated with the political party Venetia supported. Even as children we defended the cause of the party to the extent that a carpenter was told that he couldn't work on our premises if he did not support the party we supported. That sense of loyalty was instilled very early in our lives.

Going on the campaign trail was exciting for us as we went from door to door introducing potential voters to the candidates for our party and my Mom made enormous personal sacrifices to encourage the adults to vote. She was earnest in championing the political cause she believed in and was determined to be a woman of integrity, contrary to the general opinion that all politicians are dishonest. Our entire family had become advocates for her cause and attended political meetings that were held in the various nooks and crannies of the tiny districts within commuting distance to our home. Many nights we were dressed in red — the party's color, walking through the crowds, singing party songs, and rallying other young people to follow suit. As a little six-year-old it often became too much for me and many nights I couldn't remember how I got from the car to my bed. I usually ended up falling asleep on the back seat of the car with my blanket and discovered that my Dad had ever so tenderly lifted me out of the car and tucked me into bed. There were many late nights at the end of an election where the family gathered with other party supporters for the counting of the votes. The results could arouse cheers, boisterous laughter, or groans of disappointment depending on the outcome.

My mother felt that, primarily because she was a woman, she never got the recognition she deserved by the ruling party. This, however, did not dim her deep desire to leave an impact on Jamaica's educational system where she fought hard for her students. It was long in coming but eventually, her hard work was acknowledged and she was appointed one of the distinguished senators in the government. This post was a validation of the many years of sacrifice she had made for her love of country and its people.

At 10 years old I was successful in the local Common Entrance Examination and attained a place at the very prestigious, Kingston-based, St. Andrew High School for Girls. In my first year, I was enrolled as a day student, which was a rather scary experience as it was the first time I was living away home. My first host home was just outside the city and I can vividly remember walking out of the house and seeing the largest ground lizard frolicking across the lawn. Having lived in the country all my life I could not imagine there were lizards on the planet that were that large and living in my country.

Another first was having to take a public bus to school as by now I had grown accustomed to traveling everywhere by car. Neither had I ever been anywhere on my own. I had to that time always felt protected by an accompanying parent. By the second semester, I relocated to a neighborhood closer to school to the home of a very dear family friend. We referred to her as "Aunt", a common practice in the West Indian community to address older family friends even though they may not be related. She kindly offered to not only provide accommodation for two students but also to provide transportation. She made us all feel special - as though we were part of the family. She provided packed lunches and always had an encouraging word. Every morning we packed into her little Morris Minor car and off we went to school. When I reflect on those days, we had no idea of the challenges she was facing within her marriage, but we saw how resilient she was to extend herself to care for two strangers along with her own two daughters. She was truly one of my angels, a gift from God who made the incredible sacrifice for all of us, while her marriage was crumbling under the emotional trauma that infidelity brings. I loved her daughters as I would have my sisters and the feeling was mutual.

There is very little I remember about school that first year, but I do remember while we lived in that home certain activities were standard. We were all glued to the black-and-white television on Friday nights to watch *Bonanza, Dr. Kildare,* and later on, *Dallas.* There were lots of books by Mills and Boone and the Mandingo series on the bookshelves that my aunt took great pleasure in reading. As she added to her collection, the curious kid that I was, I took pleasure in reading them as well. She had no idea that I was invading her personal library and fantasizing about romance just like the characters in the stories. Not a healthy mindset to adopt at that age, but it was a happy time. It didn't take a long time to become acclimatized to this new way of life, new environment and peculiarities of the community, all at the same time, as Aunt Val made the transition easy.

After a year as a day student, I was accepted as a boarding student. High school was exciting and welcoming, offering many opportunities to meet a diverse group of students who came from many of the other Caribbean islands as well as countries outside of the region. The English principal, Ms. Dawson, was a very gifted administrator who focused not only on academics but also on etiquette. The curriculum was extensive and all students were expected to participate in academic subjects, music and sports. The creative arts were also an integral part of the curriculum and annually, several musical productions were presented to families and special guests. Standards were very high; mediocrity was not an option.

This was and still is an all-girls' school and new boarders were placed in the dormitory above the administration building. My first night in the dorm was quite bizarre. With the exception of one single bed in my dorm, all the others were bunk beds. I was assigned the bottom bed of a bunk that night. Once orientation was over, we were sent off to bed. The matron inspected the dorms as early as 7:30 pm with lights out at 8 pm. In this new environment, none of us slept very well and so there was quite a chitter-chatter before we would each fall off to sleep. That first night I was rudely awakened by water from the upper bunk. A very scared student sleeping in the bunk above me had wet her bed and as the occupant of the bunk below her, I was the recipient of her "blessing". It all worked out in my favor as I was immediately moved to the only single bed. I had come prepared with all the trimmings for my bed - a quilt, pajama case, and little comfort pillow.

The early years of High School were great fun, not only for the opportunity to develop through academics but to interact with children from various socioeconomic backgrounds, academic abilities, and oft-times the brightest ones did not come from the wealthiest families. All students wore a uniform, which comprised a maroon-colored tunic with an inner white blouse and a 'jippy-jappa' (straw) hat with a maroon colored ribbon around the crown. The hat was a requirement when arriving and departing the school grounds and the footwear was enclosed black shoes and white socks. Boarding school had very strict rules and punishment was swiftly meted out if anyone chose to be disobedient. As I had grown up in a very strict household, boarding school was not a difficult transition for me. You reported to breakfast at a specific time and the choices were few. I can still remember the faces of the girls when they were presented with the sardines, the bowls of porridge, the cold cereals, or a selection of fresh fruit. The choices were limited but no one complained as each one had a "tuck box", usually a sturdy wooden box that held all of their snacks and goodies. Parents left student allowances for the boarders in the administrative office, which helped students to learn the art of managing their finances at a very young age. The value of money was an integral part of the discipline, but it took many years for me to adopt a philosophy that I could adhere to a budget, curb my spending and save for future financial security.

Laundry was a very organized activity. Each boarder had to ensure that all their items were labeled with their names. Any soiled clothing and linen were turned into the laundry attendants who washed, starched, and ironed everything. Each girl was required to ensure she got her laundry back on time to have the right uniform for classes, after school, and sports. Boarders had to change into their afternoon/evening uniforms at 1:30 pm comprising white dresses, black shoes, and white socks and there were no plausible excuses unless you were ill. Boarders were required to go to designated "home room" at a specific time where homework was done. This could be as early as 2 pm. unless you were involved in a sporting activity and had permission to participate. Saturdays were casual days and it was the only day one was allowed to abandon the uniform and wear colored clothing so the boarders took advantage of the opportunity to walk around with rollers in their hair, shorts, tee shirts, and slippers. On occasion, they were given written permission to go off the property with a family member for a few hours. Board games such as Monopoly, playing cards and Scrabble were dusted off on weekends and the competitive edge was demonstrated when some of the games lasted the entire weekend.

I loved participating in sports because such events provided opportunities to leave in the middle of a class to participate in an extra-curricular activity. My sport of choice was lawn tennis, and so, at every opportunity, I was on the court - whether it was hard or grass. While I was not outstanding at any particular sport, I was considered an all-rounder. I captained the tennis team, played rounders, netball, and hockey but failed miserably at track and field. I also took piano lessons and on several occasions was called out of a class to practice with my instructor. I did not complain especially if it got me out of a maths class.

As I mentioned previously, my dorm was positioned directly above the administration office, a single flight from the ground. On many occasions after matron had made her rounds and we had pretty much settled into sleep mode; we could hear snickering by the window which aroused the curiosity of those of us who were not involved in the activity. We soon realized that a couple of the girls had been sneaking out to meet boys, by climbing through the window. I was fascinated to see the risk they would take as I watched it all unfold. These were images one would see on a movie screen. The girls used sheets to create a ladder so that they could climb, as stealthily as you could imagine, through a small space in the window late at night, landing on the soft shrubs below. I am yet to figure out how these girls did not get caught, but they were very determined to meet the boys and so they did.

St. Andrew students who turned 11 years old were enrolled in confirmation classes at the local Anglican Church. We tried to take classes seriously committing to a ritual that was required by all good Christians at a young age. It was more of an outing for us students and not necessarily an act that we took time to discuss, but again we just followed the rules. We were all robed on the day of confirmation in our white dresses, white scarves, and with humility, we were presented to the Bishop of the Diocese.

As we were all maturing young ladies, we were required to read, *On Becoming a Woman*. Needless to say, the hormones had started to kick in and we were beginning to notice the young men from some of the other high schools. Since St. Andrew High was considered a school for the elite and a girls-only institution, as boarders (except for those sneaking out) we only met boys at sporting events.

One of the rules of the school was that boarding students had to write letters to their parents every Sunday. For me, it was a very difficult exercise, as I didn't know what to share with my family. I can remember one summer when school would be closed for the holidays, I wrote home to tell my parents that I preferred to stay at school as I did not want to go home. I simply refused to go home. Of course, the school would be closed for maintenance and only the workers and caretakers would have been on the premises so staying there was not an option. Where would I go? Unfortunately for me, there was no other place to go but home. During this period of my life, I felt like a lost child who had no identity, no real positive connection with my family and school was a great escape.

It was obvious that this letter had a profound impact on my parents because that summer was the best summer I had ever had. I finally received some of the attention that I craved as a child and felt a sense of validation. We did activities together as a family; I was able to pursue some of the things in which I had a keen interest. I was given an easel, practiced my pencil sketching, and attended a few musical performances. This happy atmosphere was short-lived however and as soon things returned to the normal humdrum state-of-affairs.

I enjoyed music and drama in high school. My introduction to drama came about when, as a small child, my mother directed plays at the local movie theatre for years. These were large productions with props that were transported on large trucks from our home to the venue. Having completed a year at drama school in the UK she was able to fulfill one of her lifelong dreams to be a writer and executive producer of plays. This influenced my interest while I was at St. Andrew High so I became involved in the choir and several musical productions such as *West Side Story*. There are still fond memories that are conjured in my mind when I hear excerpts from this musical. One of my profound regrets is that I was not allowed to pursue my dream of pursuing any opportunity to have voice coaching, not necessarily to become a professional, but to engage in an activity I was truly passionate about. There must have been opportunities as I matured but by then the interest had waned.

I was an A/B student in my first three years in high school and then something earth-shattering happened which I cannot explain. I was assigned to a Maths class with a new teacher who was English by birth and training. For some reason, I could not connect with this teacher and my grades dropped. I went from being a grade-A student in Maths to barely getting a passing grade. Gradually, I became more insecure, lacking in confidence, and could no longer perform to the full extent of my ability. Because of the depths to which my self-esteem had sunk, when I had to do exams at school my entire body froze. Even though I knew the answers, I was incapable of recording them accurately on paper. I wish there were guidance counselors available at the time to recognize my distress and help me to overcome my dilemma.

I became quite introverted in those years, continuing to feel inadequate, insecure, really unable to collect my thoughts and unable to effectively carry out school assignments. I was in free-fall mode and no one observed this. Everyone was too busy with their agenda so I remained alone in my struggles. Having a very strong, opinionated, and confident mother who was not paying attention did not help. I kept reminding myself that I had the potential to complete assignments and accomplish amazing things but no one helped me to plumb my innate abilities. There was no individual with the gift of discernment to say this child needs help; let's rescue her.

At the end of each school term, I packed my little suitcase and took the train home leaving Kingston early in the afternoon. The train rumbled through the countryside and many rural townships for several hours before reaching its final destination. It meandered through several parishes and made several stops before I needed to disembark at the Montpelier station located in the parish of St. James and the train station nearest to Grange Hill. Riding on the train always had elements of excitement. Montpelier is about 188 km (116 miles) from Kingston and the trip was often bittersweet. One never knew what to expect going home to the little country house, but it was occupying the familiar space in the weeks ahead that made it all worthwhile. I enjoyed all the stops with various passengers coming and going with their large bags of produce to sell, live chickens for their farms, and large baskets of goods that they were taking home. Their enthusiasm was palpable and it was obvious that they enjoyed the *joie de vivre* of island living. They had access to fresh fruits, vegetables, interacted with the other villagers, and bargained for the best prices. Again, it was obvious that the women carried these heavy loads while most times the men spent much of their time after work at the rum shop, playing dominoes or just hanging out with the "fellas". Even after a hard day's work, the women cooked, scrubbed, washed clothes by hand and generally took great care of all the household chores. It seemed as though their days never ended as other wifely duties were expected late in the night.

The hooting of the train's whistle was exciting for children in the neighborhoods near to the train track. They would come running to the station when they heard the sound of the approaching train. The screeching of the wheels against the tracks was piercing to the ears as the train pulled into the stations and relief came only when the train came to a complete stop. The piercing sound of trains broke the silence of the countryside while adding a moment of excitement and anticipation for the villagers. I enjoyed those train rides as I could buy bags of freshly roasted cashew nuts and packages of hot, dried shrimps referred to by the villagers as "shwimps". "Come get you shwimps, come get you shwimps", they shouted. There was an abundance of long strings of tangerines, oranges and grapefruits available for sale and the sellers huddled at the windows of the train, each one appearing more desperate than the other to make a sale.

It was always dark by the time the train arrived at Montpelier, but my family was always there on time to meet me and that was always a pleasure, especially because they brought one of my favorite things to eat; a Tastee chicken patty sandwiched in a soft coco bread. My sister was always happy to see me and my coming home brought great joy for both of us. As we drove through the villages getting closer to our home, passing familiar buildings, I would often have a feeling of nostalgia. Despite everything, this was home.

I left St. Andrew High School with mixed emotions. I knew I had not been the high achiever my parents desired nor did I accomplish the goals I had hoped for myself. I had no idea what was ahead but the funny thing is I knew in my soul it was not a *fait accompli*. I was sent to Manning's High School, which was in Savanna-la-Mar, to repeat some subjects and it took a lot of courage for me to go there, but I had no choice. There was no counseling, no embrace, or tenderness from my parents that I can remember when they must have realized how difficult the move would have been for me. I believe Ulit and I had been intellectually bullied, which affected us in a way that was difficult to recover from. I had to search deep down inside to find that resolve to prove that I could succeed. I settled into the school very well, supported by my best friend at the time and soon found my groove which enabled me to achieve just what I longed for. Many whispered a lot about the girl who had the opportunity to go to the most prestigious girls' school on the island but had to return to another less prestigious school to complete her studies. I was shielded from much of the gossip and thankfully it did not have any effect on my future success.

One summer holiday, I joined a group of girls who attended a weekend camp way up in the hills of Manchester, a parish known for being one of the cooler or colder parts of the island depending on who you spoke to. We arrived at this large complex where all sorts of activities had been organized. We were awakened at 4 o'clock each morning to take showers under the most horrific conditions. The water was so frigid that you had to take a deep breath and muster the courage to jump under the fine spray of the jets. You shivered for the first few seconds but soon your body got accustomed to the temperature and you were able to complete the exercise no longer focusing on the discomfort you were experiencing.

After days of playing, eating and learning some survival skills, we settled in for our final sleep. That night we talked about the excitement we had experienced but we were all looking forward to going home to warm baths and fresh beds. As part of the preparation, hair rollers were put in place, clothes were ironed, bags were packed and we climbed onto our respective cots. The next morning, we discovered some very mischievous ones had been diligently painting faces with black shoe polish, lipstick, and toothpaste had been carefully spread between hair rollers. Such was the life of camping buddies and the fun times of our youth. There was no punishment meted out for the behavior however, as the counselors had also played their part.

As I grew older, I was always reflected on many things. One of the uppermost thoughts in my mind was: Why didn't my mother and I connect more as I got older even though I felt such a strong bond with her when I was a little girl? I had told her that I was going to be buried with her when she died. I can't remember her ever using the words, "I love you", but she must have demonstrated her love in a way that made me feel secure. I couldn't imagine living my life without her and I loved snuggling up to her then. I wanted to be like her in some ways, so when she went off to her board meetings, I would take the opportunity to practice what it would look like to be a fashionista like her. I would sit on the stool at her well-polished mahogany dresser, trying on her dainty pieces of jewelry, glancing often to see if her car was coming slowly up the long driveway. This was an adventure for me, beginning with her clip-on filigree earrings, her sparkling, crystal necklaces and matching bracelets and her little gold trinkets with semi-precious stones garnered during her many overseas trips. I tried on her little chignon hair-pieces, her long strings of genuine cultured pearls, and her other bangles and bracelets that were way too big for my wrists. I also tried on the hats, which obviously were also way big for my tiny head, but I wanted to mirror the image of my fashionable mother. I admired how she strategically attached different accent pieces week after week, demonstrating her creative ability to mix and match and to color-code pieces that worked for her.

Conversations about boys were off-limits for me in my household. We did not dare look longingly in the direction of a boy for much more than a quick glance. At home, there were very few discussions about what was right or wrong, instead, you were just told what not to do. As a teenager, my attention was drawn to and I developed an interest in a young man I saw in passing. One day, while I was at Manning's, I noticed a particularly good-looking young man who had a "Colgate smile". I stopped breathing. He was not the typical tall, dark, and handsome specimen women talked about but he seemed much more than that to me at the time. His parents knew my parents and so all seemed safe. My first crush was about to take full effect. As the youngest member of his family, he enjoyed the privilege of attending their private school and learning the real estate business first hand. The community had a great deal of respect for the business acumen of this family and a few of the older children were destined to carry on the family legacy.

He spoke to me one day and my heart melted when he offered to take me to school on their private school bus. The bus passed my house every morning at 5 o'clock. Why was I so willing to get ready for 5 a.m. to get on a bus to get to school two hours before classes started? There was someone on that bus who attracted my attention and whom I was eager to see. Off I would go cheerily very early each morning. In keeping with the religious practices of the young man's family, the women who attended the school were not allowed to adorn their features in any way, for example, they could not straighten their hair or wear high fashion, make-up or jewelry. In other words, de-emphasize the external and pay attention to spiritual growth and development. I decided that I would discreetly conform to those rules to make an impression on the young man and his family. I was on a mission.

Although the distance between Grange Hill and Savanna-la-Mar where Manning's was located, was only 14.1km (around 9 miles), in those days, the country roads were destined to slow things down. On the bus, we had a daily ritual where we engaged in lots of chatter and laughter. These were happy times for me and they broke the everyday monotony of life at home. I was smitten.

I suddenly began to compare myself with the girls of mixed race who were students at his school and in his circle. They were naturally pretty, boasted good figures, and appeared more suited to his family's lifestyle and image than I perceived I did. I felt intimidated by these girls and my insecurities left me feeling that I didn't measure up again. That did not stop the insatiable desire I had to be in his presence. I was drawn to him, not just for his good looks, but he was well mannered and extremely respectful of his family's house rules and applied no pressure. He displayed the qualities of an honorable man. He had a great sense of humor and we would find ourselves laughing at the simplest, silliest things. My friend was a gentleman and only visited my home when my parents were present.

Once he completed high school, he migrated to study overseas before I did and other than a photograph and the occasional letter of his progress, we lost touch with each other. Eventually, I also migrated to the USA and because we lived in different states, our connection was aborted fairly quickly. There is a saying that "absence makes the heart grow fonder" but there should be an addendum that says, "absence can make the heart wander".

Parents are very intuitive and more observant of their children's actions than their children realize. My crush was obvious to my mother and while she observed my actions she never commented. One day unknown to me, she marched into the young man's dad's office to report what she perceived was brewing between two young people. Venetia demanded that this father deal harshly with his son as she felt he was influencing her daughter's behavior, preventing her from focusing on her studies. It was infatuation but it was not affecting my studies but I didn't have a good track record with my studies so I can imagine her fear was justified. The event that took place between our parents was only exposed several years later when both the young man and I happened to be home on holiday at the same time.

During his vacation, he came to visit. His impending visit was announced by his car rumbling up the long driveway to the house on the farm and I was thrilled to see him again. It was as though time stood still as we talked and laughed just like old times. He then shared the story about my mom confronting his dad and the painful result of that confirmation. He got the spanking of his life and couldn't sit comfortably for a few days. He said he had never been "chastised like that" ever. As he shared this story, he realized that I had not been told of the meeting that had taken place between our parents. His father cross-examined him most sternly to see if he thought he was a man, wooing and pursuing a young woman. At the first opportunity to confront my mom about the "lashes" the chap received, she flatly denied having had such a conversation. She, however, expressed shock that this young man's father had taken such a radical stand but there was a silent decree issued that there was to be no communication between these young people.

It was such a very innocent, platonic relationship but one never knows given different circumstances what may have occurred. Looking back, I can see that God had a plan for my life and He allowed me to go through some mazes, some valleys, climb some mountain tops but He knew I would land on my feet. I ran as hard and as fast as I could, trying to find my place on this planet but I had a heavenly Daddy who was standing firm on His promise to neither leave me nor forsake me. He would silently control the pathway from behind the scenes, that I would go this far and no further.

When I left high school, like many other young people, I wasn't sure what I wanted to do with the rest of my life. This was not an unusual position for a youngster at my age, but where did one begin the search? There seemed to be illusions of grandeur of who I wanted to be and what I wanted to accomplish, but those thoughts were quickly erased from my mind as pipe dreams. The emotional pressure was constant and real.

My first job on graduating from high school was with my Mom, Venetia at the local primary school for a year with a group of students who were the lost children of the neighborhood. I referred to them as "my opportunity class". I relished the idea of working with those kids. We did activities that were outside the box because before they came to school, they had to work the land, care for the animals, care for younger siblings, and a host of other tasks that should have been performed by their parents. Some days they would not make it to class and were very distressed that they had missed out on the day's activities. So, my job daily was to encourage them to attend whenever they could. They had no one to encourage them in life and they lived for the times they would spend with me at school. If they missed a class, they would come to see me and explain why they were late or absent. These kids had really hard lives and had labels attached to them because very few people stood still for long enough to hear about the struggles they had. They were whipped if they did not perform their assigned chores at home and they were disappointed if they did not get to school to see me, Miss Peggy.

Working with those children provided me with an opportunity to make a difference in someone's life. The reward from working with these underprivileged children was huge for me. When they were told that I was leaving and that our classes would end, they arrived at my house with baskets of food items like yams, potatoes, avocados, breadfruit, and fruits from their gardens. They were expressing such love in their way and this moved me to tears. Just the fact that someone had taken the time to pay attention to them and to say they were valued was all they needed. I think of them now and then and wonder what paths those children's lives have taken. Their faces are a blur to me now, but I pray that some were able to escape the curse of poverty that was the consequence of their family's status.

Working with these children also triggered throughout my life many questions about how we relate to one another. How many of us ever stop to think that people behave the way they do because of circumstances, past or present? Are we sensitive to their needs or judge them without knowing the facts? Do we profile people based on ethnicity, academic achievement, residence, financial status, lighter or darker skin, or even more trivial factors? When will we appreciate the fact that we are all created equal in the sight of God and that God has no favorites? He doesn't love Billy Graham any more than He loves you or me.

After the year at my mom's school, I worked in the city and saved for my upcoming trip to relocate in the U.S. Even though I had matriculated to study at Howard University, I continued to question my ability to succeed: Did I have the confidence to work hard and prove to myself that God had created me with the potential to do this? Did I know and believe that with God all things are possible? No one had validated me to the point that I felt I could and would succeed.

There was a new transition about to unfold and with little or no preparation for what an independent lifestyle as an adult would be like, my mother and I headed off to the US on a new adventure — for better or for worse.

The year that President John F. Kennedy died, our little Caribbean island nation mourned at the reality of his passing. As children, we had no knowledge of the implications worldwide, but we listened to conversations, watched the news reports and we became engrossed in the emotional climate that surrounded us. We automatically followed the lead of the adults who shared stories about his intervention in the release of Dr. Martin Luther King, his support for the Civil Rights movement in the 60s that had given him tremendous support from the black community. Years later whenever the question was posed about where you were when JFK was assassinated, most people could relate to the time, place and the effect the news had on them.

Chapter Two

New York

My mother insisted that I save from my meager earnings to purchase my airline ticket to make my first overseas trip and although my income was very small, it was with a buzz of excitement that I eagerly sacrificed other desires to accumulate the necessary funds. There was great anticipation about traveling and the thought of exploring new horizons, but also great trepidation about what would lie ahead. What would I expect from myself and what would my parents be expecting of me?! The pressure was building. I had learned a degree of independence at boarding school, but there, I had been in a controlled environment where twenty-four-hour supervision was enforced when I was in residence. Now, there was more at stake. I would have to learn how to navigate life in a new country, find myself a job, continue with my education, foster new relationships and I would have to be the sole provider who made her own decisions about her future. I was for the first time – flying solo.

As the planes arriving from all over the world waited their turn in the lineup, they would taxi slowly on approach to the airport. The air traffic controllers guided them to their gates and the ground crew helped them maneuver to the assigned gates for disembarkation of their passengers. I wanted to appear as a seasoned traveler, so I didn't look around gazing at people and fixtures and was thankful that the butterflies in my body did not expose the fact that I was scared and excited all in the same breath. I landed at John F. Kennedy Airport in New York City with my mother and that initial feeling of emancipation soon turned to fear and trembling. Here I was, a young woman with no street smarts, no concept of what to expect, no self-confidence, and now I was being thrown into the "bowels" of one of the largest cities in the world – known as the Big Apple, the city that never sleeps. The trip to my residence was an interesting one, with police cars' sirens bellowing in the air frequently and the streets alive with activity. I could hear the subway trains rumbling above and below the ground, taxi cabs and police car horns blared through intersections constantly, while bright lights that never seemed to dim, enveloped the concrete landscape.

For me, this was a vast difference from the little sedans cruising through insignificant neighborhoods and the tune of rhythmic tapping of the hooves of the donkey carts laden with goods in Jamaica. The taxi ride from JFK airport was overwhelming and for what seemed like many days after we arrived at my new residence in The Bronx to stay with my mom's friend, I would end up crying uncontrollably. My mom stayed in NYC for that first week and then I was left completely on my own to either free-fall or fly.

On my first day out, I noticed that several restaurants and bars were open 24 hours a day, taxi drivers roamed the streets looking for fares, the newspaper/magazine vendors were alert and ready for sales all day and all night. There were booths in the subway manned throughout the night to dispense tokens for the trains, security guards were visible in the subways, homeless people were seen bundled in alleyways and on street corners, wrapped in old clothes, pieces of cardboard or anything that could provide shelter to keep them warm. So new and unfamiliar were these sights, sounds, and smells.

I should have started a program that summer at Howard University in Washington DC, however, plans changed very quickly. The students were demanding changes to the curriculum to include more studies in African American history as well as pushing the administration to make changes concerning the disciplinary practices on campus. The fiery confrontation lasted for a while and as a result, I remained in NYC from a safe vantage point where I watched with great curiosity as the events unfolded. This was a transformative era where the slogan, "Say it loud, I Am Black and I'm Proud" became the mantra for black people who were determined to make their presence, positions, and voices heard. They were fighting for equality and trying to bring awareness to racial inequality. There were freedom songs that hit the airways and the streets. Fist pumping, colorful bandanas, military/camouflage attire, became more popular than before. Large afros, beards, beads, platform shoes, bell-bottomed pants, the emergence of tattoos, and an abundance of costume jewelry all became very fashionable. Outdoor concerts were fostering the hippie movement and a lifestyle that made room for all types of drugs to be dispensed covertly, while movements of flower power, freedom, and a sexual explosion evolved among the young people.

During that first week, my mother introduced me to members of her family and friends she had not seen for some time. I was immediately struck by how many people of all ages – male, female, young, and old were smoking, exhaling the smoke into the atmosphere. This was not a habit that was prevalent in my little hometown but occasionally one may have seen a few older folk with either a cigar or a pipe. Smoking I noticed was not limited to tobacco but included cannabis which could have been purchased on any corner, harvested in the privacy of peoples' homes or their high-rise apartments. I had not been exposed to the smell of the herb as a child growing up in Jamaica, but soon I became very familiar with its pungent odor, as there were those tenants who chose to smoke it within the confines of their private spaces. You could follow the trail to that particular apartment if you had an interest and I am sure you would have been welcomed to join the party. There was a growing use of harder drugs as well and one could see some young people whose bodies were pulverized by their habit, hungover in the subway stations, on the trains, and street corners. It was very difficult for me to observe the catastrophic effect that the drugs had on these people who were trying to mask some deep-seated pain in their lives.

I said goodbye to my Mom as she returned to our homeland and as for me, it was now full-on independence. The decision was made that I would not become a full-time student in Washington and that quickly, I would need to earn my income. I sent out applications to various institutions and was eventually offered a job with an insurance company in downtown Manhattan near the World Trade Center. I still have a vivid memory of getting off the train at the Worth Street subway station, pushing and shoving through a maze of people, and barely getting off the train before the doors closed. I then had to hustle – just like all the other passengers to get on the platform and out to the sidewalk promptly. I had placed the address of the office building in my purse but then I got caught up with the traffic of pedestrians and would circle the block several times before I finally realized I had passed the entrance to the building at least three times. Fear had set in that I was going to be late for my appointment and the beads of sweat had begun to form. At this time, I didn't have any substantial work experience, that would have qualified me for any job in the big city, but I knew I had to impress this employer. I didn't have a choice; the wheels were in motion and I just had to show up. I wish I could have picked up a phone and said, "Mom, I can't do this. I am struggling! I'm coming home."

I walked into the lobby of this high-rise building and had to check the directory to find the floor I needed. I then made my way over to the reception desk and was shaking like a leaf at the prospect of this interview. It was September and the weather was just beginning to change. Everything was on such a grand scale and I honestly felt hopelessly lost but I just had to put that brave face on, right? This insurance company handled claims for some of the largest corporations in the U.S. including major firms, such as the pharmaceutical and healthcare giant, Hoffmann-La Roche. My role was to join a team of file clerks whose job was to methodically place the thousands of claim forms into oversized containers on multiple shelves stacked from floor to ceiling. It was routine work, which paid me just enough to support my immediate financial needs, while I pursued my courses at the local community college.

After the interview, I had to find my way back to the correct subway station to get back to Queens, ensuring I was at the right end of the train to get out at the right exit close to my street. For those who have traveled on the subway in NYC, you will understand the importance of this. The beads of sweat began forming again and I was very nervous this time. "Lord please help me find my way safely" was a refrain I muttered quite frequently. Thankfully, I arrived safely and would repeat that cycle many times as I was offered the job and was to start working the following day!

As the weather changed very quickly from summer to fall and then to winter, it was a shock to my system to realize what being cold actually meant. I kept piling on the layers of clothes and spent as little time as was necessary outdoors. One particular day it was extremely cold – my pillow, along with the many layers of blankets on my bed – held me as their hostage. I decided that I wasn't going to go in to work that day. I would simply remain at home and without as much as a second thought, I didn't report to my company that I was either off sick or even offer some other excuse. When I arrived at the office the following day, I was admonished by the supervisor on duty that under no circumstance could I get away with that behavior and if I were a "no show" again – I would be looking for a new job. With that said, I took seriously my choice to work or not to work and reported for duty on time every day after that until I left the company. I knew to be a filing clerk with an insurance company and going to school in the evenings was not how I intended to spend the rest of my life. I needed a compass to help me navigate my way to achieve a goal, any goal at this stage. The truth is I spent way too much time looking back at what could have been, what should have been, and at my past failures and disappointments, rather than at the unique abilities that I possessed that would help me to carve out a great, new future for myself.

While becoming acclimatized to my new residence and job, I spotted this handsome, very suave boy, Ronnie, who lived next door and soon he became a distraction. He was one of two boys born in the U.S. of Guyanese parentage but was raised by a single parent from an early age. He was full of life, very intelligent, and very focused on his education while maintaining a very flirtatious persona. He introduced me to his soon-to-be ex-girlfriend who lived around the corner and it was clear that she did not think or assume the role of an ex. You could see Ronnie coming from a mile away as he had this bounce in his step and a warm, happy but mischievous smile, wetting his lips in what seemed like a sensual or seductive way. His lady friend continued to have expectations of him and he seemed to enjoy the idea of this young woman living in hope. We never dated in the traditional sense but I would go next door to enjoy a meal made in typical Guyanese style and listen to classical music and cool jazz. The dishes were usually family favorites and as it turned out he was quite a good cook. In Ronnie's home, the traditional West Indian food that was served was more familiar to me and also far more pleasing to the palate, and as such, I enjoyed my visits, especially when his Mama was home! He was very cultured, had a terrific sense of humor, and walked with a swagger; the way he sauntered down the street was common to the young men who thought they were in demand. I enjoyed the distraction!

The kitchen, as I have mentioned before, was not one of the rooms in my home that I gravitated towards, so food preparation was viewed by me as more of means to an end, rather than a pleasurable activity. During this period, I resided in the home of my mother's friend, an American lady, born and raised. Most often, she would serve well known American dishes like, heavily battered fried chicken, collard greens, chitlins, grits, ham hocks, all dishes that were very unfamiliar to me, and that I struggled to eat. I knew I had to be polite though and still try to eat what was on offer, as I didn't want to appear disrespectful to my hostess.

I remained in the home of my mother's friend for about one year but after a while, felt stifled and began looking for more suitable accommodation. I continued my studies at night and switched colleges to a location, which was far more conducive to my transportation needs.

I had a rude awakening on my first day at college when I was to discover the aggressive nature of some of the men I came in contact with. In those days I can remember arriving on the campus of Hunter College, when two African male students who seemed to be on a recruiting drive for women from any country, approached me. I gave them all the wrong phone numbers but they remained persistent and I became afraid of these escapades and their determination. It was almost as if I was being stalked.

Some students reported how uncomfortable this behavior made them feel, but I am not sure the administration could have controlled the situation.

I was introduced to a friend of my mom at one of the regular family Sunday lunches and discovered he and I were enrolled at the same college. He was also from one of the small Caribbean islands. We had good conversations at these family lunches, but I had no interest nor did I give him the impression that that may change. We happened to be leaving campus at the same time one afternoon when I stopped to gaze through the show window of a jewelry store nearby. The chap suggested that we go in and browse. Being so young and you know the adage of diamonds being a "girl's best friend" – it didn't take much persuasion to get me to walk in. He asked me what I liked and innocently I pointed to a necklace and pendant with a cluster of three petite diamonds. We had a fun time browsing there and in some other shops in the little shopping center before parting ways to our respective homes. Several days later, I had what seemed like a chance encounter with him, and he presented me with a beautifully wrapped package. I chose to open the package when I got home, only to discover the same necklace I had identified in the store along with something else that I had admired! I was shocked, to say the least. I made the effort to find him the next day when he proceeded to tell me that he returned to the store, purchased the necklace, and was in the process of acquiring wedding rings. He had to be mad!!! He was preparing to invite me to his homeland of Trinidad to introduce me to his parents as the woman he intended to marry. When I shared this scary story with my mother, she insisted that I return the gift immediately because it sent the wrong message. The young man would not accept the necklace and he lived in hope that maybe one day I would change my mind. Next semester, a new school!

Loneliness in this big city can be very overwhelming especially if there are no close relatives with whom you can spend time, bond, share day-to-day experiences, or even enjoy a warm and comforting meal. I look back on my life through those years and I can sing praises now that God truly loved and cared for me by keeping his finger on the pulse of my life since He had a different, bigger, and much better plan for me.

From the beginning of my move to New York, adjusting to the weather was particularly difficult, to say the least. The winter, along with its characteristic cold kept me literally on my toes or in some cases, landing on my backside. I can vividly remember one morning on my way to work and my first experience with snow flurries, which no one had bothered to prepare me for. I came down the steps of the two-story apartment, in a beautiful new pair of navy blue, leather, high heeled shoes, locked the door, then turned around, and from the first step I slipped and slid right down to the bottom of the stairs. There must have been at least ten steps. My books flew in one direction, my handbag in the other and when I looked up there was a small boy who was on his way to school, who stopped and asked me, "Are you ok Miss? Do you need some help?" Torn between pain and embarrassment, I quickly got up on my feet, told him that I was ok and hustled back to my apartment to put on the appropriate footwear. I was unprepared for the weather, its dress code, and the necessary protective gear. My hostess insisted I purchase a full-length leather coat, which was the popular outer garment of that era. She proceeded to purchase a mustard-colored one from her supplier, which was not my style and nor did it suit my very small 5'4" frame, weighing in at 108 lbs. fully clothed. She insisted that it was the best cover for me during the cold winter months, however, my personality, was back then, and still is now, not to offend, so I wore it occasionally, all the while searching for a better fitting, woolen coat that was more stylish, comfortable and warm. With all the thigh-high leggings, layers of inner garments, gloves, woolen hats, and scarves, I suffered in silence, but gradually I got into a rhythm that enabled me to handle that 'artic' weather. I was so accustomed to winters where sun, sea, coconut water, fresh tropical fruit, lazing around under the mango tree, and picking any low bearing fruit, were all a part of any normal day. That is by far a more desirable winter in any language.

I quietly moved out of this residence without telling Ronnie, my next-door neighbor that I was leaving. His mother was very protective of him and rightfully so because he was, as they would say, a good catch, so the young women were all on the prowl to attract his attention. They were very intentional in trying to entice him, to venture across the threshold, but his mama wasn't having any of it. She was ever watchful and a typical Caribbean mother with a purpose and an agenda for her boys.

Jamaican couple

My next move was to share a home with a young Jamaican couple. There were some, shall we say, interesting dynamics that emerged pretty quickly after I settled in. We all got along really well, shared our spaces and chores equally as agreed. My social life at this stage was very limited, but I was quite satisfied with the way things were. I had my independence, but still liked the idea of sharing space with others and not being completely alone in the great "Big Apple". At times, we joined together for meals, which were prepared Caribbean style by my hostess who loved to cook, a benefit I enjoyed.

I had noticed a pattern developing over time that the husband would insist that his wife did not wear makeup or shape her eyebrows; she was not supposed to have her hair chemically straightened and neither was she to have any fancy hairdos. She should remain completely *au natural* just the way he liked it, or so he said. There would be no fancy attire for her – just an ordinary, ultra-conservative image that would of course not attract other males. She never resisted but always complied with his rules and without argument. She was the submissive wife, just the way he wanted it. I was soon to discover, much to my horror, that he was living a double life. He was seeing someone else, outside the marriage, someone who had all the trappings and trimmings he didn't want for his wife! She was very fashionably dressed, well made-up, with the rings and things representing the complete opposite image of his wife. As I watched this disaster churning right in front of me, I felt a deep sense of sadness for his wife, who was clueless to her husband's antics.

The summers in New York City can be brutal with temperatures known to rise to as high as 104 degrees Fahrenheit. As such, while I occupied my private space in the apartment it was not unusual for me to sleep scantily dressed. It was late one hot summer night while I was sleeping in my room that I had the sense that someone was in the room with me. Do you ever get the feeling that someone is watching you? Well, this happened while I was sleeping. When I opened my eyes, the husband was standing in the doorway to my room, gazing at my barely covered body. I was so horrified at this sight and he too was shocked that he had been caught. I was in a daze and fear gripped my very being while I wondered how long had he been engaging in that behavior unbeknownst to me. These were people who I had grown accustomed to and whom I trusted. I had been very careful to remain respectful and allow them their privacy as I assumed, they would have done the same for me, so what was this all about? Once again, I knew it was time to find myself new accommodation and this time there was a sense of urgency to the search. I would leave no stone unturned over the next 48 hours.

There seemed to be a thread woven into the tapestry of my existence that predators would seek me out and make their sordid, unsolicited "intimate" advances that would always be promptly rebuked. Adopted seemed to have always been a theme in my life.

Maxine

I had to move quite quickly to find another apartment and soon found what seemed to be the ideal situation, to share an apartment with another young Caribbean woman. Maxine's parents were moving out of the state and had hoped to find her a roommate, so she wouldn't have to be on her own in this great big, scary world. The city was very fast-paced and young, single, vulnerable women would always be a target for all sorts of unhealthy situations.

Maxine was a beautiful, highly intelligent, creative, black woman, who was well on her way to graduating from the New York Fashion Institute when I met her. We got along wonderfully. She was the first black woman I had ever seen who made a fashion statement by cutting all of her hair off to wear a very low, boy-cut-style afro. With her prominent chiseled cheekbones and her flawless skin, she represented the young black generation beautifully, as a 'fashionista' of her time and her humility made her even more attractive.

Once I met her parents, they shared that as a result of a job attachment due to a career change, they had to relocate to another state. They were concerned with whether or not to move her, as she was well established in her academic career and they preferred not to uproot her from NYC. She was so close to completing her studies, that they were desperate for her to get a roommate that they would be comfortable with. As God would orchestrate it, I met their need and they met mine.

This was the beginning of a wonderful friendship. I left the insurance company at the end of my first year of employment once I was entitled to my first vacation. I started a job as a nursing assistant at a hospital downtown Manhattan working the night shift so that I could advance my education by enrolling in daytime classes. The arrangement was perfect for Maxine and me, as she would be at home at night while I was at work, so rarely were we in each other's space. In those days having come out of my strict family background, I wanted the best of both worlds. It seemed that because I was in one of the lowest-paid positions in the hospital, I was always assigned to work the weekends, so time and time again I would call in sick. I lacked discipline in those days because here I had the opportunity to do what I wanted to, with no parents hovering in the background, and yet I still felt trapped. It seemed that all of the best activities were happening at night when I was scheduled to work. I reasoned that since I was young I needed to enjoy my life and partying was part of that equation. There were no rules to live by so what was there to stop me doing my own thing?

During the time in this residence, a friend of Maxine came by one day and we all hung out together. Ricky was his name and he became a regular visitor to our home but he was Maxine's friend. He developed an interest in me but I refused his overtures, as his personal style seemed repulsive to me at the time. He had the largest afro, sported a full beard, and was a Marlboro smoker. He was always late when he came to visit us and that I found very annoying and disrespectful. I would continue to refuse his advances many times before finally laying down my ground rules, which were – to be clean-shaven, have a low haircut, i.e no large afro and punctuality was a must.

One evening, Ricky arrived at the apartment, and when I looked through the peephole of our door and didn't recognize the person on the other side of the door! When he announced himself and I opened the door, I almost fainted at the sight of this well-shaven man, with a low 'fro' and very clean cut. That to me was the indication of a man on a mission to win over a woman's heart.

My roommate, Maxine was a beautiful, black woman and I felt as though I lived in her shadow. Her features were so striking and "modelesque" that I couldn't even begin to imagine trying to measure up to her. Like most young women, a sense of inadequacy became something I identified with, even after a year of independent living in New York. She could have been featured on the cover of any magazine except that in those days it was not the politically correct thing for mainstream magazines to feature black women. Fortunately, with the emergence of magazines like Jet, Essence, and Ebony, amazingly smart and beautiful black women would finally go on to be showcased for all the world to see.

Sharing the apartment was perfect, as I've said; we occupied the accommodation at different times so we hardly saw each other. Maxine started dating a very handsome man from another country who appeared to be as suave as Sydney Poitier. He looked like a model. He was tall, dark, and handsome and spoke with a spellbinding foreign accent. His voice was magic to her ears and she was completely swept off her feet, not breathing long enough to even touch the ground. They spent lots of time together, especially while I was away from the house. He was always in her space but they never seemed to go out on dates, not to the movies or even for a meal, but whatever he did – he made her happy.

As her relationship developed with her guy, my relationship began slowly with my suitor but really without purpose or any actual long-term plan. We just seemed to meander our way through some interesting patterns of behavior but in my heart, I wasn't sure that it was what I really wanted. Loneliness, when you live in a big city, can cloud your mind and cause you to modify your standards to become more accepting of situations which under different circumstances you might reject. Did I know what I really wanted or was I just settling out of convenience because someone had made himself available to me and I had no one around to suggest otherwise? I wish there was someone around in those days to knock me across my head and say, "You don't have to settle!" There are so many of us who talk ourselves into relationships out of desperation, infatuation, or simply lust, hoping that things will work out because we desire romance so badly that we allow our minds to deceive us into thinking the other party does too. Unfortunately, that's not always the case.

Maxine's love affair continued to progress rapidly with her man and then the unpredictable happened. I got a frantic call from her one evening to say she had just discovered that she was pregnant. She had been feeling really ill and went to the doctor for what she thought was a routine check-up only to discover, much to her horror, that she was with child. It was more than a nightmare for her, as a young woman, not sure what she would do next or how she could possibly find a way to tell her parents. The disappointment of it all was too much for her to bear.

There were several things to consider at this critical time in her life but thank God I was there to support her – even if I didn't have the answers. I could only offer an ear, as I was none the wiser. She was still in school and being supported by her parents and she felt that there was no way to tell them of her plight. When she told her boyfriend, the expectant father, the same charismatic man who lavished her with all the attention, he suddenly became a stranger and was very quick to announce that she couldn't have the baby.

What we would soon discover was that he was married and lived in another borough with a wife and children. We would never have guessed that the rogue was a married man because after all, he had spent so many countless hours in our apartment, cooking, listening to music, hanging out, and romancing my friend. He insisted she have an abortion, which was illegal in NYC in those days and the risks involved were huge. How does one arrange to have an abortion in a State, where it is an illegal activity punishable by law and which would result in "quality time" in the lockup?

Maxine went out and did what I thought was unthinkable at the time. She had an abortion. How did she know where to go? With whom did she consult? I knew nothing about the abortion until I got a call from a hospital late at night saying that Maxine needed me to come urgently as she had a medical "situation". The administration/police were very interested to know who had carried out the abortion so they could prosecute. Of course, I could offer no assistance to them, as I knew nothing. In those days, there could have been criminal charges launched against persons caught committing what back then was considered a crime and was punishable by law. When she got home, she rested for a few weeks before she recovered from this most horrific ordeal. I was there to take care of her the best way I could, while the boyfriend disappeared to a place unknown. This was a very challenging time for both of us as the medical implications could have been very serious. Thank God she recovered and continued to live a normal, healthy, and successful life.

The long-term emotional impact of an abortion can be devastating for anyone and we were young and uninformed of the spiritual ramifications of such an action. She felt her whole world collapsing and became so distraught that she wanted to drop out of school, much to the horror of her parents. They, of course, had no idea what had transpired but they became very concerned about their daughter's lack of enthusiasm for life or even her education. They had invested so much in her and were convinced she was well on her way to major success. Why was she willing to give up everything? What had happened to cause this sudden change in her?

It took a while to convince her that she couldn't put her life on hold anymore for a predator whose selfish intentions were exposed. She finally agreed to stay the course and return to complete her studies. During these moments, one realizes how important it is to surround yourself with authentic people who have your best interest at heart. She was like a sister to me and I felt compelled to support her in any way I could. With only two semesters left to graduate with a promising career in the world of fashion design, she had to stay the course. It all paid off in the end, as she managed to establish herself as one of the leading wardrobe mistresses working on such Broadway productions as *The King and I* with Jul Brenner, honing her skills and ultimately carving a very successful future for herself. Maxine's remuneration was lucrative enough to allow her to work six months of the year and travel the other six. She knew she had a choice to either wallow in self-pity or stand up and be counted as one of the successful, creative women of her time and she made the sensible choice to renew her mind and soul. She knew success meant commitment and hard work and that she did.

With the passing of time, Maxine would resume her normal lifestyle, but unfortunately, she continued to make very bad choices with the men she came in to contact with. They viewed her as one of a group of young professional women who were so desperate for male companionship that they were willing to settle and they gave freely of their financial resources. They took advantage of her earning power to satisfy their own extravagant lifestyles, occupying expensive apartments in the city and driving luxury cars around town. We lost touch with each other over the years but I pray she finally had her epiphany and shed some of that baggage.

Angela Davis

There was a moment in the early 60s in the USA when the nation was thrown into turmoil overnight, as a young black woman named Angela Davis, who was born in Birmingham Alabama, became a prominent figure in the Breaking News stories. She grew up in an area predominantly occupied by black families whose homes were constantly attacked and even bombed by the Ku Klux Klan. That level of violence escalated and created perpetual fear in the lives of the people in several impoverished neighborhoods and after a while, Angela's mother, who had grown weary of the frequent near-misses, made the decision to relocate her family to New York City. Any parent would have considered the ramifications of such a drastic move but it proved to be the right decision and as a result, it enabled the furthering of her daughter's education.

Having had the opportunity to study in France and Germany, Angela excelled in her French studies and she became a household name, as the world was riveted by the escapades of this young black woman who had become notorious as the first chairman of the Black Panther Party. The party fought for equal rights and prison reform which affected mostly the black population. I was impressed by Angela's strength and determination to fight for what she and her movement believed in and I recognized that same strength (on a very different scale) in my mother. I have tremendous admiration for women with the fortitude to demand change for the betterment of their communities and their nations. They tend to act on their convictions and find ways to solicit the necessary resources needed to accomplish their goals. They are very intentional in their purpose. Growing up in a household with a strong woman who fought daily for her rights, taught me what it would take to be a catalyst for change.

I was captivated by these events in the 60s and 70s as they unfolded but was relieved at the end that a story had been told. I learned if nothing else, as did the rest of the world, the deep despair the black communities suffered by being marginalized, brutalized, and ostracized just for being black. Angela Davis was determined to see justice served, as she viewed it. Despite her best efforts, she spent approximately 16 months in prison while she attempted to claim her innocence in the courtroom. There were several acts of violence her movement was accused of, but most significantly, the kidnapping of Patty Hearst, the daughter of the founder of the Hearst Foundation.

Anxiety and fear gripped the nation – as it did me when numerous sightings were reported of the victim and the growing support for the radical group. There were no other stories on the air that commanded the attention of listeners as televisions were on full blast as soon as a sighting was announced and regardless of where you were you had to catch a glimpse at the closest television. The question on everyone's mind was how this group could outrun, outmaneuver the FBI and all other law enforcement agencies assigned to the case for so long. Patty Hearst was finally released safe and sound to her family and in the end, justice prevailed. After many years of being blacklisted, Angela Davis was able to redeem herself and later reinstated as an influential professor at Berkeley University in the USA.

Ricky

My friend Maxine was fully engaged in her workload and I was now tip-toeing into a relationship. Once I agreed to date Maxine's friend who had now cleaned up his image, it was a life of constant partying on my days off. My compass was directed to wherever the action was, so the weekends were for partying, calling in sick from work, or not showing up to work at all. There was this internal conflict, knowing that I needed to earn money to sustain my living expenses, but at the same time trying to juggle those crazy hours at work to allow for playtime.

On weekends, it would be dancing at the clubs all night, enjoying my drink of choice – Brandy Alexander – and having friends over at 4 am for breakfast. I was the world's worst cook but wanted to impress my friends so much that I decided one morning that I was going to make Jamaican dumplings. I bought the flour, added all the ingredients into a bowl, and proceeded to put the water to boil. Once the water came to a full boil, I carefully rolled the batter into tiny balls and dropped them one at a time in the pot. When I returned to check on the pot I realized that the dumplings were floating at the top of the pot. I was horrified at the sight and checked the bag with the flour only to discover that I had purchased self-rising flour and I had also added baking powder to the dry ingredients!

Embarrassment took hold of me and I threw the dumplings into the garbage before anyone in the house could have a good laugh at my expense.

There was never a weekend that my suitor and I were not on the road going somewhere. We made several trips to see friends in Toronto leaving NYC after the rush hour some Friday nights just to enjoy a good party. We would return to NYC at 7 am Monday, just in time to shower, change, and get to work at the bank at 9 am. Several cups of coffee later I was on a count-down to see how close we were to closing time. We lived a very carefree life in those days and didn't stop to consider any consequences of our actions except to convince ourselves that we were young.

On one occasion we rented a Mark 3 vehicle and took off, just the two of us, to a fete in Toronto. It was late one Friday evening and up ahead was a long stretch of highway with nothing interesting to see most of the way. There was very little traffic with the exception of the large 18-wheelers that passed you as though you were motionless. We listened to cool jazz and chatted incessantly about what we intended to do once we arrived. It was an eight-hour trip and about five hours into our journey, we heard police sirens blaring in the distance but gradually getting louder. We suddenly realized that it was a police car indicating that we should pull over. We responded immediately and were told that we had exceeded the speed limit and had to report to the highway court promptly.

We followed the policeman to the court a few yards away and were fined some outrageous amount that we could not pay. We were not allowed to leave until the money was paid so we called our friends in Toronto who took the three-hour drive to meet us and pay the fine. Needless to say, it was a very costly trip but that didn't deter us from other adventures. There was no repeat performance on the return journey.

Ricky's mother was initially very thrilled he had met a woman who had influenced him to clean up his image. When I was introduced to her the reception was far from what I expected. Here I was, an average, dark-skinned woman who spoke the Queen's English, was cultured, polished, and polite; but clearly not what she had envisioned or was accustomed to. She didn't attempt to hide her disappointment and it was soon obvious to me that she would have preferred her son to date a woman of lighter complexion, with straight or curly hair. There was and still is a stigma among some, that light-skinned women (called "red women" in Caribbean parlance) were always a better choice, partly because it was assumed that those women would produce "beautiful" children. She was determined that her son was to marry such a woman and it didn't matter if the woman had the mouth of a pirate or not. Ricky became enamored with one such woman and found himself in a predicament trying to decide to whom he should commit; the woman his mother thought was better suited for him or the simple, generous, cultured woman he had come to know and love.

I knew nothing of the struggle he was having at the time until his mother revealed to me that he met someone else whom she felt suited him more. She may have been right by that, but I was too young, naive, and inexperienced to know how to extract myself from the situation.

Since childhood, I was exposed to seeing black women measured and marginalized but to be placed in a competition like this was unexpected at such a young age. I was compared with someone who was tall, lean, light-skinned, long, flowing soft hair, the ideal candidate as far as this mother was concerned. The power that some of these women wielded was, and is still, an interesting dynamic even today when one observes how some men respond to fairer-skinned women. So entrenched is this "complexion complex", that skin bleaching has become a phenomenon even in some very poor districts in my own country.

Our relationship continued to develop despite the interference and one afternoon, we took off to visit a relative who resided in Queens, one of the Boroughs in New York City, when we had a very strange encounter. We were traveling at the designated speed limit through the neighborhood and as soon as we made a turn at an intersection, we heard police sirens behind us. We responded swiftly, pulled over quickly and two police officers hopped out of their vehicle with guns drawn and demanded that the driver get out with hands raised, to turn around and place his hands on the car. We were shocked, to say the least. The officer said we had driven through a stop sign and so they were issuing a traffic ticket. If that were the case, why then the need to have guns drawn? We never got an explanation and dared not ask a question. There were certain neighborhoods in the city that black people were not expected to be venturing into and could be stopped at any time by the authorities even if they lived there. The police patrolled the areas, they questioned anyone they considered "suspicious" and there were times when men were arrested purely on suspicion even though no crime was committed. This was the 1970s.

Ricky and I had a very active social life and several unusual events transpired in those very early months of getting to know each other. There were always people around with schemes and ideas they wanted to lure you into and I had my share. One evening we were at a local club just listening to some music when a man introduced himself to me as a producer/ photographer of a magazine. He didn't say what type of magazine nor did I ask but he suggested that I audition for his magazine to possibly become one of his print models. I was flattered but opted to decline the offer and politely walked away from that conversation, giggling. I took his number pretending to be interested but never called. My gentleman in tow was not impressed and totally rejected the idea, which sealed the deal that it wasn't happening. He was extremely jealous anyway so his borders were re-enforced. Who knows where that invitation could have transitioned to a life of decadence, sold to the highest bidder, prostitution, or even drug addiction?

Life with Ricky was tumultuous. He was so misguided, insecure, too carefree, very controlled by his mother, incapable of making smart decisions, and had no goals for a future. He was certainly not a man on a mission for a better quality of life. He was totally at the mercy of his mother and as often as she dictated, he wanted nothing more than to please her, risking everything else to accomplish that purpose. No decisions were made without her approval and she was the commander and controller.

Things changed the summer after we met when I became pregnant and was thrown into a whirlwind of emotions. What would I do with myself?! Already I felt my mother was not proud of my non-accomplishments so how do I now call home and say, "Guess what Mom, I am pregnant." Out of sheer desperation, I contemplated having an abortion simply because I couldn't imagine how I could support a child when I could hardly take care of myself. I didn't even have the funds to have an abortion and was challenged with the emotion of wanting to have my baby.

My partner wanted me to have the baby but I felt he was too unstable to be even considering this idea. We talked it through and after much deliberation, we discussed getting married to legitimize our relationship and move forward to share the responsibility of caring for our newborn.

There was always the lingering thought of abortion as an easy way out but having walked through the experience with my friend Maxine, I knew it was not an option. By now abortions had been legalized in NYC so one could easily have walked into any registered, local establishment and had the termination completed within a couple of hours.

To be married in NY State, both parties had to be 21 years old or have the written consent of their parents. As neither of us had reached that age, Ricky approached his mother to get the necessary permission but she flatly refused. I then had to muster the courage to tell my mother via snail mail. Of course, she was disappointed but she realized the deed was already done and miraculously she offered her unwavering support and consent for the marriage. My mother flew from Jamaica to NYC in the hope of trying to convince Ricky's mother, hoping that by speaking some wisdom into the ear of this supposedly mature, Cuban woman, she would consent. She still stubbornly resisted. Time was of the essence so we did some research and discovered that a few other states had more relaxed laws, so I flew to another state that allowed the marriage of 19-20-year-old youngsters but we couldn't make it happen there either. There were some clauses in their judicial system that were not favorable to us so we had no choice but to wait until we both turned 21 to get married.

My dad had by now relocated to New York City having completed his studies in the state of Indiana. He acquired a beautiful apartment in Brooklyn, on the 8th floor of a building that had spectacular views of rooftops and the city's skyline. When he first met Ricky, his reaction was priceless, really one for the ages, an Oscar-winning moment. He belted out without hesitation, "My daughter has a lot of nerve!" You see, Ricky stood tall at 6'4" and if he stood in front of me no one would see my tiny 5'4" frame fully hidden behind him. That summer I moved in with my dad and it was the best decision I could have made at that time in my life. It was a very precious time of bonding and healing while sharing some of the struggles I had experienced as a child living in the home with himself and Venetia. These were very mature conversations, just being able to give vent without being judged. My dad never spoke ill of my mom even though he would have had his own share of drama. It was a safe environment and he was very kind, gentle, and supportive during those months. There was nothing I needed that he didn't provide for me. During those years in

NYC, his plan was to earn adequate money to make a greater contribution (which was long overdue) to the household back home. This was a chance to prove himself worthy of the title, husband, and provider.

The pregnancy was uneventful and I was taken to Brooklyn Downtown hospital to deliver my first child. Oh, what pain we mothers have to bear. Returning home from the hospital and spending quality time with my dad was like every girl's dream. I was pampered and spoilt while he poured his energy into ensuring I had a good diet, rested, and all the while creating long-lasting, wonderful memories. He was always the gentleman and very discreet about how he defined the family dynamic. I knew he loved me through the process and was even more tender than I had ever seen him throughout the years we grew together as a family. I realized with time though that he was not particularly enamored with Ricky but he recognized my desire to be with him and released me to go to live with him after the baby was born. I moved with Ricky under his mother's roof, if one could imagine that. What were the chances of that even being a consideration? There were so many promises and I hung onto them with great expectations.

As a young woman trying to discover her identity, her value if any, her future, sift through her hopes and dreams, life was getting more confusing each day. It was a period of deception at the spiritual level where, if anyone showed me a little care and attention, I immediately felt special, which I hoped could develop into love or so I thought. There is such a thing as falling for the counterfeit and that is what I fell for. I wasn't able to discern how to evaluate the sincerity of these gestures, as my worldview was naïve and superficial.

I had no idea that there were such things as weapons of warfare being waged against me and that the intention of the adversary was that I should have self-destructed. There were early signs that the enemy was "temporarily" winning as I was losing myself in the palm of yet another, far more sinister dysfunctional family. But God had a bigger plan and fought for my safety and security and protected me against those who sought my demise. My heavenly father sent his angels to war for my soul and he determined that I would not be reduced to that of a lesser mortal enslaved in a cage. I was not created to survive in a state of mental disability by becoming a non-functioning victim of witchcraft.

If only I could have understood that back then, but God allowed that experience as part of my testimony. We do have and do make choices in our lives that will have a huge impact on our future and during those years I was totally oblivious to the violent streak that was well concealed in Ricky's mindset. Later in life, that experience would enable me to be empathetic to women who are going through the experience of physical and emotional abuse. I made the choice to stay and God allowed it. If only I could have seen the mountain-top experience God intended for me while I was in the valley, instead I went looking for answers "in the valley". It was as though I was saying; "Not now God, we can talk later."

I had no knowledge of the Cuban culture and the dominance mothers had over the lives of their children, but my mother-in-law was extremely possessive of all of hers. No one was good enough. She methodically and successfully destroyed all the relationships of four of her five children and only one escaped her venom and remained married for many years. I can clearly remember her calling Ricky at all hours of the day and night to run errands for her, whether or not it was convenient for him. Here was a mother who could not let go of her children, especially this son, whom she had full control over without any care or concern for his family. She believed wholeheartedly that there was a force (witchcraft) that would provide her with favor in everything and if it affected anyone else, *c'est la vie.*

There are people you will meet in life who have the ability to easily alter the trajectory of your journey. It is not easy as a youngster to discern who those people are, but the sooner one can make that discovery or can identify situations that are not compatible with your lifestyle, you can strengthen your resolve not fall prey to the coercion of others. Know who you are and stand firm on what you believe; in other words, be true to yourself.

There are several people on my journey who left their mark. My mother introduced me to a friend of hers who was a brilliant, creative, self-taught dressmaker. She lived as an illegal immigrant in the city and for many years she was constantly "looking over her shoulder" in the hope that she would not have been identified and deported. When I was introduced to her, she was "dating" a reputable, doctor who at the time, was married and resided at a very exclusive location in the Hamptons, New York. This location was and still is home for many well-known celebrities for their weekend getaways from the maddening crowd of the city. They would party, golf, go yachting, indulge in the best seafood, and enjoy each other's company. My mom's friend, however, was never invited to participate in any of those activities but rather, she had a designated rendezvous time once a week with this gentleman. They would start by meeting, early in the afternoon for a meal together at a fine dining restaurant, which was then followed by dessert in her apartment. As a reward at the end of each visit, he would leave an envelope with cash. She looked forward to her weekly visits and tried to lure me into this kind of lifestyle as she felt the extra cash could be very handy. That was not how I planned on living my life, so I promptly refused.

My contact with this lady became less frequent and my mother couldn't understand why I was isolating myself from her. After months of being chastised for not seeing the benefit of maintaining a good friendship with this woman, I had to enlighten my mother and watched her expression change as the truth was exposed. My mom made a conscious decision to maintain a friendship with the lady, but I walked away. I had no idea at the time how useful that connection would prove to be until later in life as unknown to me the lady had sustained a long-standing relationship with my husband.

While my baby grew well and was loved by everyone, the over-controlling mother-in-law's behavior took on greater meaning. She was determined to have her way and so I suffered under the dictatorship, with no voice, while I occupied my space in her home. During this time my life took a major nosedive when I discovered that my husband was drinking quite heavily and frequently smoking marijuana. He began exhibiting streaks of violence and on more than one occasion, hitting me in fits of unexplained rage with no regard for his strength. My face would be bruised and even though I shouted, hoping that his mother would hustle up the stairs to call a truce, there was no response from her. I couldn't fathom how a mother could be present in a home, hear her son physically abusing his partner, and not make any effort to intervene. There was not even a whisper from her or any attempt to help curtail this violence, but rather to pretend it wasn't happening. This behavior continued for several months and on one occasion I went to work with a pair of big, black sunglasses to cover the black eye. How could I think my work colleagues did not recognize what was happening to me? Still, no one asked, no one intervened and no one tried to help. I didn't just walk into a door or knock my face against the nightstand. Some people I am sure felt it was not their problem, or they were too scared to ask and didn't want to get involved. I looked back at those days and wondered about my childhood. I had never seen my parents have a physical fight. They quarreled and screamed at each other, rather, my mother screamed at my father more often than not. We got lashes with belts and brushes as children but nothing prepared me for the lifestyle of verbal and physical abuse I was now experiencing.

My friend Gail.

My American-born sister-in-law Gail is also a survivor of the harsh reality of a mother-in-law with no conscience. She not only endured the pain and anguish of being totally disrespected but also by God's grace, has been able to carve out a very successful career and livelihood. God has truly redeemed all that she lost and more. To her, I am eternally grateful for holding my hand when all seemed totally out of control.

Gail opened her home to my family so that we could occupy the apartment at the lower level of her house. She was educated, ambitious and she really spent time trying to offer the comfort I needed at the time. She worked tirelessly to build some structure in her home and to motivate her husband to be the successful businessman she thought he could be. She was a high achiever and a cheerleader any husband could wish for but like me endured the wrath and major stress from our mother-in-law who felt that we were not good enough for her sons and our complexion too dark to qualify for a position in her family. The irony was that this American woman was far more intelligent and ambitious than her son was. She was successful in her own right and was the driving force in the union. They had two children together before she too had to relocate from the state in order to carve her own niche and fulfill her goals and dreams. Angels truly walk among us and she was one of mine.

My life in this household lasted a bit longer than it should have, but I kept fooling myself into thinking that he really loved me. I endured this torture for a few more years thinking that after each episode and the subsequent apology, the gifts, the hugging, the caressing, that things would get better and he would change. After all, he said he loved me and I convinced myself that it was so because that is what I longed for. Funny thing with us humans is, there comes a time in your life when you know, that you know that you have had enough. That time finally came and I made a conscious decision to gather the funds I would need to transition into a new safe space. I devised a plan, which I proposed to my husband and he agreed that we should send our son to spend some time in my homeland with my parents so that we could reorganize our lives and try to make our marriage work.

It's sad but true that many people in abusive relationships allow themselves to be manipulated by the person who appears to have more power. The abused person often has very low self-esteem and as a result lacks the skills, strength, and courage to walk away. There are also those who are not abused physically but are emotionally crippled with fear of the unknown. There are those familiar yet agonizing thoughts: "How will I survive? Where will the funds come from to support me? I am afraid to venture out". We become stressed with having to finally make that decision. The idea that no one else would want to be with them, care for them, or love them because they have been brainwashed to believe that they are not worthy. They tell themselves that they are unattractive, unqualified, have no value, and low self-esteem becomes the accepted norm and mindset. Even when they are in a safe place, they feel invisible.

2nd pregnancy.

While this emotional and physical battle was raging in my life, I faced the reality that I was living very recklessly with a monster and found out I was again pregnant. This time I knew I had made a catastrophic mistake and could not manage life under those circumstances. Without hesitation, I enlisted the services of the local hospital to have an abortion. All the while I knew it was wrong but I felt compelled to take the risk. I cannot recall the excuse I gave that allowed me to go through this procedure but it all happened very quickly with the injection of a saline solution. Somehow my husband discovered what was happening and rushed to the hospital to try to prevent it, but it was too late. I couldn't imagine living in this abusive lifestyle for the long haul; I would not have survived.

Steve goes to Jamaica

Once the reality was faced head-on that there was not going to be another child, we were able to move past the abortion drama and decided there were some drastic changes that needed to take place. My husband relished the idea of getting the support for our son Steve, so the arrangements were made, the date set and off we went on this new adventure. My son was excited to make this trip with his mom, but my heart was aching at the thought of not being there for him. I could not imagine the change in my mother that she agreed to take and care for my son! She really had a nurturing spirit that fueled her existence and this was obvious when we arrived at the airport. My parents were anxiously awaiting the meet-and-greet of their first grandchild and their reaction was surprising and priceless.

We spent a wonderful time bonding with the family on this incredible, vast farm where the only noises were those of the birds, the crickets, and the wind whistling through the trees. Occasionally the dogs would bark or you might have heard the little public buses rumbling along, blowing their horns to announce their arrival in the villages away off in the distance. My sister with whom I grew up and who I will always love for her gentle spirit and calming nature, still lived at home at the time and was happy to have a little one to care for who would provide some entertainment and curb her evenings of boredom. My son was just two years old at the time and bonded very quickly with the family. Just to be outdoors, enjoy nature at its best, play with the animals in close proximity was love overload. He was spoilt during his short sojourn as everyone indulged him in all sorts of activities to satisfy his curious spirit and sense of adventure.

When the time came for me to return to the US, I had to conceal my emotion so it was not obvious to my son. Leaving him behind was one of the most difficult decisions I have ever had to make, but I needed to rescue myself. He was and still is a loving, gentle individual with a big, beautiful smile. He loved to give tender little hugs, which made you feel special. I had to compose myself on the day of my departure as I didn't know how to say goodbye to him. I had to sneak away so I wouldn't have to see his tears and feel his little heart, tugging for the embrace of his mother. I felt so guilty about leaving him behind but my life was in shambles and I needed to find myself and purpose while trying not to impose that level of trauma on him.

As you will discover this was a cycle that was repeating itself in my family. It would seem to be a generational curse but what could I have done differently given the circumstance? Would my son feel abandoned? Although it was not an adoption, it was still the reality of handing over a child to someone who had rescued a child before. My son was happy on that beautiful farm with his grandparents and his aunt so now it was time to put my life in order.

I knew I needed not only to make a move mentally but also to move physically. It was not easy to convince my husband that the game was over. It was a 'you love me so you can't leave me' struggle but my 'aha' moment had come. There comes a time in everyone's life where you must think of yourself and what is meaningful to you as an individual. If you are unhealthy mentally, emotionally, and physically, everything and everyone around you suffers. A new me was emerging and I finally felt a sense of freedom from harm and danger and desperate to get my life back in order. Before long, I found my ideal apartment, walking distance from the subway, and in a central location with a large shopping center two blocks away from my residence.

The phone calls from my ex became persistent; more frequent and desperate in an attempt to restore the relationship and so he kept begging for us to talk about things. The state of loneliness began to raise its ugly head and foolishly, I allowed him to visit on occasion and listened to all his promises that he had changed and we could have a wonderful life together. When you have been abused and were not privileged to have counseling to strengthen your resolve to keep moving, you can succumb to moments of weakness. My life at this stage was on a steady incline and I was regaining some confidence and practicing my interior decorating skills, which had been dormant. The separation had created the time I needed away from this man and each day felt better than the day before especially because I could return to my home at the end of the day and feel safe.

When his overtures didn't work, his mother started calling me more often than she ever had, asking if she could to see me. I agreed to see her against my better judgment. She offered to renovate her home so her son and I could have our own quarters and begged that I take him back as he was on a rapid downward spiral. He was living in a section of her home, his alcohol consumption was totally out of control and she thought there might have been other drugs on his list. He seemed to have been consuming a significant amount of unknown substances and was destroying his body and his mind. She told me that she had checked various parts of the house and that she had found numerous, empty bottles of various types of alcohol which he had consumed in a relatively short period of time.

I informed her in the most polite way that I was sorry to hear of his plight but my negative response was not what she wanted to hear. I was quick to remind her that he had already destroyed several years of my youth and I was no longer prepared to endure that lifestyle of torture. I needed to make a success of my life and being with him was not the path that would take me there. I was surprisingly very firm with her much to her surprise but reminded her that I had never been her first choice for her son so why now? When I told her that I had been exposed to arguing and shouting in my home as a child but the level of brutality I had suffered in her home and in her presence was totally foreign and unacceptable, she squirmed but had no rebuttal for those comments.

Through this period of turmoil, she reported to me that her son had lost an excessive amount of weight and I think she was scared that he would have died of a disease or committed suicide. None of her pleas had an impact on me as she hoped. I knew I had no choice but to keep moving in a direction that did not include this family. My response was the same and again still not received very well. That was the beginning of a new onslaught on my person and my life.

His mother had taken up the charge of calling persistently and seemed desperate to persuade me, pretending she had not heard my decision. There were times I felt I was being stalked, causing me to be looking over my shoulders on the street and in the subway. I was very proud of the fact that I was finally able to fend off his overtures and not to be enticed into harm's way once more. God was clearly on my side.

There were some dark days to follow. I would go through a period of depression after the breakup especially as the winter months approached and I suddenly felt so alone. Some of my own fears of feeling unworthy, unattractive, not valued caused some of my old struggles to overtake me. When I walked through the streets, traveled on the subway, I gazed into the faces of other people to try to read their minds solely based on their expressions. What did they see in my face? Did evidence of the pain in my mind and my heart appear on my face? Did they see the result of a failed relationship and that no one would be interested in me? Could they see the loneliness in my face? Would they care or reject me because of my flat nose and small ankles? It's amazing that as women we have this capacity to focus on every single detail we consider negative because of what people have said or what the commercials suggest that beauty and success should look like. This added pressure could only result in a person suffering from an inferior complex, stifling their full potential. I believe I created a façade and even thought that I wore my mask well.

No one could see my pain, as everyone was too busy dealing with their own stuff and trying to navigate through their own spaces, hiding their own scars behind their own masks. It was really about the survival of the fittest at whatever cost. People were just trying to make ends meet, trying to hang on to their own relationships, sheltering from their own storms, growing in their spaces, learning, or hopefully living their dreams. They had no time to stop and say to me, "Hey, I see the sadness and pain in your eyes; how can I help?"

I wasn't the only one in my circle struggling with issues, but most were too proud to share theirs. Let's just pretend that the walls around me are not falling, and then I would appear to be successful. There were a few in safe spaces but many were going through tumultuous times during that season. I was introduced to a young woman whose husband had been deployed to serve in the war. This was a season when young men in the US were drafted to serve in one of the armed services as long as they satisfied the required screening tests. Other than mental or physical limitations, there were only a few exceptions, like that of religious affiliations. This young lady was pretty, sophisticated, elegant, and determined to acquire the finer things in life. All of us young women wanted the ideal man who could support us financially but some wanted that more than others. She had met this very handsome man who stood at about 5'9". He was tall and could have graced the cover of any GQ magazine. He had dark hair, a thick black mustache, and a very charming personality. They seemed well suited for each other, but things changed dramatically after he was drafted. His tour of duty spanned many months and he suffered like a lot of veterans, returning home damaged emotionally and mentally having served as a soldier in Vietnam, a war that claimed many fatalities. He really had a hard time readjusting to normal civilian life and as a result, my friend struggled to maintain a basic lifestyle, but thankfully with the support of friends and family, she made it through. Her husband's behavior patterns became very erratic and in time that would become progressively worse. He wasn't violent but became more irresponsible, more isolated, leaving home for days on end without an explanation. When he returned home his silence was deafening. I supported my friend as best as I could during many tearful nights as she struggled to ensure the best life for her young daughter.

The Vietnam War caused incredible, irreparable, physical, and psychological damage to a lot of the soldiers who served, and several endured mental and emotional issues long after they returned home. PTSD is how it is now defined but financially the families suffered significantly in the aftermath as well, because the compensation they deserved was very slow in coming and that put a huge strain on many relationships. My friend felt the full brunt of the damage not only for her daily needs but her inability to continue to live that certain lifestyle that she had grown accustomed to. It took a few years for my friend, but she came out on the other side.

I was never extravagant in my spending and knew that I had to be careful and to exercise wisdom, knowing that I had no one else to rely upon for financial support but myself. It has always been important for me to support my friends in their trying times as best as one could if only to lend an ear, offer that shoulder to lean on, or even share a word of encouragement. To stay focused, I realized that I had to block the temptation of the well crafted and clever marketing tools suggested by commercials, to influence viewers into unrealistic spending practices. Some young women succumbed to the temptation and became obsessed with shopping in stores that were clearly way above their income bracket.

A clever marketing strategy for some of the large department stores like Macys, Bloomingdales, Lord & Taylor and Saks Fifth Avenue was to easily trap customers by offering store credit cards persons had not applied for, to lure them in. The ladies needed to be accessorized with the Gucci or Fendi bags, which seemed to be a major accomplishment in those days. I never craved the latest designer gear, to be seen at the finest restaurants, to see the latest shows on Broadway, and have exotic vacations, as those activities were not in my budget. I enjoyed the simple life.

I realized back then that I was not as easily influenced by the people around me to engage in a lifestyle I couldn't afford, just to feel equal. There were many lessons that my childhood had prepared me for and as much as I rebelled as a youngster and considered the restrictions inhumane, I had seen enough modeled about finances to make smart decisions and adopt lifestyle behavior patterns that may have saved me from bankruptcy. Seeds of wisdom had been planted very early in my life and it all made sense as life evolved. The years under Venetia's rule did have some positive impact after all, as the Bible says, "All things work together for the good of those who love the Lord and are called according to His purpose." I believe back then I was called to His purpose but was not aware of it.

I watched as young women were lured into excessive spending habits and forced to hide from the creditors and block their phone calls. Most young, single women desired to have men in their lives who are accomplished with successful businesses, secure assets, were kind and generous and who could easily provide for them. They wanted all the trappings of the good life and it would even be better if they didn't have to work for it. The hope was for that knight in shining armor who would come along, sweep them off their feet and place them in a house with the white picket fence. I felt as though I was living in a parallel universe back then, not ever aspiring for many of those things.

The Anglican priest.

While my creative juices were flowing again, I felt it was time to give attention to my spiritual and interior designer focus. I made a decision to return to my Anglican roots and found a church in my new neighborhood just two blocks away from my apartment. The idea was to become more involved and I offered my services to work with the children who frequently attended. I reasoned it was time to try to make a difference in someone else's life in an attempt at self-healing and worth. I dutifully signed the guest book at the entrance on my first visit to the church and later that day received a phone call welcoming me as a visitor. Within a few days, I got another call but this time from the resident priest, personally welcoming me to his parish and asking if I worked in the area. I innocently mentioned that I was employed by a company in lower Manhattan and gave him the name. That week he called my job to say he was in the area and could we meet for lunch! This took me completely by surprise and of course, without hesitation, I refused the invitation. Days later the doorbell in the lobby of my apartment building rang and when I responded it was the same priest who was inviting himself upstairs to my apartment. That was the end of my attendance at that church. I tried to evaluate exactly what was going on in my life with these men. Did I look desperate? What vibe was I giving off? Not only was this man a priest, but a husband and a father. Looking back I can see how cleverly the enemy tried to lure me into unfamiliar territory, but God knew and said no. All along God had a plan and was shielding me from the snare of the enemy however; I still made irresponsible choices that I would pay the price for many years later.

My school friend - Patsy

I unexpectedly connected with an old school mate who happened to live just a few blocks away. We stayed in touch often and she soon introduced me to her boyfriend and his best friend who had also become a friend of hers. She was dating this very handsome young man at the time who was years younger than she was, but age didn't matter as she was completely smitten by this man. He was often physically abusive to her, but she forgave him time and again and stayed with him anyway. She was just obsessed with this love of her life and nothing or no one could tell her otherwise.

Very late one night in the middle of winter, I heard the buzzer screeching from the lobby of my apartment building. I hopped out of bed to respond to the desperate alarm to hear my female friend frantically asking me to let her in. I buzzed her in immediately, and when she got to my apartment I noticed she was in her nightgown, with no shoes or a coat on and it was a cold winter's night. She fell on the couch and I was off to the kitchen to make her a hot drink. She told me that she had a fight with her man, he hit her a few times and she fled to the only place she thought would be safe. I have never understood why she would have had a second thought about going back to this man but that's the influence abusers have to capture the minds of their victims. I understood her plight and immediately went into care mode to assist her for the remainder of the night but first thing in the morning she took a taxi to the man's sister's home. It was her attempt to remain close to this man, to forgive him for his abusive behavior and not surprisingly before long, they reconciled and continued their relationship for years to come. With time I lost track of her and often wondered what life has been like for her.

While this turmoil was unveiling, I was introduced to Patsy's gentleman's best friend who was a male registered nurse. He was very charming, very tender, and generous. I had never met a male nurse before and was very curious to hear the stories of his daily adventures at work. We went out to dinner on a few occasions and after a party at a sister's house one night, he became too intoxicated to drive me home, so I got behind the wheel of his big black Mercedes Benz (with no driver's license) and drove back to my apartment. What a risk-taker I was. The next day I had a real headache trying to figure out what I had done. In that short time, I knew this man, he was very impressive showering me with flowers, chocolates, and jewelry. He had a plan. Ricky, on the other hand, was grieving the loss of there being any relationship and was finally coming to grips with the idea that there was no chance of reconciliation and he needed to move on.

My new-found companion felt very comfortable hanging out at my place and one day asked if I would mind him borrowing my house key so he could be there when I got home. Innocently I agreed, as he had been very kind to me up to that moment. When I got home from work earlier than expected one afternoon he announced that he had to go out on a mission. He had to "make a drop", he said. Of course, I had no clue what that meant. He opened the closet in my entrance hallway and took out one of the largest, black garbage bags you could find which was stuffed with marijuana leaves. I was shocked to discover that he was a courier for the drug and he was using my apartment to hide his stock. There are no words to describe the horror and terror that coursed through my veins and to think of the possible consequences of his actions and the risk to me. That was such a wakeup call for me. The door lock was changed and his visits ended with immediate effect. Again, I can only say God was determined that I would not be swept away in this valley of the shadow of death and established the protection I needed to avoid a disastrous future.

My nature is to nurture people who are experiencing difficulty and so I often became the sidebar counselor trying to help everyone through hard times. I would walk through the pain with them and be their champion until they were strong enough to once again stand. With my own events as they were unfolding daily, my body and mind collapsed under the pressure I placed on myself. Not only was I having my own identity crisis for all the years I had been taking on other people's drama, but soon I also found myself having a meltdown and had to be hospitalized. I was conscious of my surroundings and knew what was happening but had no control over my emotions or my actions. While I was there, I looked around at the patients to see what I could identify with, in them; what did we have in common? Some were heavily sedated and appeared comatose. Some wandered around the ward aimlessly, others had to be strapped to their beds, some appeared normal and I knew I didn't belong there but had no control over the situation. I spent a couple of weeks in the hospital where I met with counselors who helped me to deal with my insecurities and my thoughts. It was just what I needed to come to grips with my emotional condition and to be able to appreciate that we all have issues/struggles in our lives that we are uncomfortable with, but need the correct tools to overcome and not be overwhelmed by them.

I had no idea that demonic activity was real and it would take many years for me to understand that the enemy's intention is to steal, kill and destroy and that I had definitely been marked for destruction in that season. God, however, had a different plan for my life. He has given each one of us gifts and talents and the enemy will certainly come against you in an attempt to thwart God's plan. But guess what? God is supreme, omnipotent, omniscient, and omnipresent and He will not only protect but will fight for us. Many are called but few are chosen. I thank God every day that He chose me. When I was released from the hospital, I relocated to a new apartment and started my life all over. This was not just a choice but a necessity.

Time began to heal my wounds and recovery was now possible. My son was being cared for by my family and I was able to gather my thoughts to see how I could put the pieces of the jigsaw puzzle of my life back together. My in-laws were stunned that I would have had the courage to pursue that sneaky end to the relationship. I believe that they saw in me a weak woman whom they could have easily manipulated all those years to satisfy their own devious desires. They thought they had found a lamb that they could lead to the slaughter and they tried.

Ricky goes to Jamaica

Ricky, in a final desperate attempt to win me back, flew to Jamaica, and not explaining to my parents what was actually going on brought my son back to NY. I am sure that his mother orchestrated the whole thing as she was a strategist who believed she had all the answers to every situation. While at work one day, Ricky called and asked me to stop by his house after work so he could show me something. Reluctantly, I agreed and went there that evening. With much fear and trepidation, I climbed the stairs to the front door. As I ascended a flight of about 10 steps, I looked up and saw my son at the top of the stairs. I am not sure how I managed not to faint on the spot. I gripped the banister so as not to fall in front of the child, who by now, I am sure, had no idea what was going on. This was the most deplorable effort to coerce or try to force me back into the relationship. In his rather disturbed and mangled mind, he hoped that would have convinced me to return to the matrimonial home. As much as I loved my son, there was no way I was going to return to that traumatic lifestyle. I had already decided that my life could have been at stake. The plans the family had for me did not materialize as they expected as I made another radical decision to let my son remain with his dad.

When the chips are down, one always feels that there is nowhere to go but home when you need to regroup. I gave up my apartment in Queens and returned to my family home on the Prospect Farm in Jamaica. That was a dramatic turn of events for me to return to my home country, but the plan was not to stay on the farm but to enroll at the university in the city. My parents had bought a farm of 112 acres in a remote part of the Westmoreland. The main house was situated on a hill and the views were different depending on the time of day. There was a river flowing through the center and if you were close enough you could hear the gentle gurgling of the ripples meandering through the shrubs. It was so remote and although we were connected to the public electrical supply there was no telephone service. Running water was supplied by tanks, which collected rainwater from the roof of the house into catchments to supply the household's needs. Hundreds of fruit trees of all varieties were easily accessible. One could go outside, reach out and pick navel oranges, tangerines, pull pineapples, pick any variety of mango, pink-centered grapefruits, star apples, or plums. Then there were the flowerbeds; the roses of different colors, gerberas, the ferns, the bougainvillea, the crotons, the June roses, the plumbago plants and so many more. We would stay up late to see the night-blooming cirrus, bloom one night of the year.

The river cascaded through the property and my father built a dam to create a waterfall where he would bathe every day. Each morning he strolled down to the river with his soap and towel in hand and would disappear for some time while he communed with nature. I ventured there on one occasion and once my toes touched the frigid water, I knew that this was my last experience. It was so serene with the foliage growing along the river, the river-stones smooth and clean and the air infused with the sweet fragrances of the varied lilies that were strewn along the riverbanks. It was such a picturesque image that has left me with fond memories of all those years ago.

On the farm we reared cows and chickens tended to by a faithful, committed overseer. He resided at a house at the entrance to the farm and as such he also served as a watchman and gate attendant to see who was coming and going. He was very good at his job and clearly had the patience to cope with my mom. She was extremely strict, bossy, and intolerant of certain behaviors and worth mentioning, she demanded to be respected at all times. Some people were afraid of her. Her command of the English language was impeccable and she could reduce your self-esteem to the lowest ebb in just one short phrase with little consideration for the impact her words had. She said what she felt and that was that.

We often had two housekeepers: one would do the cleaning and the laundry and the other the cooking. Even though my mom was a reasonably good cook, her busy lifestyle demanded that she sought help to maintain the household. In addition, she employed a full-time gardener/farmhand, to assist with the many garden beds and fruit trees on the farm, to help with the cattle and any other odd jobs as required around the house. A jack-of-all-trades was necessary at the time as my father wasn't much of a handyman.

There was very little theft in those days except for the odd item that the maid would consider her own, thinking it would not be missed. They didn't know how well my mom knew her things and therefore that maid would be gone in no time. There were the usual house pets, the cats and dogs around all the time, and they too enjoyed the spaces that allowed them to wander freely throughout the immediate property and in the house. The cats were quite happy to give birth in my sister's closet, but as I wasn't and still am not a cat lover, I think they knew better.

I was enjoying some childhood memories, like seeing the preservation of various pieces of antique furniture made from the mahogany, mahoe, lignum vitae trees that grew on the island. My favorite piece was a beautiful antique mahogany dresser in her bedroom in which she kept all her bits and pieces of jewelry. I reflected on the times when she was out I would sit on the stool and try on the pieces and just gaze at myself in the mirror. What were the thoughts going through my head? I have no idea. Did I want to be as strong as she appeared to be? I had never seen my mom cry. I had seen her very angry and throw things, destroy things, but not cry. Most of her anger was directed at my dad for not being the man she wanted him to be —strong, assertive, ambitious, committed, helpful on the farm, be more responsible with his money and prove to be more of a leader in the household. The irony is that she wanted that but she wouldn't give him room to become that person. She completely dominated him and all he would say was that he didn't respond because he wanted a quiet life. It was better if he didn't respond, as we all would have suffered the fall out from it. Nothing he said would have been acceptable to her, so, most times silence was his response.

While in this meditative state, I continued to come to grips with what my future should be. It was a very difficult decision to make, as there is no way under the sun I could envision myself returning to this remote lifestyle on a farm. I had become a city girl, who needed the bright lights, the fashion, the various types of cuisine, the television with multiple channels, and all the trappings that go with city living. My parents were very concerned as you can imagine and so my mom suggested that I spend some time with a very close friend of the family whom I had felt very close to for many years. On the flip side, life on a farm must be thrilling if you are a country girl. I loved the idea of having access to all the fresh fruit I could want by simply going outside and being able to pick my favorite from any tree at any time but the downside to this lifestyle was having water piped from an overhead tank, cold water showers, and no telecommunications to contact the world beyond the farm. Unless someone was brave enough to wind their way through the village up the steep incline to find you – you were on your own. Unfortunately, this was not going to be my reality.

The family friend - Leon

I grabbed the opportunity to register at the university to complete my studies and especially having the support of my parents was huge for me. The situation with my son was at the top of all our minds but it was a matter that could not have been easily resolved. It was complicated. My mom suggested while I had free time I could assist a family friend in his business. It seemed like a brilliant idea to me as I would earn a stipend to help support my next move. I had known of and visited this friend and his family over the years but up until that time had not really connected with them since I had been away but when we did meet we always had a good laugh. During our short conversations, I found him very easy to talk to and shared a lot of the issues I had endured, after all, he could have been family. Leon, as he was familiarly known, was a well-established psychologist with a successful practice. He had a good reputation as far as I was aware of in the community and I looked forward to working with him. It all seemed so civilized at the time because I saw him as a modern man with whom I could share some of my struggles in past relationships and the struggles with my mother. Basically, conversations I couldn't have had with my parents.

My first day in his office, which was surprisingly modest in its décor, went well, carrying out basic responsibilities like answering the phone, making calls, scheduling appointments, etc. A few days later, he suggested that we have lunch at a Chinese restaurant close by. Chinese food happens to be one of my favorite meals, so I was thrilled.

After a delicious meal, he announced that he had an appointment with a client so he suggested that I go with him. It was a lovely, sunny day and I gazed at the sea as we drove along the shore for about 20 minutes. What could have been better than this? Here I was in the tropics in the company of someone whose company I was beginning to enjoy, a father figure and a full stomach. He took a detour off the main road and drove past a small rum shop heading towards the beach. I began to wonder where this client lived, as there were no buildings beyond the rum shop. I became confused at that moment but could not have envisioned what was to happen next. Suddenly Leon took a sharp left turn and started driving into a densely, heavily vegetated brush where the car was almost totally submerged in trees and bush. I was alarmed and dumbfounded as to what exactly was happening. He turned the engine off and then proceeded to lean into my body, placing his hand on my left leg and grabbing my breast. To say I was shocked is not an adequate enough word to describe what I was sensing at that moment. I yelled at him to move away but to no avail. He continued to try to force himself on me but I continued to resist him. I then without hesitation dug my teeth into his right arm with all the strength and determination I could muster and was prepared to keep biting until he realized that I was not going to be one of his victims. I was 5'4" and weighed 108 lbs and knew I had to be brave and strong to fight against this rapist. During this force of will, his watch fell off his arm and he knew and recognized that I was not the weak little princess he expected who would fold under his advances. He gave up when he realized I was not giving up or giving in, so he decided to return to his position at the wheel, put the car in reverse and we headed back to civilization.

I was very pensive on the way back as we drove along the road, which was parallel to the sea. As we traveled mostly in silence, the few words he spoke were, "They say that people who love the sea are crazy, and I love the sea." As we were not related, having an "affair" with me he thought, was not a problem if it was consensual, but it, in this case, it was not. Here is a man I valued as an adult up to that time, with whom I had conversations about anything and everything. I was now amid a full-on conundrum, my mind was racing with mixed emotions and shocked by the fact that all along I was confiding in and entertaining a potential rapist, and who knows, there could well have been others.

I was a guest in his home, which he shared with his wife and children. That night we sat around the table as a "family", had dinner, chatted and he behaved normally. Later that night, I went off to bed in the guest room which I occupied, but my brain was working overtime, reflecting on the very bizarre activity of the day and could not make any sense of what had transpired. I felt betrayed, victimized, and shaken to the core. I must have dozed off before long; only to be rudely awakened by a physical assault with hands caressing my body determined to arouse a response. I woke immediately and demanded that unless the act stopped I would scream "rape!" loudly enough for the neighbors to hear. With that threat, this crazy man fled from the room. The bedroom door had no lock so I had to push the dressing table behind it to be sure I had no further sexual assault during the night.

The bell rang that breakfast was being served at the usual time the following morning, so we all assembled in the dining room. The housekeeper/cook had prepared one of the typical Jamaican breakfasts with lots of my favorite dishes and succulent fresh fruit from their garden. My host's wife had specialized in home economics and so she relished the idea of providing scrumptious meals for her family and guests. My host/family "friend" was also an ordained minister at his church, thanked the Lord for the meal, and proceeded to chit-chat while we ate. One could not have imagined the sequence of events that had taken place the day and night before, as everything appeared normal. Thankfully I was able to find refuge at a friend's house for two days following this incident. I made no contact with the family during that time, as I desperately needed to gather my thoughts. Who could I share my horrific experience with? My mother would not have understood and how could I even consider divulging to my hostess what evil deeds her husband was up to? I was disgusted by the whole experience, sick to my stomach, unable to eat, but also felt trapped like a caged animal. My soul was in turmoil and I ached inside. How could this be happening to me?

While I was having my misadventure, Ricky renewed his determination to fight for what he thought were his rights as a husband and so he remained in New York pleading for my return. I tried to process it all and knew that

I had to make a decision and quickly, for my safety and my future. What was the better of these two evils? At the time, I didn't dare to explain the truth of the situation to my mother as to my sudden need to flee from this household. There have been numerous stories of young people exposed to similar situations who because they were too afraid to fight would end up giving in to the predator or even causing themselves bodily harm. Some have lived with the shame of the experience for many years without any form of intervention to deliver them from the scourge of rape. I consider myself fortunate to have had the strength, will, and courage to put up a fight and push back against the aggressor. I thank God that it was not one of the scars I had to live with for the rest of my life.

I crashed with the school friend who asked no questions but allowed me the space to gather my thoughts desperate to make the right decision. After two days I returned to Leon's house, having made my decision that I was going to have to return to NYC. When I returned to the house, his wife chose to reprimand me for my disappearance as her husband was "frantic" that I had taken off and nobody knew where I had gone. I was always considered a little rebellious so I suppose I was being true to form in their eyes. When I announced that I would return to the US they were quite frankly outraged that I had made such a decision given the reasons I left in the first place and suggested that the proper thing to do was to let my parents know before I departed. They made no effort to hide how disappointed they were that I was not going to stay in Jamaica and complete my studies. I accepted their advice that it would be the right thing to inform my parents and I agreed to return to the farm which was a five-hour drive away, to break the news to them.

Leon insisted he would take me on the long journey. It was a drive that would take us through the countryside and some of the most amazing vistas most of which would be unseen by the tourists visiting the island. The rambling hills were vast and pronounced as though they were reaching for the stars. It was early morning and the dew was still on the ground. There were signs of laborers rising with the morning sun to greet their day before the intensity of the sun became overbearing. The vendors were busy getting stalls ready to display their produce in strategic ways to attract the passersby.

His offer was conditional. I informed him that I would not hesitate to fight again, more vigorously this time, if he dared to attempt to assault me in any way, form, or fashion. He agreed to be "a gentleman" and so I accepted the offer to make the journey to the country with him. Once again, I was gripped with fear at the prospect of having to tell my parents my plan as they had genuinely looked forward to having me back in their lives and to help me chart my new path. It was not an easy visit and one I wished dearly I didn't have to make but I had accepted the fact that it was the best thing for me to do given the circumstances. It is difficult to describe the scene as it unfolded in the presence of these two older folks. Amidst the tears, the harsh words, the inability to voice the truth, to expose the predator sitting so close to me; the idea that I had let them down again was truly heartbreaking for them. I was told that if this was my decision, I would be disowned, abandoned, and that it would be final. I was also told that I would not have their stamp of approval to return to NYC.

The conversation with my mom grew even more "interesting" as her fury escalated over my decision. I was ungrateful; I was self-destructive and other words that are even now too painful to repeat. It grieved me that I didn't have it in me to reveal the truth of the matter. How could I say, "Did you know Leon attempted to rape me and therefore I cannot stay?" She was so hurt by my decision that her thoughts and actions became irrational and she kept repeating that I would be disinherited and would not be listed in her will. I listened to her emotional rant, helpless and unable to defend myself, unable to look into the eyes of my attacker as he sat there in silence. Did he think I would change my mind? He had selfishly destroyed an opportunity for me to get my life back in order, having found hope after living in a very dark place. He had taken advantage of my pain and vulnerability and instead of offering compassion and refuge, he pounced like a wild animal seeking to conquer its prey. I have no idea what went through his mind in those moments but as painful as it was I nonetheless thanked my mother and father for all they had done for me. My father appeared motionless throughout this conversation and I have no recollection of anything he may have contributed to the conversation. It was not unusual for him to remain silent, he seemed frozen, he had no voice and if he did it was never loud enough. He was probably worried that anything he said would not have been received well by the lady of the house. His language of silence by then had become his coping mechanism. As I said my goodbyes I knew how hurt my parents were about my decision, but I also knew that the episode had to be kept as my secret and observing the perpetrator sitting silently across the table while listening to the dialog, is painful even on reflection. I had neither nerve nor courage to expose the situation for what it was. How would my mother have received it?

Even though my mother was an educator with all her academic achievements and years of experience as a social worker, she had no clue what was happening in the minds and lives of the children right there in her own home. She had not built a trusting and comfortable environment for my sister and me – where we could share openly about the things that were happening in our lives. When one becomes a parent, it becomes so very important to ensure there is an open line of communication between our children and ourselves as they are exposed to peer pressure and so many other influences in their environment. I am guilty of not taking enough time to stay close with my children to allow them to share personal, intimate experiences without me wanting to fix things. As I matured and decided that they were old enough to understand, I was able to share some of my challenges with them. This level of transparency has allowed me to foster more open and meaningful communication with them.

I became aware also, that there exists a group of reprobate men who consider themselves privileged enough to assume a free pass to conquer any woman they desire and decency and respect are irrelevant. My encounter with the predator, a trusted family friend, was no different. He wanted what he wanted and how dare I resist his overtures. God gave me the strength and resilience to push back while I was determined not to be taken advantage of.

Leon honored his word and we left my parent's house heading back to his house in the city. We retraced the journey through the hills and valleys and the tension was palpable with very few words spoken while we drove throughout the countryside. I was very somber, scared and a sense of hopelessness started to creep into my thoughts. The city was looming in the distance and I could feel the anxiety rising in me, my heart racing, palms sweating as it was action time once again. What do I do next with my life? One morning I got up and decided that was the day I would leave the island. The housekeeper had been told that if she discovered that I was planning to leave the house again, she was ordered to call Leon the moment she suspected I was getting ready to leave. Well, money talks all the time, so once I had confirmed the arrangements, I got dressed and booked the taxi. Fortunately, the housekeeper happily accepted the US currency I offered her to be quiet and she would make the call after my flight would have departed. This gave me enough time to escape with no interference.

I had no idea what awaited me when I returned to the big city because it seemed I was running away from one situation and into another unhealthy one. Out of the pot and into the fire, as the locals would say. It seemed like sheer brutality on either side of the ocean but how strong would I be to withstand it all? I knew I could pray but did I truly understand what that meant? Would God come through for me again and if so, when and how would I see the manifestation of that?

Returned to the U.SA.

I was separated from the in-laws but still received a string of consistent calls from my husband. On my return to the US, I began proceedings for a divorce and after repeated costly trips to the courthouse in my borough and my husband's decision not to show up, I was finally granted the divorce. There was no celebration but instead a sense of relief that a new chapter had turned in my life. All along I still yearned to be part of a family, where love was first and foremost in our lives. I wanted to have that older brother who could care for me and I hoped he would respond in a minute if I needed him. The desire was to have a nuclear family to wake up with, travel with, dine with, have fun together, and love.

HARLEM ....

My next move was to Manhattan and I settled into a lovely apartment on one of the safest, most rustic sections of Harlem and within walking distance of the City College of New York. I could breathe again! My life was falling into place – finally.

Walking alone can be the norm for a single person living in a big city like New York. The funny thing is that there are millions of people living in the city, some with whom you interact daily and yet it can be a cold and lonely place. How many of us have been in a room full of people and still felt lonely? In a big city like this one, that feeling is magnified and it becomes important for individuals to develop special interests to stay healthy mentally, emotionally, spiritually, and physically. I was at a place where I was finally taking more responsibility for my actions and making better choices. For the first time I could look into the mirror, see me and tell myself, you are going to make it. As the months passed, I could enjoy my one-bedroom apartment, later transferring into a three-bedroom apartment – again within walking distance of the subway.

I would periodically visit mediums who read tarot cards, tea leaves, crystal balls - cheap and easy. This seed had been planted as a child with Madam X and the crystal ball and so it continued. It meant finding a person who I thought would be able to advise me where my fortune was; what I was doing wrong or why my marriage didn't work; was there any chance I would meet a good man one day and I listened attentively to hear what they suggested was in my future? There was always a degree of skepticism as to what I heard and how much of it I deemed correct at the time. I allowed myself to be bamboozled and would frequently need to "check-in" to see what was the latest news flash concerning any situation I was involved in. I can distinctly remember one psychic telling me we should switch chairs, as she was not able to tell me anything I didn't already know. What did that mean? That was my lame attempt at being spiritually connected. It is recorded in the Bible that God is a jealous God and we should honor no other God but Him! It all seemed such an innocent act at the time.

I changed jobs many times during my early years while I lived in New York. I just didn't know what career I wanted to pursue. Several things filtered through my mind that seemed interesting and that could bring a sense of satisfaction emotionally and financially, but I lacked the courage to get the training I needed to venture into any of those areas with confidence. I needed to come to grips with the realization that I desired to be recognized by people, but in fact, that was not their role and most people were too busy trying to navigate their own purpose. To be loved and to feel loved is all I wanted more than anything else. If only I could find that someone who desired to be with me for me and not for what I could do or give.

Having survived an abusive marriage, the thought of entering into another partnership seemed way off in the distance. I had become somewhat cynical about relationships, putting up all the walls to prevent myself from engaging in anything short-term or uncommitted for the sake of companionship. The risk of getting hurt again was always on the top of my mind. I never wavered from my simple Christian beliefs during this time but on the other hand, neither did I engage in any practices that would have strengthened my faith or spiritual growth. Amid my drama, there must have been a shield of protection around me that prevented me from straying into a destructive lifestyle, such as addiction, gambling, or prostitution – all the easily available behaviors.

While I was with my husband, I had developed a taste for cigarettes from merely lighting his for him. The taste of Marlboro was not at all appealing but I continued to smoke them because it had become a cool look, giving the impression that you were a regular girl. I was so naïve that I did not know back then that there were people who were street smart and who could have easily injected normal cigarettes with lethal drugs. Thankfully that was not part of my story.

Post the divorce, I was granted full custody of my son who had returned from enjoying special moments with his grandparents on that peaceful Caribbean island. He had far more privileges there than I had when I was a child, but that lifestyle was about to change. My apartment was very spacious with plenty of room for my son to join me at just the right time. My lifestyle was very simple with few friends, but still no serious attempt to develop spiritually or to add regular attendance at a church as a part of my weekly activities. I think what was being modeled in the Christian communities was not attractive to me so instead of trying to draw closer to find God and build a relationship with Him to gain some direction in my life and my future – I stayed in that dark place looking for answers in all the wrong places.

The corner apartment was situated in the ideal location at the end of the corridor on the third floor of the building which had a front view of the tree-lined street and a tiny glimpse of some businesses from the east side.

This was the fourth borough I had resided in, in NYC as life began in the Bronx, then Brooklyn with my dad and finally Queens with a husband.

There were so many negative reports on Harlem but many people ignored some interesting facts about the district. It was predominantly occupied by Jews in the 19th century but later on, there was a great migration of African Americans and gradually the Jews moved out. To appreciate Harlem one would need to explore its deep roots and therefore recognize the value that this neighborhood has had especially to the entertainment industry. My experience of living in Harlem was one of seeing the tangible impact of the long history of crime, drugs, and violence but I was soon to learn there was so much more to discover. The neighborhood boasted some of the best intimate jazz clubs, a strong sense of the African-American heritage, and was home to many great restaurants with exceptional soul food. A major landmark was and still is, the iconic Apollo Theatre located on 125th Street, home to many entertainers and featured Top Billing for many who were already world-renowned artistes. The theater created a platform in the early years for mainly black artistes to sing, dance, and deliver comedic performances. Some of the legends known to have performed there were Ella Fitzgerald, James Brown, Richard Pryor, The Supremes, The Temptations. Michael Jackson, Stevie Wonder, Aretha Franklin, Steve Harvey just to name a few. If you were a talented artist and were allowed to perform at The Apollo, you knew you were on your way to becoming a star. This was also a forum where up-and-coming artistes were privileged to showcase and hone their craft under the tutelage of the masters in the field. There were numerous times when walking the streets near the Apollo, one would catch a glimpse of a celebrity fully clad in his or her costume, stepping out of a long, black stretch limousine and heading into the theater.

It seemed like another cultural shift for me – having lived in other quieter neighborhoods in New York. This neighborhood was always alive with activity – like the loud street vendors, jostling for your attention or men selling their oils and incense from their little square foldaway tables on the streets. On any given day you could easily bump into a young, clean-shaven Muslim man bedecked with his jacket and black bow tie, trying to engage anybody who would stop for a minute to listen as he tried to persuade them to listen to what he considered to be sound doctrine.

Some friends of mine were horrified to learn that I had moved there as it didn't appear to be an affluent neighborhood and it was also perceived as a dangerous address to have. Initially, I didn't mention the address for fear of unnecessary scrutiny; I just said I lived in Manhattan on the upper west side. That sounded grander. I enjoyed its diversity and of course the proximity to public transportation. The subway was two blocks away and there were public buses on every corner. There was a much larger population of blacks and lesser proportions of Hispanics and whites in my area. The businesses I frequented were mostly on the corner of the main street where the Colombian hairdresser provided the services of applying chemical relaxers and securing large plastic rollers to the hair of customers. There were peculiar odors that emanated from the salon depending on the chemicals that were being used on the various textures of hair, but no one complained. There was a shoe repair shop next door and another where one could purchase wooden masks of varying sizes, mostly imported from Haiti, artifacts depicting the African heritage. There was no shortage of locations to purchase oils and spices for cooking or hair products that were developed and sold specifically to the black population to soften and make the hair more manageable. I frequented that shop to buy the Dax and Bergamot hairdressings to improve the texture and condition of my very thick mane. A staple in the black communities was also the shoeshine man who took immense pride in polishing his customers' shoes with such passion that it became a regular stop for anyone who wanted that prim and proper, well-groomed look.

Food is one way the community integrated and I can't forget the smell of the crispy, deep-fried chicken coming from the cook shops in the area, served with a side of collard greens and cornbread. The smell and taste, were intoxicating and irresistible, making it difficult not to succumb to the craving that is evoked as you passed by. As a young woman growing up in a very proper household where table manners were essential, I could imagine how horrified my mother would have been to see me walking down the street chomping on a chicken leg or a slice of pizza with the melted cheese dripping down to my elbow. That's what freedom looked like.

There were many abandoned commercial and residential buildings around as those who had been able to carve a better life for themselves, opted to move to other boroughs or out of town, leaving behind a trail of despair, dust, and debris. Also, it was sad to see the human element of destruction of some of the young people, mostly male, who had succumbed to the scourge of illegal drugs or alcohol – laying wasted at the side of the road or begging for a dollar to buy something to eat. The majority of people coming out the subway just stepped passed them as though they were invisible or fixtures they needed to avoid. There was no expression of compassion towards them, including me, unfortunately. What could we do?

In the Caribbean, it is commonplace to be greeted by total strangers on any given day with a "Hello!", "Good morning" or "How are you?" and that often caught visitors by surprise. This was not the case in this big city. Everyone was hustling to get to their destination and certainly not interested in making polite conversation. In the apartment buildings I lived in for many years, I knew the names of only a handful of people who resided in the same multi-story complex. I would get an occasional nod as I went by, from the residents with whom I made eye contact in the foyer of the building or a wave if they recognized me as a familiar face. Passersby didn't engage you in conversation unless there was a problem, which affected all of us. They would barely grunt a good morning even if you saw them often and up close. My apartment was secure as most are in NYC, outfitted by the tenants with several heavy-duty locks to prevent unwanted visitors. I felt very safe and secure in that building so much so that I went to bed a few nights unknowingly leaving my keys hanging outside the door but thankful when my immediate neighbor would hand them back to me.

The sounds of the sirens and subway rumbling 24/7 were the ongoing background noise one lived with, in this city, but after a few months, it seemed not to matter. We can and do become acclimatized in a relatively short period to our environment.

After all the drama surrounding my son, we were happy to develop a routine that satisfied both our needs; and I had a great routine. When he left school, he could walk to our neighbor's, at a landmark residence on the corner of our street, at 72 Hamilton Terrace. This street is located in Hamilton Heights in Harlem, just around the corner from the home of the famous American statesman, Alexander Hamilton. Next door to the residence was a small museum that we often visited housing artifacts depicting the history of the neighborhood and the Hamilton legacy. There was a church that offered refuge for many people, most of whom were immigrants that needed help. I would collect my son after my day's work and immediately go into caregiver mode with the dinner, bath, and homework. His father didn't play much of a role in his life in those days but had visitation rights any weekend he wanted to spend time with him. Needless to say, my son spent more weekends with me than he did with his dad.

AMERICAN HEALTH FOUNDATION (AHF)

I managed to complete a course in medical assisting which proved very useful in my next job when I joined the team at **The American Health Foundation**. It would take a series of interviews before a decision was made and then I was appointed. After weeks of training sessions, my job description and standard operating procedures were finalized. It was a huge turning point in my life. Having worked in organizations before in positions I did not enjoy or where I hadn't achieved any measure of success, I joined a company where I felt gratified for the opportunity to learn and gain a peep into the window of the human psyche. Breaking old habits was far more challenging than I realized, as human nature is to settle and become comfortable in a place or situation, and deciding to change could take years. I have heard the expression that it is better to stay with the devil you know but that premise should be debunked as it is often the fear of change that causes us to be trapped in toxic situations, relationships, unhealthy eating, poor financial management, obsessive negative thinking, lack of self-control, unforgiveness and more.

I developed a friendship at AHF with one of my co-workers named Carl who moved from a small township upstate New York to the city. As different as our family history was, we enjoyed sharing about our upbringing, some moderately priced restaurants, and had some good laughs. He was very kind, caring, and a good listener. Within six months of my assignment, he decided to follow into the footsteps of some of his family members by joining the New York Police Department. On his recommendation, I was promoted to a senior member of the Health Counseling team. Although Carl had left the company, we continued to meet from time to time for lunch and talk about social issues, professional challenges, and the latest events in the lives of our families. There is nothing better than having a good friend with whom you can share your struggles and they still have your back. Carl was a white American and during our many outings, we were never subjected to any racial slurs, which was quite amazing for that era. Once I established with him that I had no romantic interest, he reluctantly accepted and agreed that we would remain friends. We could call on each other any time and that's how special platonic relationships should be. It is said that one cannot have a friendship with the opposite sex, but I believe that once the ground rules and boundaries are established, contacts are in a public place, conversations don't cross the line, it is possible and so it was with us.

During my tenure with the **AHF**, I finally began to discover who I was as a human being. There was a resident psychologist whose role on the project was to help each of us identify our strengths and weaknesses, external influences, and discuss methods of conflict resolution among other behavioral attributes. This level of training for the staff initially, prepared us all to be able to counsel and treat the participants in the program.

The training was extensive and intense. My job description as a medical technician included conducting stress testing, electrocardiograms, and venipuncture, measuring and recording basic vital signs and smoking cessation clinics. The transition into this role was quite easy and I looked forward to what each day had in store.

The AHF study was the first of its kind to be conducted in the US. The first requirement was to screen 10,000 men between the ages of 35-57 years old, in the New York City area, who were at a 10% risk of heart attacks. It was a voluntary program funded by the National Institute of Health. The incentive for the men was to have free annual check-ups with a qualified medical team of doctors, nurses, technicians, and counselors, so the response was great. The study was scheduled to span eight years with a group of 400 men in the study group and 400 in a control group. It took two years just to select the 800 candidates for the study and to ensure their availability to participate in the seven-year process. The team selected for the experimental group would be seen bi-monthly and the control group would be seen once per year.

The screening centers were set up in various neighborhoods; on college campuses, police precincts, and other specially selected locations across the city. The areas were selected to allow for easy access to the center for the participants due to the frequency of the required visits. The group was very diverse with blacks, Hispanics, whites, Italians – a true mixture of all ethnic groups. The behavior patterns among the blue-collar and white-collar participants were very similar as all the men wanted to achieve a measure of success; job security, to provide for their families, safety, and to be in good health. There were distinct differences we discovered as it related to some of the men in their effort or lack thereof, to discipline themselves to achieve success. When the initial screening was completed, we deduced that eating habits were the most difficult areas to change. Those who were determined, willing, and adhered to the guidelines to make the necessary changes became the stars of the program.

Once the participants had risk factors that were associated with heart disease such as; high blood pressure, high cholesterol; were overweight, and were smokers, they were eligible for the program. The change was not easy for most of these men and very early, through the required counseling sessions, we discovered how significant the impact of one's self-control, ethnic and cultural history, peer pressure, and lifestyle had on one's ability or desire to make the necessary changes.

We also saw first hand that old habits were very difficult to break or modify. The physiologist would schedule meetings with those participants who were struggling the most to make lasting change. There were many interesting characters who we came into contact with but one participant made a real impact on all of us when he announced that he struggled to make the necessary changes primarily because of his lifestyle. He informed us that he and his wife agreed to an open relationship, which meant that they could engage in intimate relationships with other people. With time the emotional and physical demands of this arrangement had proved to be too challenging for them and his marriage suffered as a result. He lost interest in the program, was desperate to salvage his marriage, but while he was determined to put the pieces of his life back together, a health plan was not of immediate importance. Interestingly enough he would brag about his ménage a trois in the group sessions and other participants appeared fascinated to learn more.

There were so many lessons I learned daily, listening to these men share openly about their childhood, which affected them in significant ways but also mirrored some of my own experiences. It would have been inappropriate to share my personal experiences with them but if only they knew the impact of some of those conversations on me. Some of these sessions helped me have a better understanding of some of my insecurities.

We conducted smoking cessation clinics daily, which I assisted with and advised them of the health benefits of not smoking. Some were taken to clinics where they were shown the before and after images of smokers vs. non-smokers. This, however, was not enough for some to quit right away. Even though we thought those were extreme measures to take, you could quite often hear, "I am not ready to quit". For the first six months, they had learned to recognize the triggers and put boundaries in place to counteract them, but the struggle for some was real and they felt as though they were drowning. I was proud of who remained firm, determined to conquer this battle. For them, success was guaranteed. Many businessmen traveled for work and needed greater contact to maintain their schedule so that service was also provided. There was a well-structured follow-up program, which was just as intense as walking though the in-house sessions. The same rules would apply; remove all ashtrays from their desks, homes and hotel rooms, and substitute the craving for the cigarette with fresh fruit or raw vegetables after meals. They were asked to avoid parties or friends who were habitual smokers or places where there would be a temptation to smoke, even if the activity was job-related. One fear most people had was the weight gain, a known side effect of quitting. A smoker develops an unconscious desire to frequently have something in their mouth so they needed to find a substitute.

In the early 70s, people were becoming more health-conscious and tobacco companies were required to put warning labels on cigarette packages. There was much more conversation in the public domain also about the effect of butter and eggs on cholesterol levels as well as salt on elevating blood pressure. The study was designed to see what the results would be if intervention took place early and regularly in those who were at high risk, so it was incumbent on us to keep encouraging the participants. There was a lot of emphasis on exercise as part of their daily routine;

walking a few extra steps, taking the stairs instead of the elevator, parking a little further than they needed to, etc.

While I was committed to the success of the program, I was very careful to conceal a regular activity, safeguarding my big secret, as I remained a cigarette smoker. At the end of the smoking cessation clinics, I would dash off to the ladies' room to enjoy a few puffs of my Marlboro. Of course, the chance of being caught was slim as the program was exclusively for men so they would not be barging into the ladies' room. After several years of this deception, I realized that I too had to put myself through the program, and I did! It happened on a winter's night when I discovered that I had one cigarette left in the box. I would take a puff and put it out, light up again until there was no more. The next morning, I had no cigarette to have with my coffee and suddenly remembered that I was on a mission to quit smoking. Every subway station in New York City has a kiosk that sells newspapers, candy, and cigarettes, so the temptation was all around. We were not allowed to smoke on the job for obvious reasons so that helped to reduce the temptation at least during the working hours. To achieve my goal, I had to remove all triggers – ashtrays, and matches from my home and monitor my activity with friends who smoked. After years of quitting I realized that I was suddenly repelled by the smell of cigarette smoke and its lingering odor in my surroundings.

As part of the training for this job, all staff needed to participate in counseling sessions for themselves, scheduled weekly. This was the first time I discovered much to my surprise that I was not the only one on the planet who had mental and emotional issues to overcome. What a relief to know that I was not alone. Everyone has some kind of skeleton in his or her closet that they prefer not to have exposed or they may not even recognize their need for help. We all make mistakes, make bad choices, we tell little white lies to get ourselves out of situations and sometimes even try to mimic the behavior of other people. We exalt ourselves to cover these flaws or cast blame on someone or some situations that we claim was responsible for our actions. It's a mindset we all easily adopt. It's where our comfort level lies. The counselor was able to tap into my past and identify circumstances that affected how I responded to situations. I was overwhelmed at some of the revelations but was also assured that so many people have had similar experiences and worse. Listening to some of the participants in the program brought tears to my eyes when they spoke about some of the secrets they kept for years; behavior they were not proud of, damage through childhood experiences and they never got the opportunity to benefit from counseling or deliverance. If only there wasn't the stigma associated with mental health counseling and treatment.

During my counseling sessions, I was reminded of many choices I made that resulted in a consistent pattern of failure and disappointment. My entire life was consumed with questions about how to navigate the hurdles as they presented themselves. I learned how easy it was to admire an individual who seemed to have achieved some measure of success but oblivious to the hurdles they had to jump over to get there. I have judged people based on what is visible to the naked eye, be it positive or negative, which is not a fair assessment of who they are. Were their decisions based on their interests or what others expected of them? Did they feel like failures or did they feel a sense of fulfillment? Several people have gifts and talents locked up inside and they had no opportunity to bring them to fruition. There were those persons who were pressured into certain careers, which they didn't feel satisfied in but felt compelled to stay the course. They are so many variables that affect our state of wellness.

I became even more empowered during this period of my life and accepted the fact that life will have lots of ups and downs but we need to be strong, to be grounded in something, and not someone to get us through. These were life lessons to ponder, but how easily we forget when adversity comes our way. Several of the men had low self-esteem and simply wanted to be valued by someone, anyone. I had not yet developed a deep personal relationship with God – He was still a foreign entity in my mind who I prayed to and who I hoped would work things out on my behalf – but He needed to respond sooner rather than later.

There were many nationalities and personalities on staff at AHF offering a great melting pot of styles and cultural interests. There was the young Jewish woman who desperately wanted to get married, there was the Slovenian woman who had her nose job and came to work with the bandages on her nose, and then there were those who surprised all of us by declaring they were homosexual. This was a reality of the 70s, where some people were trying to find themselves by experimenting with the latest drug of choice, as an avenue they hoped would get them the peace they longed for. I rarely socialized with the company personnel except for the occasional Friday night when a small group of us would go to the nearby restaurant for happy hour. You would order a drink and enjoy a full meal from the snacks that were served. The spread was extensive – from chicken wings to raw vegetables with dips, nuts, mini meatballs, crackers, cheese, and a variety of olives. Smoking was permitted in the restaurants in those days so it was a great outlet to be able to publicly enjoy a smoke with friends; a refreshing glass of wine and some snacks.

As I always had a special interest in being fashionably dressed, I eventually gave in to the designer choices and bought my first Gucci bag. I felt I deserved to show that I had "arrived" as a professional woman living in the big city. You were judged by your dress, your address, your vacation locations, the Broadway shows you saw and could brag about, and I felt that I was now on my way to being recognized as an achiever. It was my turn. I convinced myself that I was not trying to compete with anyone else but I was setting my standard of what was pleasing and attractive to me, or so I thought. On reflection, I was trying to fit in, make my own statement, and not to feel lesser than my peers. Up to this time, I was pretty much a loner, "standoff-ish", one may say, but the tide was turning and I was becoming more confident.

My desire to improve my image spilled over to my big son. I sauntered into the children's department of Saks Fifth Avenue to discover that I could provide him with quality clothing without overextending myself. Under normal circumstances, there was no way that I could have shopped in stores such as that. I realized that I had foolish pride to think that I didn't deserve to shop in those stores, failing to realize that there were opportunities to purchase garments at affordable prices but I had become intimidated by the labels of luxury designer brands not knowing that there were out of season collections, that were affordable. We donated bags of clothing to the Salvation Army which provided a collection service. This activity was also a good lesson to teach my son the meaning of sharing the items that were still in excellent condition to people in need. In addition to this humanitarian effort, it allowed me to clear my closet of things that were no longer fashionable, and thereby, I could acquire more stuff – every woman's dream activity.

At this time in my life, setting funds apart for my future was so far from my mind. I spent as I earned, so saving was only necessary if I was on a mission to do something special. There was no budget but I was controlled enough not to find myself in a state of bankruptcy. I took advantage of the store's layaway plans and adopted a very valuable lesson from a wealthy aunt whose philosophy was not to purchase items unless they were on sale. Just be patient and wait was her mantra; wise words from a millionaire.

One balmy summer afternoon as I was leaving work at the AHF located in the Ford Foundation building, across from the United Nations, I was hustling to get home to unwind in the comfort of my apartment. It was customary that everyone rushed to the subway before the traffic build-up with the commuters pushing and shoving to get a seat on the first train entering the station. A gentleman, who was parked at the entrance to my office building, approached me with a laser focus on getting my attention. I was very polite, said hello, and kept moving. During that period, I was introspective while I held my head high and stayed focused on my primary goal. I was very fashion conscious, posing the right questions to shop assistants to improve/pursue my image and self-imposed journey to empowerment. I thought at the time this gentleman had done this before so I didn't feel particularly special about his approach. I remained very curt with just a mere hello each time I would see him, however, I ensured that I was tastefully color-coordinated every day. New Yorkers are very good at being suspicious of strangers and I had become a New Yorker.

This gentleman, however, was very persistent and seemed to be in the same location each evening as I walked along Second Avenue to the subway station. One evening I politely stopped, he said hello and asked if I worked in the area to which I replied in the affirmative. He handed me his business card and I continued along to my destination without even glancing at the details on the card. There were so many issues and emotions I was dealing with at the time that I was not giving much credence to these advances. For someone to present his credentials so easily to a woman on the street of New York City was not impressive to me at the time. Little did I know.

Several weeks after my chance encounter with the man in the black beamer, I found the business card he had offered, tucked away in my purse and decided to see the name and the details. The driver had permission to park in the area designated strictly for diplomats or officials working in the area. This 'no parking zone' was constantly under surveillance by the traffic police and violation of the rules would automatically result in a traffic ticket or the vehicle jacked up and towed away. Curiosity began creeping in as to who this seemingly important individual was. Although major issues were pending in my life, my curiosity was not piqued enough to investigate further – just yet. I must have appeared aloof as I made no attempt to connect with this distinguished gentleman and he may have assumed that having presented his business card with the contact details, that I would follow up with a call.

I began taking a different route to the subway station for a few weeks in order not to be confronted by this gentleman, but a few weeks later, I would receive a phone call from the building telephone operator that someone was trying to locate me. It seemed impossible that in this great big city I could randomly meet someone from my past. The building operator was the mother of the same cute neighbor from the Bronx, Ronnie. Expecting to be all about business, I took the call. Much to my surprise the same stranger, with the black BMW, with the business card, from the sidewalk, had tracked me down. He had done his research. I have to admit that I was impressed that someone was so eager to find me.

He had been searching for a little while and I must say I was flattered. He seemed very persistent in meeting me and so I agreed to have lunch. Always the fashionista, I had to create a positive image whether I was interested in this man or not. One way I could make an impression I thought was to be fashionably dressed, to apply flawless, natural makeup, and accent the outfit with complementary accessories; that made me feel special. It helps if your date extends thoughtful compliments so your efforts to be pleasing to the eye are confirmed. How often do we do things just to create an illusion that we are happy, grounded, secure, savvy, and successful in our own right? If we are honest with ourselves, we do this often.

I discovered on our first meeting that he loved to sing, was a regular church chorister, was single, and it was obvious he had a job. He was a gentleman who exhibited the social graces like opening doors, pulling the chair for me, standing when I approached, and even escorted me back to my office. These were behaviors modeled by my dad, so this gentleman was scoring high on many fronts. He was interested in meeting again and I thought, why not. I was still very cautious as I tried to navigate the emotions of a lifelong string of disappointments and to determine if I was ready to engage in something or someone new. I was careful not to send mixed messages to complicate his life or mine.

I returned to my studies and was determined to press forward to gain my degree and not allow myself to be sidetracked again. I had already completed courses in microbiology and psychology but was not clear which direction I wanted to go with my education. I leaned towards the arts but still, I had a passion for the sciences. I was fighting to overcome the fear of failure but miraculously, I excelled beyond my expectation, and gradually layers of insecurity were slowly beginning to peel away.

That summer I agreed to meet the gentleman for lunch and continued on many occasions as we visited numerous restaurants within walking distance of our respective workplaces which coincidentally were in adjoining buildings. It was wonderful to try various cuisines in the neighborhood from restaurants that specialized in fish dishes, Indian, Chinese, Thai, and many other ethnic hot spots. In an attempt to impress I was also invited to join him for lunch on a few occasions at the United Nations' restaurant which was a special treat. This lifestyle was becoming a regular part of my weekly routine, but as long as it was not impacting my figure, it was a bonus.

During this period, I enjoyed the attention, which made me feel special, cared for, and that someone desired to be in my company. It took a few months of convincing myself it was time to let go and try again, so after some time a relationship developed. I was particularly sensitive towards my son, wanting to protect his little mind and emotions, so bringing a stranger into the home was not ideal. Single parents struggle with decisions like these as it is important to protect the stability of the children and what the little people are exposed to in the home is the learned behavior they will pattern as they become adults. As a result, every effort was made to only introduce my son when I thought the time was right and I felt there might have been a future in a relationship. He had not been exposed to another male in our home except his father, so all my decisions needed to be in his best interest. My close circle of friends was very small and my days of late-night partying and dancing until the wee hours of the morning had become a distant memory.

I was inconsistent with following up on homework, so I had to solicit the help of others to support what my son needed. I believe that rather than have regrets about not doing more with or for children academically; the key is to find someone who can. We should avoid the pitfall of chastising ourselves for our failures and lean on those with the strengths to gain the support needed to harness the gift and talents in our children. Even though I was by now slowly emerging from my discombobulated past, I continued to waste time looking at what others had achieved and not recognizing that I too had worth. I didn't seem to have the impetus to press through enough with him in some areas, but I did provide a comfortable, safe, peaceful, fun home for him and we had good times together.

Many parents look into the rearview mirror of their lives wishing they could rewrite the script and not feel as though they failed their children in so many ways by things they may have said or exposed them to. We can only pray that with time and honest communication with our children we can explain the various aspects of our journey and know that they may only understand when they too become parents. I desperately wanted my son to grow up in a healthy environment while I processed my issues. I did not fully comprehend that "God knew everything" and that He had a purpose for my existence and that He created me in His image. I can remember watching the televangelist Jimmy Swaggart and when others would laugh and blatantly ridicule him I knew there were things he was saying that had started a stirring in my spirit. I knew then that even though I was not attending church, he had inspired me that God existed and He was orchestrating and allowing things to take place in my life to get my attention. I could not have imagined there was a God who could have allowed those things: the good, the bad, and the ugly – to take place with or without my consent. As funny as it may seem, tears flowed down my cheeks once in a while as Jimmy Swaggart was preaching. Something touched my spirit. Pastor Swaggart, unfortunately, fell from grace when he allowed the enemy to lure him into a dark place, disgracing himself, his family, and his church. There is a grace however that God gives all of us and that is, He is always willing to forgive us if we repent of our sins.

He served his time, repented, and returned to his ministry having had the counseling and deliverance he needed to make things right with God.

While this awakening was gradually emerging, my relationship with the new man was developing and we spent a lot more time together. We loved the same genre of music, he loved to cook and which woman doesn't appreciate a man who cooks. I must have told him very early that the kitchen was not my favorite room in the house, but that wasn't an issue for him. I was the woman who would make your home esthetically pleasing and cozy; a place you longed to come home to. That was my forte. He appeared to be a good catch, as they say, but for me, it was not about being a good catch, it was about whether or not this man was committed to a serious, long-term relationship with me and eventually with my son. Would he be respectful, tender, loving, and kind? Would he support my visions and dreams? Would he be willing to be a father figure for my son? Did he expect me to challenge his intellect? Did we complement each other? Did we have the same values? Would this relationship lead to marriage and did we want to have children together? The fact is that some couples don't have that discussion until they are thrown into a situation and then have to figure it out much later.

I had a dream that I found my way to an apartment building and when I stopped at the entrance, the security guard directed me to the fifth floor of the building. I was guided to walk along the corridor to the last apartment on the left where someone would meet me and hand me the keys for that door. He said that would be my apartment. In the dream, I opened the door and it was beautifully decorated with furniture strategically placed and a small, cozy patio overlooking the parking lot. I was so excited and started to fantasize about having this wonderful new apartment I was going to occupy. It was ideal and quite different from the one I currently occupied. There was a change coming.

After several months of enjoying fancy restaurants, the gentleman invited me to dinner at his residence and he was cooking. Taking a leap of faith, I accepted the invitation, followed the directions and found my way to his apartment. When I approached the building, I told the doorman who I was going to see and he directed me to take the elevator to the fifth floor and go down the corridor to the last door on the left. As I approached the door, the gentleman came out and greeted me very warmly. Can you imagine my shock when I entered the room to see the furniture positioned exactly as I had seen it in the dream, with the small patio at the end of the living room? Everything was laid out as I had dreamt. Do you believe God had a plan? I was in such shock, I think I was speechless for a moment, but could not mention it to my host. He would not have understood.

It took quite a while for me to comprehend the enormity of the dream unfolding. I was very excited when I first had the dream as I thought I was moving into an apartment of my own with my son, not into someone else's place. I was puzzled as to what it all meant because this was early times yet in the relationship and I wasn't even sure there was going to be a relationship. As time passed and we experienced the normal upheavals couples face in the early days, we continued to share more of each others' space. I continued by consultations on the situation to see if this was where I needed to be. During those days God was not central to my daily routine but guiding I am sure from the wings.

I had another dream one night that I was in this room looking into a crib and there I saw a beautiful baby girl wrapped in a pink blanket. Standing off to the side of her crib was this man I was dating looking on at the scene. Confused by this dream which I couldn't describe or share with anyone, I was immediately jolted out of my sleep. I dismissed the thought, as having another child seemed so far-fetched to me that I could not envision being pregnant again.

My partner by this time had relocated and was sent on assignment to another country for several months. During that period of separation, we too had an emotional break and I soon discovered that I was indeed pregnant. My life was full and I was happy and enjoyed a wonderful pregnancy. I seemed so carefree during those months not at all calculating what the future had in store. I reflected on the dream of having a baby girl and I was very healthy, glowing, getting great comments from everyone around me. It was magical to think I would have a girl to spoil and to love and my son was excited at the idea of becoming a big brother.

The pregnancy went well with no issues and I was taken to the hospital at the moment of truth, stopping along the way to have a Big Mac and a large, thick, milkshake. My baby girl was born after a very dramatic turn of events which forced me to have to endure an epidural. This was administered when I was fully dilated and thank God it was not a long process. My best friend who is a qualified nurse was at my side to hold my hand and turned out to be the great surrogate that I needed at the time.

My daughter Lisa was so beautiful and I immediately knew that my life was about to change again for the better and forever. Here I had my little princess whom I could cuddle and take care of. I now had my little family to love and to cherish till death do us part. My son was over the moon to show off his little sister as if she were a toy. We were all happy and enjoyed the time I wasn't working, to be able to bond. To be able to dress my children especially my little girl was special. What are little girls made of – sugar and spice and everything nice. Many friends gave her clothes so her wardrobe was more extensive than mine with outfits and accessories befitting a little princess. As a little girl, it was important to have that boost of confidence instilled in her at an early stage. She needed to know she was fearfully and wonderfully made. She needed to be loved and to feel loved, so what I felt I lacked, I poured generously into my daughter. Those were happy days.

Once my maternity leave was over I returned to work and had the luxury of having built-in babysitting services, which allowed me to continue my career, while caring for my young family. My son adored his little sister and was very protective of her – while my daughter's personality captured the hearts of many and she was never lacking for hugs or kisses. Everyone loved her. When her dad returned from his assignment and met her for the first time, he was thrilled and curious about everything she did and every sound she made. It was such a pleasure to see how invested he was in his little girl and asked numerous questions about her daily activity. This was a new beginning for him too.

The Kidnapping.

My son doted on his little sister and it was always fun to watch them interact; the older, big brother and the little princess. As my little family was making all the adjustments that came along with the expansion, we methodically continued with our daily lives. One evening our lives were shaken by the act of one selfish individual. My son arrived at the after-school care at the residence across the street from our home which was customary. For some reason that day I had a quiver in my stomach and a premonition that something unusual was about to happen. When I approached the after-school center, the door was unlocked so I ran up the stairs as I usually did and called his name, but there was no response. His care-sitter was to announce that his father had taken him to get ice-cream. I was hysterical, as we had no prior arrangement for that to take place and when I tried calling his father's house there was no answer. Suddenly I was consumed with fear. Panic set in so I called my friend, the law enforcement officer who was fortunately attached to a division of the New York City Police Department (NYPD), in the same borough where I lived. Together we drove to my son's father's family house and much to my delight when I knocked on the door, my son answered. I invited him to come with me and he willingly came without question.

There was such a sense of relief for me at that moment and I am not sure what my son felt as a little boy in the middle of this tug-o-war. I didn't even dare to ask as I didn't want to stir any negative thoughts in his young mind. I just didn't know how to respond to that situation. Children in these situations can be easily swayed by the non-resident parent who offers treats to get their attention and affection. The parent who has primary care is normally the disciplinarian, while the visiting parent offers all the "fun things" so the child becomes confused about what is real and what is not. I couldn't offer treats often but I could offer love and safety.

Once we were safely home I instructed the after-school sitter that under no circumstance should my son be allowed in the future to answer the telephone or respond to anyone knocking on the front door. He was not allowed to leave the premises without consulting me and gaining my permission. Several weeks later when everyone had dismissed the situation, there was another moment of déjà vu. I followed my normal routine and went to collect my son and he was gone again. There was no one this time who could explain how and when he had disappeared. This was the beginning of my nightmare.

Again, we returned to my ex-husband's residence but on this occasion, no one answered the door and no one answered the phone. There was a total blackout from the family. We did as much investigation as we could, including checking for valid driver's licenses through the police department without any positive leads. Finances would not allow for the legal investigations that may have flushed them out of their hiding place, so

I relied on my contact in the NYPD to locate the family. During the long agonizing months following the incident, I leaned heavily on my current relationship to keep myself sane. Time went by, the tears flowed and the prayers continued even if it all seemed like the impossible was happening. There seemed to be no hope of finding my child. I knew he was with his father and not a stranger but that did not diminish the worry I had for his wellbeing. If the wicked grandmother had anything to do with his relocation, I feared for the type of man he would become and that my child would grow up to be totally dependent on her and damaged like his father. During the period of complete blackout of information about Steve's location, I could only pray in my simple fashion hoping that God would shake heaven and earth to reveal his whereabouts. It seemed to be the only action I could take as everything else was out of my control. All those years I continued to send Birthday and Christmas cards to the family house in Queens, New York.

The years kept rolling along and I had to keep believing the day would come when I would reconnect with my boy. Through some divine intervention, my mom connected with her friend the dressmaker who happened to be well informed as to the status and location of my son and his father. Armed with this information, my mom took a trip and arrived at the residence in Florida. Can you imagine my horror when my phone rang one day and mom asked me if I could guess where she was calling from? Of course, I had no idea. She was in the home of my son's grandmother, the evil woman who had invested so much time in trying to destroy my life. One more shock was in store when she asked me to hold on and she handed the phone to my son who by now was a grown man. It was emotional and awkward at the same time but the joy in knowing he was alive and well was fulfilling. It had been about 12 years since his kidnapping. The assertiveness and ability to negotiate that my mother employed in her roles as principal and an active politician in the past, certainly helped her to advance a conversation with the grandmother who agreed for her to visit. Her communication skills certainly came in handy in this scenario.

Despite the heavy emotional weight I endured, God carried me through it all. I had no idea how my family would recover and truthfully, I look back on those days and know that I must have been helped the whole time. My early childhood education and lack of affirmation made it easy to allow those feelings of guilt to creep into my mind. The negative thoughts came fast and furiously: Was I not a good enough mother? Was I responsible for all this? Did my son prefer to be with his dad? Would his life have been better with his dad? Would he have been happier with his dad? Would his physical needs have been better satisfied with his dad? Where did I fall short? Was this a malicious act by my in-laws to make me pay for rejecting their advances? What could I have done differently? My church upbringing had taught me that if you train up a child the way he should go he would not depart from it. I had done the best I could for the short period I had with my son in the early days so I had to trust God that he would be ok. I had strayed far from my upbringing; hit a lot of bumps in the road, but God was patient along the journey. It was well with my soul. I had to let go.

God was diligent in his pursuit of me. He never gave up on me when I gave up on myself. He always had His hands firmly planted on me and with His divine protection outstretched as if to say to the enemy, "You can't have this one; she belongs to me." What would I have done differently if I had understood that God had a plan for me and was working on my behalf? Would I have said, "Yes Lord, I hear you? I will patiently wait for you"? I doubt it. I would probably have continued trying to do things my way, making irresponsible decisions, pressing through with toxic relationships, failing at many things, continuously comparing myself to those I thought were in a better place than I was, and allowing people to take advantage of my kindness. I had to endure rejection, humiliation, adultery, and other painful experiences before I finally called on God to fill that space that only He could fill in my life. I slowly began to put trust in God. It took a long time to finally submit to God's will and His way.

I had many conversations with my son before I finally reconnected with him in person at the Miami International Airport. We agreed to meet when I had a five-hour layover and as we had not seen each other for ages, we were not sure who to look for. It was agreed that he would page me soon after my flight landed but for one hour, we were paging each other from different levels of the airport.

Imagine, there I was waiting anxiously for my boy, trying to focus on a magazine when I heard, "Hi mom." in this low baritone voice. I turned to look and there he was – a man 6"3" mirroring the image of his father – looking down at me. There are no words to describe the emotion for both of us. We hugged for what seemed like ages, but could find no words for the several minutes besides saying, "Look at you, oh, and look at you." My son had arrived in a long, sleek black limousine with flowers in hand and off we went to have lunch for my favorite meal at a Chinese restaurant. This was a moment of truth as I was finally able to share the pain of the kidnapping and pretty much set the record straight as I knew he would have been told many disparaging things over that time to convince him I was not a stable mother.

He shared very cautiously about what life had been like for him and the pain that he had also suffered from a father whom he loved but recognized deficiencies that were out of control. Of course, as I expected, our account of the kidnapping was vastly different. There were times he felt abandoned and unloved while other members of his immediate family seemed to thrive. He has exhibited the character traits of a very compassionate, kind, generous loving big brother and with time I believe there will be greater opportunities for healing in all areas. Time stood still for us at that meeting, but again I could see how God carefully orchestrated the reunion at His designated time. God is always on time. A lesson learned during this miraculous ending is that it didn't matter how simple my prayer was, God was observing my heart and that my actions throughout this journey were genuine.

⁂

Venetia … Liberia

Venetia had a great opportunity to be seconded to a school in Liberia, West Africa, to conduct teacher training for close to a year. It was a unique experience for her but she relished the idea of giving back and advancing the quality of the educational system wherever she was appointed. She told many stories of the conditions under which she had to live and the unusual food choices that she never really got used to. She managed to develop some friendships that proved to be essential as the mode and frequency of transportation were very unreliable. There were the physical needs she required to satisfy her, as well as her desire to go to church at least a few times each month. Arrangements had to be made well in advance to accomplish these activities.

At the end of a successful tour of duty, I believe she was ready to get back to a normal routine and enjoy some familiar faces and cuisine. She wrote to say that she planned to live in NYC for a while, therefore she demanded that I found an apartment large enough to accommodate the family and she determined in advance that this would be a reality. As we had resident status, there was no challenge with immigration so anything was possible. Or so she thought. There were no questions such as, "Would you like to?" or "How do you feel about the idea?" It was – just make it happen. At that time, I occupied a small cozy one-bedroom apartment but had the option of moving into a larger apartment in the same building. I went into a tailspin at the thought of reliving my childhood, when I had literally "escaped the net". This is the same individual who had disinherited me several years previously because I disappointed her by abruptly departing my homeland.

Carmen's help with Venetia

Of all the members of my adopted family, there was only one person who was always willing to listen and support in any way she could. She had a big heart and made a huge impact on my life. Carmen was born in Panama in July 1924 and her family migrated to the USA where she studied medicine and resided in the very same apartment in NYC for over 40 years. She never married nor did she have any children of her own, but she had cared for all her relatives' children throughout her life. She was the only person who made contact and frequently reached out to me to inquire about my wellbeing. I remember vividly when she offered me a haven of rest in her cozy residence on Charles St. in Greenwich Village, downtown Manhattan. I stayed with her as long as I needed at a time when I was most vulnerable and desperate for support.

I needed her again on this occasion as she knew how traumatized I was and these life experiences were coming full circle. The situation loomed large so she immediately went into research mode. She again offered the nurturing I desperately needed at a moment in time and came up with a solution in short order. She knew I had suffered enough under that very authoritative rule and needed to help. She also knew my mother and her reputation very well. She was very compassionate about the situation and scheduled a series of appointments for me to share with a colleague of hers who was a psychologist. I was frantic about my mother coming back into my space and what she would have expected of me. I had numerous visits with this professional who gave me valuable tools to handle the imminent situation. So often we humans need some professional help to identify our issues to become healed from our struggles, but the stigma attached to therapy is just as real today. Thank God that I was in the right place, at the right time, with the right answers.

The flight lands from Liberia

I was very bold in asking my companion to take me to the airport to meet my mom and I felt real anxiety en-route to the airport to meet her. The flight from Liberia landed and my heart began racing, my mind was in flux and my companion was oblivious as to whom he was about to come face to face with. On that fatal day, I wondered if the old Venetia would show up and embarrass me one more time. I dreaded each moment as she emerged from the arrival lounge. I slowly walked forward to meet her and introduced her to my companion. "Mom, this is Wendell. Wendell, this is my mom ..." Would she surprise me and be civil on this occasion? That may have been asking too much. "Well," she said, "another Wendell?" How does one respond to that? There were no surprises there.

She had been traveling for close to one calendar year so she had accumulated a lot of personal effects. Along with her many suitcases, she brought out a very large batik print that was already framed on a wooden stretcher. This piece of artwork was way too big to fit inside the vehicle but she proceeded to tell my companion to place it on the roof of the car! The image of the family of the Beverley Hillbillies came alive. Here we were emerging from JFK International Airport! Allow me to paint the picture. Here we have the diplomat, driving his brand new, sleek, black, well valeted BMW with his important CD plates, legally parked in a zone reserved especially for diplomats and other VIPS at the airport. Here he is with his new girlfriend, obviously wanting to impress her mother and he is on his very best behavior when her mother says what? "Tie this large canvas which I have brought home to the top of your car." Well, so as not to disappoint, he dutifully struggled to tie the painting to the top of the car. In those days it was fairly common to see passengers arriving from other countries with large bundles tied in sheets. I pleaded for the earth to open and swallow me. We found our positions in the car after some maneuvering but in the meanwhile, the gentleman tried not to damage the radio antenna. Once the painting was secure Venetia exclaims, "Wait, the car can't drive if the antenna doesn't work?" Do you laugh, crouch below the seat, or cry!!!! Would this man stay the course or would he dash off in another direction, I wondered?

It was not an uncommon occurrence for Venetia to create a scene. She would have her way at the expense of any and everybody. We arrived at our destination at my apartment in Harlem and she promptly alighted the car, handbag in hand, and walked away to visit friends in a building across the street, while we, her waiting staff, carried all her luggage to the apartment. That was my mama. The Queen had arrived. I knew at that moment that I had made the right decision not to consider getting that three-bedroom apartment she insisted on for the family. I could not imagine what my companion was thinking and didn't dare to ask. I am not sure I could deal with a discussion about the behavior I knew all too well. How does one even begin to explain?

When my mom returned to the apartment, I told her that I would be gone for the weekend. In preparation for her arrival, I had provided just about everything she could need during her stay. The apartment was not adequate for two women who struggled to communicate with each other. I gave her a key and said goodbye. How dare you be so bold? I thought to myself. The tools I had been given empowered me to take charge of my life, space, make my decisions, and stick with them.

When I returned home the following Monday after work, I found that she had left and went to seek solace at some relatives in another borough of New York. The early morning phone calls began; 6 am was the norm. I politely asked her not to call that early, especially on a day I was not working. I was making my rights known for the first time, truly taking control of my space without being rude or disrespectful. I was chastised in so many words that I was disrespectful to have left her alone in the apartment to go gallivanting. All this time I was trying to take control of my own life and not allow myself to be bullied once more.

She became extremely belligerent and decided that since I didn't want to live with her, she would return to Jamaica where she would feel valued and continue with her passion as an educator and make her contribution to her country. There was so much acrimony that I decided it was best not to accompany her to the airport. Once she settled back into her routine at home, she began sending letters quite frequently. There was no internet in those days so it had to be "snail mail". She expressed herself in the meanest, most graphic ways with total disregard for my feelings, needs as a person, or emotional stability. The first few letters left me shaking with similar emotions I felt as a child. There were no words of encouragement, praise, empowerment, love, compassion, or care but the comparison was made to Mr. X or Mrs. Y's child. I just wanted to be me. Deep in my heart, I knew at an early age who I wanted to become but that was not encouraged, so I became very despondent and felt lost at times. Speak when you are spoken to and no "backchat". It was really not "backchat", just me trying to have a voice.

The contents of the letters would sear into my consciousness and after a while, I just couldn't read them when they arrived in the mail. I was so shaken with anticipation of what would be said that I stopped opening or reading them so they were tossed in the bin. It may have been as much as a year that passed before I communicated with my mother and that was to tell her that I had given birth to her second grandchild, my daughter. I wish I could have been a fly on the wall to see her reaction to the news. In those days there were still no telephones at our house on the farm so mail took a few weeks in either direction. She eventually responded to the news, but none of that conversation I can remember. It took a while to resume any civil communication, but with time, my Mom grew eager to meet her new granddaughter.

There was a tug-o-war to discover if God truly existed. It was a recurring thought that just wasn't going away. Do you believe or don't you believe? There was a real struggle trying to understand the magnitude of God's presence and power and passion to have a relationship with me. What exactly did it even mean to have a relationship with God anyway? Going to church was a ritual that I endured because that was what was expected. There was no one around with the passion or anointing to guide or educate me on the things of God. There was no teaching about "resisting the enemy and he will flee". There was no one sharing about denouncing Satan and asking Jesus into my life so he can set me free. There was no teaching on repentance or forgiveness so it was all superficial knowledge. I knew there was so much for me to accomplish but was not resolute enough in my faith or ability to pursue my dreams but there were always those moments that my faith would be stirred.

There is an older brother.

As I relaxed in the quiet of my apartment late in the fall, I received a phone call from a woman whose name I recognized from my childhood. It had been several years since I had any contact with her or her family and even then the contact was distant. After the formal greetings and words of reflection on who she was, she proceeded to announce that my brother was in New York City and wanted to meet me. I grew up with an adopted sister of Indian heritage and that's all I knew. After many questions and much disbelief, curiosity took over. I asked all the questions that came to mind and before the end of the conversation; I got a phone number and pondered upon the idea of calling that number.

It took a few days to make the call and the excitement at the other end of the line was so strange to me that I felt uncomfortable not being able to respond with the same level of excitement. We talked for a while and scheduled a time to meet.

Some time had passed before I finally decided to face the situation and got on the train, followed the directions, and knocked on the door of an unfamiliar house. A deep, male voice responded and then unlocked bolts before opening the door with great enthusiasm. Here was this stranger lifting me off the ground, wrapping his arms around me and hugging me in a loving, warm embrace. It was the older brother I never knew existed.

We talked for hours during which he informed of relatives I never knew. I had a biological mother and siblings who remained in the land of my birth and he proceeded to give me a short yet comprehensive brief about another family. It was all seemed like a blur by the time I got home. By now I was 30 years old and for the first time discovering that I wasn't who I thought I was. Wow! I had been adopted by Venetia and Russell.

What I discovered on that night was that I had seven siblings on my mother's side, who all knew of my existence and I had no idea of theirs. They all were born, raised, and spent their formative years in Jamaica. It took me a while to internalize this information and I walked in a daze for days trying to understand what the entire process meant to me and the rest of the family. During this process, my mother Venetia had no idea that this contact had been made and I was not sure how she would have dealt with the revelation. There were so many questions unanswered in my mind and there are no words to describe my state of mind at that time. It all seemed surreal - too much to absorb. The ironic part of the story is that the same woman who adopted me was the same woman who accepted the responsibility of caring for my son during those turbulent times. It's fascinating how our lives can come full circle.

The questions were endless: How did this all come about? Why was I the one chosen to be adopted? When did all of this happen? Why was this not disclosed sooner? Who else outside the family knew? How did my biological mother come to grips with the decision? Who was my biological father? Where was he?

I maintained contact with my newly found brother however, I was feeling a sense of guilt that I was not feeling the same sense of urgency to reunite with a family I didn't know because I was in shock/denial and I am sure it was visible for some time. I believe he understood my position and remained very patient as I tried to navigate through all the emotions encapsulated in my heart during that time. My mind was racing as I reflected on my life from my childhood and I tried to ascertain if there were any clues that I would have missed. I can remember being called names such as having a flat butt and Chinese eyes but none of that could have prepared me for the reality that my biological father was half-Chinese. The funny thing is that I kept wondering why as a young girl I was so attracted to the young Chinese men in my community. Separate and apart from the business acumen of the race, I was fascinated with how close-knit they were and I envied the comradery they shared which I didn't feel within my own family. It appeared that the success of each family was contingent on the efforts of the established families and their strategy worked.

My brother had observed the lifestyle of those families all his life and shared many stories of what he observed even as a child, confirming what

I had seen that the families never attended church services nor integrated with any other race in the communities.

This is how my older brother Hopeton briefly described his situation: -

He recalls that he attended the same primary school as I did, but the principal of the school, Venetia told him that under no circumstance was he allowed to have any contact with me. It was decided and he agreed to keep his distance. He was a child, just a few years older than I was but knew there would have been harsh consequences if he violated the rule. She manipulated the situation to the extent that both children never attended the same classes and were assigned to different sections of the school where possible. How that was even possible as the building was very small and classes were held in a very confined space? There was no stone left unturned to ensure that there was no human contact with each other as siblings. The effort it must have taken to carry out this mandate must have been stressful and relentless.

Throughout his early years, he desired to pursue a career as a pilot, to develop the ability to fly across continents, to see the world, and to have new experiences was what he craved. He never had that opportunity realized as he had neither the courage, the resources or the support to engage in a field of study. He never thought he was good enough to dream that big. He eventually joined the Police Department in Jamaica where he felt accomplished as a human being before migrating to the USA on the invitation of a friend, hoping like so many to seek a better life. Once in the US, he remained focused on his primary goals of searching for steady employment and finding his younger sister. He managed to make contact with a woman from our district who also had migrated to the US, who had my contact details. My brother has been able to carve a niche for himself and is enjoying a very comfortable life both in the US and Jamaica while still carrying the mantle for maintaining the relationships with family members. He is a proud husband, father, and grandfather.

Meeting my younger sister Dawn.

While I believed for a resolution to the situation with my son, my life continued to take many twists and turns including the day I got a call from another member of the family, a sister I had not yet met. Dawn acquired a posting from her government in Jamaica to NYC and had settled in for a while when we first met. We connected immediately and there was no doubt that we were related. There was chemistry, a sense of humor, and a comfort level that was undeniably free and easy. We talked, we laughed, we shared and it was amazing how it seemed that there was never any distance between us.

I was so happy to see how pretty she was with healthy hair, beautiful teeth, and flawless skin, first impressions that are important to me. She had a very vibrant personality and talked incessantly, and still does today. Anything in the world I wanted, I am sure she would have given me. There was an immediate love attraction. I learned many more things about my family in the upcoming weeks and I tried to process it all one step at a time as I grappled with the details of the mysteries of the discovery as they unfolded so many years later. Dawn who is 10 years my junior, had heard all the stories about me even though I didn't know of her existence. She lived with our mother, a different father than mine, and other siblings. Our lives were very different, but over the years, she said she kept abreast of all my movements. I was so gripped with pride to get to know her that I had a determined curiosity to find out my history, so we spoke for hours and hours trying to put the pieces of the jigsaw puzzle together. I am sure many stories were repeated ad nauseam but it didn't matter to us as were sisters trying to bring healing to a fractured situation. Dawn was fortunate in some way to have spent her early childhood with both of her parents, however, the toxic environment proved to be difficult and left an edible imprint on her life.

These are my sister's thoughts

> *"As far back as I can recall, the name Peggy was seared into my consciousness — the sister who was adopted. I had no idea my mother kept up with every milestone in her life, but we knew when she won a scholarship to the elite girls' school, St. Andrews High, when she migrated to the US and when she got married. We knew a lot but we just couldn't reach her. As a young girl, I romanticized her - my older sister, who I imagined to be very pretty, poised, and polished. I even*

dreamt of going to St. Andrews High School, because she did. I wanted to be like her long before I met her.

My mother's firstborn migrated to the US. His first order of business was to find his/our sister. The news of him locating her felt like we all had won the lottery. I remember where I was and how I felt when the news broke; we were delirious. Finally! Pictures followed, showing a charming, young woman, poised as I imagined, pretty and refined. Her resemblance to what we knew – was a younger version of my mother, which was startling. Mom was pleased and relieved. It was obvious her adopted mother had given her the life my mother had hoped she would have. Peggy and I finally met in the early 1980s when I migrated to the US and lived at the Beverley Hotel. My anxiety level was sky high and I felt like an ingénue. When she finally entered the room, it was a relief. She hugged me and put me at ease. I tried not to stare, but I was thinking, wow! She is the younger more attractive version of my mother – petite and classy. Specific details of our meeting remain etched in my mind like the Diane Von Furstenberg wrap dress she wore with the expensive two-tone flats and chunky accessories.

Thirty years later, my sister is still my role model. I have been there to observe the intimate details of her many transitions and her resilience and resourcefulness to rise above life's curveballs".

My sister has enjoyed a very successful career while living in the USA and is a graduate of prestigious universities. She is the doting mother of one son.

It was an interesting period for me and I became very sensitive and a bit scared concerning the whole situation and the future. How was I supposed to feel about a mother I never knew? How would the mother I knew, feel about me reconnecting with a woman who had given me up for adoption? Did she ever imagine the day would come when I would make that connection? Why was I not told and had to discover these facts in what seemed like a very sinister fashion? I knew the time would come when I had to meet the other members of my biological family but had no idea when that would have happened.

The American Health Foundation had completed the study 10 years after the inception and the data was forwarded to the National Institute of Health. My career as a medical technician came to a close and there were many mixed emotions for all of us who had worked together for the entire period and held hands through some tumultuous times. As a team, we had gained a lot of knowledge about the importance of early detection and intervention for the medical issues associated with heart disease. There was an excessive amount of literature to be read, healthy recipes to taste test, perfecting one's skills in testing, and counseling the clients to gain their trust. As most of the members of the team were female, it was also important for us to recognize the boundaries necessary when ladies counseled the men to ensure professionalism at all times. There were numerous awards granted to the President of the AHF for his vision and dedication to the completion and success of the study. With the contribution of various partners, a book of recipes was published to be of great value especially to those who were considered at high risk of heart disease.

The months that followed allowed me to get some much-needed rest while I enjoyed time with my daughter who was growing up quickly and bringing me pleasure daily. There were several decisions to be made going forward and I had to become realistic about the changes I needed to make.

After many serious conversations about my situation, my daughter's dad and I decided to get married so we could start a family, but it meant moving to the country to which he was assigned. There were huge emotional and financial costs involved before making the final move and I had to carefully calculate the prospects/risks of re-entering that deep level of commitment again. By this time, I had given birth to two amazing children whom I cherished and even though I was estranged from one, they both held such a special place in my heart that I felt satisfied that I had done my best. It had to be a part of God's plan for us to be a family, so we prepared for the big move.

Chapter Three

Canada

The move took place after some dramatic events were settled and I transitioned into my new role as a homemaker. It was initially difficult for me to conform to a life of financial dependency, having been independent for such a long time, but my focus was on creating a happy home for my family. We settled into the fully furnished house that was assigned to us, but sadly there was not much opportunity for me to exercise my interior decorating skills. Everything was provided, so it would not have been prudent to invest in additional amenities. Canada was quite different to me than New York was in several ways, like the physical environment, the warmth of the people and the opportunity and desire to engage in more outdoor activities. Both the US and Canada have been allies for many years and the Canadians have always been very receptive to foreigners visiting their nation.

I spent the majority of my time caring for our daughter and often pondering and praying that my son was safe. I played indoor tennis, went snowshoeing with a group referred to as the "Foreign Wives' Club", enjoyed special breakfasts, and indulged in afternoon tea in the various homes. In this diplomatic community, I found it fascinating to hear the conversations that primarily revolved around exotic vacations and acquisitions that were mostly material stuff. No one talked about service to his or her communities or giving back. I am sure at the governmental level there would be an emphasis on developing better communities on a broad scale, but my experience in these gatherings was that there were no conversations on a personal level of anyone expressing interest in reaching persons in need. I suppose it's my passion for people that causes me to look for the same passion in people that I meet, especially if they have the resources to lend a hand. We are all not the same and that's a fact I must accept.

Surprising, I enjoyed much of the great outdoors in the winter months, attending events like the Winterlude, which took place in the Confederation Park downtown the capital city of Ottawa. This annual festival, which has existed for the last 40 years, is held for three weeks in February as an international ice-carving competition, attracting artists from countries around the world. They descend on the city with their carving tools and the blocks of ice they would have commissioned to diligently create exquisite sculptures; masterpieces from the ice. It was hard to believe any of that was possible until you saw it unfolding before your eyes. Most of the masterpieces took days and the viewing audience increased as the days progressed and as the images became more pronounced, while the fascination grew.

Several of the free activities took place around this festival along the Rideau Canal, referred to as the world's largest natural frozen ice-skating rink. This waterway connects Ottawa, which is the capital of Canada, to Lake Ontario and the Saint Lawrence River in Kingston. This is the oldest operating canal in North America and its value and beauty were highlighted as a UNESCO World Heritage Property in 2007. Another attraction unique to this city is the display of the miles of garden beds strewn with tulips of all the colors of the rainbow. They were imported from Holland and the artistry in the way they are displayed created a generous kaleidoscope of color and symmetry. God's creation was so evident that it was impossible to miss, but still, most people wouldn't recognize it as such. No human being could have created or even designed those beautiful flowers with such an impressive variety of colors that were on display.

This diplomatic community was very diverse with several ethnic groups from around the world represented. There were a few experiences that I didn't have to wrestle with while residing in New York City, but was compelled to figure out solutions to fairly quickly. For example, every woman needs to have a hairdresser she can trust and especially with black hair that needed someone who was a specialist. Making those connections in the 1980s in Ottawa was a challenge to me, as I needed a hairdresser who knew how to apply a chemical agent to relax and straighten the thick hair of a black woman. I desperately needed help. None of my contacts provided any suitable recommendations so I took a chance and wandered into a well-established hair salon one day on the main street downtown. I thought I would start with a simple "Wash and Set" to test the skills of the stylist. I was warmly welcomed, was covered with the apron, placed by a sink and I waited until the water was at a comfortable temperature. There was a little chatter in the distance but I pretended not to be interested in the conversation. My hair was washed and conditioned and then transferred to another chair where this young, white gentleman stylist attempted to blow dry my hair. I reflected on the very skilled French–Canadian hairdresser, Guillaume who had mastered the art of treating and blow drying my hair in New York, so there was no apprehension that this stylist couldn't do as good a job. After several attempts of this man trying to detangle my hair, I realized that it was an exercise in futility and I was becoming quite frustrated and concerned about the condition of my hair. I had to make a bold decision recognizing that I was clearly in the wrong establishment. I decided to take the gentleman out of his misery as I am sure that under his garments beads of sweat were dying to escape and create a pattern on his outer garments. I politely made an excuse, said I needed to leave, paid my bill, thanked him, and promptly departed. It was a somewhat embarrassing situation, but it was best for both of us that I gracefully made my exit.

As I walked out the door it occurred to me that even though we think we are all the same in God's image, there are real differences that we would either have to work hard to understand and improve or just agree that we cannot satisfy each other's needs on all occasions. It would be good to note that God's word says he has made each of us different as well so we have different skill sets to work with. Isn't that a thought? I am sure that gentleman was very relieved when I decided to hop out of his chair and leave so he would not have destroyed my hair and the reputation of his salon. I wish I was a fly on the wall that day to hear the conversation that transpired after I left and who made it first to the closest bar for happy hour. One bit of advice to the ladies is that if a hairdresser says they are not equipped to treat "black hair", trust what they say and move on. Don't insist that it is easy as it's only easy for those who know how!

Our marriage was intended to be a very simple, low budget affair with just a few close friends. The one unspoken caveat was that our parents were not invited. We never had any discussion as to why we didn't include our parents at our wedding and I have wondered how I would process the idea of my children getting married and I was not part of their celebration. We agreed not to be married in a church although we were both regular attendees of the local Anglican Church. It was not going to be the traditional event and I was not wearing a traditional wedding dress. As it turned out I was able to purchase a dress from a sale rack that I paid the hefty sum of US$50 from the prestigious Bergdorf Goodman store. This was a store I visited maybe once in my life before then but somehow wandered in there on a whim. This dress had been specifically designed for me, as it was the perfect fit at size 3. The pattern was embellished with ecru lace, very sheer with no inner lining but was accessorized with a flesh-colored bodice to conceal just enough. The composition of the dress piqued the curiosity of onlookers as they begged the question, "Is she or isn't she wearing anything underneath?" I dared to be daring in those days, showing off my petite frame. I got dressed at a friend's home and she, on cue, supplied me with a very small, ecru colored lace, Chinese umbrella - the identical color of the dress. She had no idea what I was going to be wearing so it all came as a complete surprise to all of us. A Chinese umbrella … was that significant to my heritage?

Our wedding was held on a beautiful afternoon in an especially secluded area along the Ottawa River. The attendees were the priest, the four witnesses, and a photographer. The ceremony was brief with the traditional vows used at most weddings and the "for better or worse" promises recited as is customary. The following day we held a champagne reception with close friends in our home and looking back at the photos, it was a beautiful and fun evening with lots of laughter. There was a conga-line around our living room and our daughter was, of course, an integral part of the celebration joining in with her little movements. There were all indications that this was the start of a wonderful new, long life together with my little nuclear family. We didn't go on a honeymoon following the event as my husband's work schedule didn't allow the time back then, but life was good.

I developed a relationship with one very special couple, Connie and Jack who were my new neighbors. They were an elderly couple somewhere in their 70s at the time who had relocated from Britain. Jack was attached to a new company that had expanded to Canada and he was deployed as the best candidate to help facilitate the move. They spent most of their spare time engaging in their favorite activity – entertaining.

Our chance meeting was a fascinating story. I arrived home one day to find an unusual package at my front door. It was a small plant that had been carefully placed so we could not miss it on our way in. At the time we were not sure if someone had left it there by mistake so we left it there just in case. We couldn't figure out how it got there until several days later it became clear that someone was seeking to befriend us. A little nine-year-old named Emily had "borrowed" one of her grandmother's plants and left it at our door.

This had seemed like such a simple act but there was a reason for this encounter and I had no idea at the time what was about to unfold. Emily returned the following evening to ask if she could join us for dinner. I sent her to enquire if her grandmother would allow her to sit with us, as we were strangers to the neighborhood and her family. We agreed to have her join us only if she was given permission. She did return and we had a lovely time with her that evening. Quite often she would return to play with our daughter who was less than half her age. Soon after, I got to meet her grandparents, I discovered that Emily's mother Heather had been adopted by this couple. Heather had been a runaway child and Connie and Jack just wanted to give her a new life, with hope for a good future. They gave her the best of everything – the best education, clothing, whatever she desired, as they had no children of their own. It didn't take them long to learn that

Heather had mental issues. She was a very troubled child and the couple was called to her school on numerous occasions for her bad behavior and threat of expulsion. She managed to graduate eventually and soon after, left their home for another Province without as much as telling them where she was going or what she planned to do with the rest of her life.

Connie, Jack, and I bonded well and we believed that the misfortunes we experienced as a result of the adoption process created that simpatico between us. There were numerous stories of the emotional upheaval one can endure during adoption. They were clueless about Heather's whereabouts until she arrived on their doorstep one day with this child who was by now about five years old. This elderly couple was no match for the wit of this young child and they were neither physically nor emotionally equipped to cope with her antics. Heather left the child in this elderly couple's care, but the government child services division visited the home on numerous occasions threatening to remove her from the household if her behavior did not improve. My husband and I did whatever we could without getting too involved, but it was to no avail. Emily eventually abandoned them just like her mother had done and went in search of her mother who by now had gotten married.

Connie was completely distraught by her inability to improve the situation and shed many tears for days on end. During that time, it was very difficult to watch her suffer in silence. There were just no words one could express to bring comfort to her during those times. How does one console the broken-hearted mother who had given her all? The pain they felt for the disappointment in the young woman they had invested so much in was real. They were treated unimaginably. Heather exhibited such disdain for them, cursing them like a pirate and ridiculing them for as long as she was in their presence. All they wanted was to love and be loved. That was the last time we saw Emily's mother. It was indeed a very sad day when Emily and Heather left but it may have been the best thing for this very fragile couple. They had been subjected to the fierce onslaught and tongue-lashing with the venomous words from this young mother's lips for way too long.

I sometimes wondered if my adopted mother had been as devoted and passionate about my wellbeing as I saw portrayed by this couple. Had I disappointed her by not achieving all she had hoped for? Did I take time to express enough gratitude to my adopted parents? Was this my story too? I know for sure that there was never any disrespect on my part towards them and the colorful language Heather used did not bare any resemblance to my vocabulary. I spent a lot of time with Connie and Jack while we lived in Ottawa and tried to shower them with as much affection as I could muster in a vain attempt to cushion the blow of the rejection and pain they were experiencing. Heather prohibited Emily from visiting her grandparents for a long time and that was the only family they had left at their old age. While we lived next door, I spent as much time as I could with them and took them out on many jaunts around the city. I loved on them as best as I could.

Connie and Jack hosted several musical evenings where they had sing-a-longs, prepared meals, and enjoyed lots of laughter as a way of coping with their situation. They were extremely generous and the most caring couple I had ever met. They had developed a small circle of friends and we were the first and only people of African descent with whom they had ever developed such a meaningful relationship. My empathy towards them was indescribable.

It was interesting to see how people responded to us when we were out and about with them and we had fun with it. Quite often as a young black woman, I would tease onlookers when seen in public with Jack, this elderly white man, as we went on errands like going to the bank or shopping together. I can remember a couple of really funny times when we were in the bank and I would go to the cashier and say, "Jack, hon, how much should I take out?" We would then watch the reaction of the cashiers as they would glance at each other and squirm. We would then walk out the bank hand in hand, having a good laugh in the car.

There is another funny story where Connie and I go into one of the large department stores and I said to her, "Connie, you know you are not happy that I married your son". This little chatter was purposely done to observe the expressions on the faces of those within earshot. It was hilarious to watch – the naughty side of my character was in full bloom. The reaction of people to black and white friendship was always remarkable to me and people are quite often not sure how to respond and this was true on both sides of the spectrum. Reports continue to indicate that racism is alive and well but in those days it was more likely exhibited in very subtle ways.

As I compared my adoption experience to Heather's, I tried to rationalize why she would have treated her parents in that unforgivable manner. The only plausible conclusion was that she was struggling with an undiagnosed mental condition that nobody recognized. My mother was so much more military in her style of communication than Connie, who was very gentle, mild-mannered and soft-spoken. She was caring, generous, loving, and wanted only the best for her daughter. I was exposed to a much harsher lifestyle but had the restraint not to overstep the boundaries or be rude. Connie and Jack were neither judgmental nor condescending in any way to their daughter and willingly shared anything and everything they had with her. They understood her history, that she was abandoned and neglected but were sensitive to how fragile her mind and thoughts were. They did not fathom that their investment to nurture and care for this child would have gone completely wrong. My mother was also very generous and kind but had demanded such a high, unrealistic return on her investment with those in her care that people ran away too. Connie and Jack always exhibited unconditional kindness to me and transported me when I needed it while my husband was at work. They would offer to babysit for us from time to time and even on those occasions when I would sneak away to take driving lessons so I could surprise my husband.

My spiritual connection was dormant but I still believed there was a God. I didn't have the confidence to share my faith with them, but I fostered a very genuine relationship with them so they could feel loved. They adopted my family and we adopted them. I began to see that the state of adoption has a "spirit" of its own and not everyone has mastered the tools to make it work emotionally, spiritually, or financially. It was a sad day when the time came to leave this wonderful, couple behind who had come to mean so much to me. They were getting older and had no other family members to care for them so they more than likely have had to move to assisted living facilities. The year after we relocated they happily came to spend time with our family and that was the closing of another chapter in our families' lives.

God will put people in your life to provide the support you need in a season by dispatching his angels to come in all forms and all ages. These were my angels for the time I lived in their country and on reflection, I was truly blessed to have them so close to me. I could share from my heart without feeling judged, without shame, without any threat because they were on the opposite end of the struggle that I had.

Our lives are dictated by parents, teachers, priests, and counselors and as adults by our bosses and even our partners. I wanted to be free to shout from the rooftop that the world was my oyster and nothing or no one was going to prevent me from achieving my goals. You may say I can't, but my heart and soul said, "Yes, you can"! When you have failed often enough, you will one day awaken to the realization that one day, things can and will get better. If you are bold enough to look in the mirror and tell yourself there must be another way, a better way, to get things done, by George, God will open the windows of heaven and make it happen for you. Once you make that bold admission, you should dare to start thinking differently, to try something new, speak what is not as though it is, trust your instincts. Your gifts are just waiting to be unleashed.

I have been in situations where I felt intimidated by the people around me and remained silent when a question was posed that I had the correct answer to, but was afraid to speak. I was gripped with fear that I may not get it right, so I remained quiet. The confident people, on the other hand, were loud, blurting out an answer even if it was incorrect and didn't seem to get embarrassed. Far too often, I stifled my ability to progress because my mind had been incarcerated and oppressed by years of authoritative rule. If you share that sentiment, take heart, it's your turn coming up next. Remember you are not a mistake, because God designed you to be exactly who you are. He created us equal, He has no favorites and you have the right to exist and succeed just like everyone else.

I remain amazed when I realize that all along God was watching me side-stepping His will. He gave me the ability to choose and I was exercising that right to do what I thought was right for me. In the meanwhile, God's hand was directing my path as though he was saying, "This far and no further." As a result of these boundaries when I wasn't paying Him any attention or caring that He was watching, I reflect on my life and remain forever grateful that He did not give up on me. I am also grateful that He did not give me everything I asked for. He knew best.

While in Canada I used the opportunity when I was not playing tennis or experimenting with cooking, to create a cookbook from several recipes that I had discovered. This new adventure, however, did not increase my desire to spend more time than was necessary in the kitchen, to improve my skills.

In our quiet residential neighborhood, the townhouses were attached duplexes designed to accommodate families only and no businesses could operate in the development. It was far different from life in the Big Apple; a much more peaceful lifestyle and more conducive to family life. Ottawa is considered one of the coldest cities in the world and so each home was outfitted with a designated electrical plug to keep the vehicles engines warm enough overnight, to ensure that they would respond with the first turn of the key each morning. The designs of the homes were similar, with a bonus feature of a fireplace in the family room on the ground floor. Our home was furnished with plush couches and high pile rugs, creating a very cozy atmosphere. The sliding doors opened onto a small backyard through which you could watch the snow falling in the winter months. From the windows on the first floor, you could watch each day as the icicles increased in numbers, creating images of their own on the well-established trees on the property. It was magical to watch the daily transformation of the landscape. It was a far cry from the solid, concrete jungle of towering buildings of New York City. Far off in the distance on a rare occasion, one could hear the sound of police sirens but there was no rumbling sound of subways or heavy traffic to contend with. One could appreciate instead the rustling of the wind occasionally whistling through the trees breaking the sound of silence. Our home was close to one of the highways so one would hear just a murmur of vehicles during the rush hour, but that was not enough to pollute the stillness of the afternoon.

Most days were filled with the duties of a housewife and with a new circle of friends extending invitations at will. Life was quite stress-free in those days when one day the most unimaginable event took place when I was about six months pregnant. It was just after 4 pm and my daughter was lying in my bed, glued to the television watching her favorite show, *Sesame Street*. I grabbed the opportunity to take a shower with the door ajar as I was still maintaining a listening ear to my daughter when I heard footsteps racing up the stairs up to my floor. I had just stepped out of the shower and found it strange that my husband was home so early and running up the stairs. What was the excitement, I wondered? I was partially dressed when I opened the door to come face to face with a very young, white boy with ginger-colored hair at the top of the stairs. I screamed at him, "What are you doing here in my house?" He was so shocked to see me that he darted back down the stairs through the family room through the now opened sliding glass doors and escaped.

My daughter was so focused on the program that she was oblivious to what had transpired. I mustered enough courage to call the police, gave them a description, and then called my husband. The response from the RCMP (Royal Canadian Mounted Police) was immediate and since the information given was accurate enough, they caught the culprits (there were four) running along the highway. What I did not know at the time was that there had been a series of break-ins in the same neighborhood, but no arrests had been made as the occupants could not identify the thieves

It took a while to get over the shock of it all and how different the outcome could have been. For days I was shaking, checking, and rechecking doors and windows to ensure they were secure. The police reported that the boys had developed a pattern of knocking on the front doors of the homes and if there was no response, they assumed no one was home and would then force back doors open. We were truly protected by divine intervention because not only was there was no personal harm, but they were only able to grab a very small item from the stereo system. They anticipated that the home was unoccupied so they had no time to rummage through the bedrooms to see if there was any valuable loot to be retrieved. They seemed to have had an interest in items that they could get rid of quickly and with no real distinguishing marks or labels. It all happened so quickly that it all seemed like a blur. As there were four of them in the house, they seemed to have spread out with one on each floor to cover all the bases as speedily as they could.

Once the police completed their investigation and determined that they were the same group breaking into the area, I was asked to go to the police station to identify at least one of the boys whom I had confronted. I was petrified at the thought of exposing myself to a line of questioning. I objected of course and under diplomatic status could not have been compelled to do so. As it was my legal right, I continued to object. The police officers were very persuasive however and pleaded with me to assist them in finally putting the young criminals behind bars. There was no adrenaline rush to travel to the station and peer through a glass window to identify the young men. It was one of the most nerve-racking experiences of my life. There were a few people lined up in a row and I was scared that I might make a mistake and identify the wrong boy. After sweating and doing a few deep breathing exercises, I pointed to the one I felt closely matched the description of the intruder I confronted at the top of the stairs. I was told at a later date that the four were imprisoned for nine months so justice was served and the neighborhood was safer for it.

My younger sister came to visit and this was the first time we would be sharing space in my home and those were very special moments of bonding. That weekend I was able to introduce her to my little family, to the city, and continuing the endless stories of our family history. She reminded me that my biological family assumed that I had enjoyed a wonderful life of glitz and glamour, but slowly I was able to expose some of the challenges I had endured in a very transparent way.

Birth of my third child

My husband and I had not discussed, thought of, nor planned on having more children. It just never happened to be part of any conversation we had when we were alone or with friends. Much to our surprise one chilly day in the fall, it was confirmed that I was pregnant. I am not sure how we both felt at the time regarding having another child, but the excitement grew as time progressed. I enjoyed my pregnancies as there had been no complications and I managed well while my skin glowed and my hair grew into large thick braids, almost unmanageable. I have little memory of how my daughter felt about having a brother or sister, but like her parents, we all became excited.

My pregnancy was fairly uneventful in the first two trimesters, however, things began to change soon after. The birth of my youngest child proved to be the most difficult of all and even life-threatening. After routine trips to the doctor, I was told that my blood pressure was becoming out of control. I had to be hospitalized two months before the delivery due date. During those weeks spent on bed rest, you begin to feel comfortable in the space, getting to know the staff and saying goodbye to other mothers who had delivered their bouncing babies and went home happily.

As the weeks went by, my stay became longer and longer as I awaited the arrival of my baby boy. The obstetrician became more concerned with each passing day as the blood pressure was not responding as they would have liked so a decision had to be made urgently. Six weeks before the delivery date, I was rushed to the theater where emergency surgery was performed at 4 am. Once the procedure was complete, I was returned to my hospital bed. My obstetrician was Haitian and demonstrated kindness, gentleness, and displayed a great bedside manner, which allowed me to feel very safe in his care. I was sedated throughout the surgery, while the nurse was checking my vital signs, I can remember distinctly saying to her, "I don't think I am going to make it." Can you imagine a patient coming out of surgery making such a statement to the nursing staff? Can you see a white person turning white? She turned as white as a sheet and the next recollection was awaking in the intensive care unit with tubes everywhere. I believe that was God again sending out an alert to save my life, which the enemy wanted to end. I stayed secured to a bed in the ICU and did not see my son for four days.

My husband was summoned many times throughout those days to come to the hospital not knowing what to expect on each of those occasions. I can only imagine how he must have suffered in silence as he went through this challenging period of waiting and the urgency to respond to each call. Considering the trauma endured post-surgery, my recovery was fairly quick and I was able to return home after a week of observation. Our newborn, on the other hand, born at a meager 3 ½ pounds had to remain hospitalized until he was at least five pounds before he could be released. During his stay, he remained in an incubator in the early days and as a result, his very fragile body had to be tube-fed. We visited the hospital often but with restricted hours, as they needed to maintain a sterile environment for our baby. However, when we were allowed in we had to be decked with robes and masks. It was amusing to view the little man through the glass walls of the nursery. He was the smallest child and yet the most active. There were 8, 9, and 10-lb babies lying in their beds sleeping soundly and barely moving, yet our son was always busy, busy. How could that be?

He was named Sacha after the son of my obstetrician's son and once he had gained the required weight, passed all the necessary tests, he was released and was on his way home to share a life with his big sister. She was extremely excited, curious, and attentive to him and very fussy that she now had a playmate. Physical therapy began immediately for our baby boy and continued for several months to improve his motor skills while we thankfully enjoyed the benefit of the great health care services Canada had to offer. We could only thank God that we had the most qualified doctor to be able to get all the care that we both needed. My son is alive having survived such a dramatic entrance to the world so I believe there is a special purpose for his life and I look forward to the day when he walks in the presence and power of God into his destiny and to fulfill his purpose.

We watched him being taught basic things: to roll over, to get on his knees, to creep, and eventually, to walk. It was wonderful to see the interaction between my daughter and her little brother and although she was a great, big, protective sister for a while, she at times became fretful that he was getting so much attention. She didn't quite understand how important it was to nurture and give the undivided attention to him as we supported him through the various stages of his development.

The ambivalence my daughter felt towards her brother was visible sometimes and she had to demonstrate it one way or the other to make her point. One day she was in her room and I thought for a while that she was unusually quiet so I went to find out what was going on, only to see that she had cut a huge chunk of hair at the front of her head. I assumed it was an attention-seeking moment – a tantrum of sorts. At this rebellious moment, I was drained, my energy level was zapped and other matters were arising that took my focus away from the situation. She settled down quickly as we were able to figure out how to cope. My ability to discern or some may say feminine intuition was very active and the discoveries challenged the status of my household.

There was a time when I felt guilty that I had not given my children my all, but I was a broken woman who didn't know she was broken. I was trying to keep my head above water while I navigated the role of a wife, mother, daughter, and friend. There was a lot to process, many rocky roads to travel, emotional scars to heal to try to sustain a good quality of life and a healthy lifestyle. One good thing was that the support I got, in a strange country from new friends, was very much evident and very much appreciated. The lessons I learned from that time in my life were mostly to take time to heal, take time for myself, and if possible help anyone I could along the way.

For several months while I lived in Canada I didn't share my childhood experiences with persons I had become familiar with. I believe that I was either embarrassed by my situation or was ashamed that I would not measure up to those around me if they knew. In the meantime, there was always a feeling of not being "good enough" and therefore I camouflaged my insecurities by paying closer attention to my external image. I made sure I was always well dressed, well-coordinated, my hair was well-coiffed and I wore complimentary accessories. Having a slim frame made it very easy to purchase affordable clothing, having discovered early that wearing designer clothing was not an essential detail to be fashionably dressed. On the flip side, I became aware that most designers selected more durable fabrics, well constructed for a better fit, and opted to ensure the colors chosen were symbolic of the trend for each season.

I wanted to use this time to explore as many forms of entertainment in the winter as I could to stay active. I played indoor tennis fairly regularly although it became a new experience having to play under ceiling lights and I also went snowshoeing, a strange new activity which I got used to very quickly. It seemed weird to have tennis rackets strapped to your feet, but it was fun and became a weekly event scheduled for the diplomats' wives prior to attending the teas organized at different homes. It certainly was one way of keeping busy, learning from others and being entertained by an eclectic group of women who were also foreigners.

In Canada, there are numerous bicycle paths and it was refreshing to be able to take my daughter riding along those secure pathways close to our home. This also encouraged me to go out and enjoy the wonderful outdoors, the crisp, fresh air, while allowing her to pick some wildflowers. She made little bouquets to give to some of our neighbors, before arranging the remainder in her little vase at home. This was a daily routine that we both looked forward to once the weather was favorable.

In those days, other forms of "grown-up" entertainment included visits to friends' homes for Sunday lunches, dinner parties, cocktails, enjoyed good conversation, while trying to change the world. The West Indian communities regularly hosted events, celebrating milestones from their various countries, played cricket and dominoes, and readily offered a spread of their native cuisine at every opportunity they got. They were very hospitable, frequently entertaining persons who were considered "new arrivals", helping them to settle and become acclimatized as quickly as possible.

After giving birth to our adorable son, like some mothers, I dealt with the agony of postpartum depression. This is a real condition that many mothers across the globe have had to cope with which most often goes undiagnosed. I wasn't aware at the time that I was experiencing the dramatic effects of this condition, until I had visitors in my home soon after the birth of my son. I was extremely sensitive to many things around me and there could be no other explanation for my behavior. My female house guest whom I had known since childhood, behaved in a very disrespectful manner and my response was harsh and swift. She probably realized much later that her actions were insensitive, but I must admit mine was extreme. That situation made me realize just how easily one can become unrecognizable when responding to an incident where they feel threatened. There was a certain level of tolerance that I would accept especially after the trauma of childbirth as I did, which left me emotionally fragile.

We all have moments when we behave in insensitive ways, but to be able to recognize it and to forgive yourself and the other party, can sometimes take several years. I am not sure that apologizing was the correct posture during that particular incident because there is a protocol one should adopt when you are a guest in someone's home. There are certain rules of etiquette that you do not violate if you wish to be invited back; be sure to observe how your host manages the household, see how they conduct themselves in their environment and let that be your guide. There are often unspoken rules.

Here is what I have learned about postpartum depression, which can be triggered by many things and a few symptoms are:

- Feeling irritated and angry
- Lack of patience
- Everything annoys you
- Resentment towards your partner or others close to you
- You feel people are judging you

These are just a few of the symptoms that I was experiencing which may explain my volatile response to the houseguest at that time.

During the months that followed, my son continued growing by leaps and bounds and by now responding very well to the therapy. He was a fighter and seemed eager to get going. There seemed to be little concern from his care providers as he was developing at a satisfactory rate. He had a wonderful personality and people were drawn to him regardless.

One of my favorite seasons has always been Christmas and being in Canada was no different. It was always a wonderful time in our home and every effort was made to make it special. We put our pine tree up, had it well decorated with strings of colored lights, and lots of gifts were placed below it, mostly for the children. We watched with glee the sight of snowflakes just outside our glass doors with the lights, filtering through from the street and the houses nearby. There was a constant reflection of the multicolored lights on the icicles and snowflakes, which served as a wintry backdrop. It was a very picturesque sight indeed and so we often left the curtains open so we could embrace the beauty of the outdoors night after night. We loved to watch our daughter open her gifts on Christmas morning while we sat on the floor and watched the glow in her eyes as each package was methodically torn apart.

We were still in our nightwear early one Christmas morning enjoying that intimate moment together when suddenly there was a rapid knocking on the front door. Winter in Canada was cold and could be brutal, so I wondered who dared to leave their warm bed to venture out. We had not extended any invitations to visitors so this was a surprise. When I opened the door there was this young woman, standing there with a gift in her hand stating that she brought a gift for our daughter!!!! I gather she expected to be invited in, but that was not a part of my Christmas morning plan. I had a vague idea who she was but I was not sure what her mission was. I was not very gracious I must admit and dismissed her, not in the most polite way, before slamming the door shut, offering no semblance of Caribbean hospitality.

It was amazing how God will often disclose some things supernaturally. I became acutely aware of things that under normal circumstances, I should not have been privy to. One may ask, "How did you know this or that?" I could only respond by saying I just knew. Maybe one day men will realize that women "know" things so any deceptive activity that they think they have mastered, just know that the woman already knows. God helped me navigate this journey and I will be forever grateful to Him. I implore you to trust Him as I did, accepting that you too can have a close and direct relationship with Him because that is exactly what He desires.

Barbados/Jamaican vacation from Canada

The wheels were in motion for me to finally make contact with other members of the family so on our first family vacation together we jetted off to the first part of the journey to my husband's homeland, Barbados before heading to my homeland. The Barbados portion of the trip was to introduce me to the island and for him to reconnect with friends and family in anticipation of his relocation the following year. It was different but we experienced no major drama traveling with two small children thankfully, apart from the expected earache as we engaged in the descent. It was a pleasant trip with a few anxious moments about what to expect.

We enjoyed two weeks in Barbados and the last week was spent with Venetia in Jamaica. I prayed long and hard throughout hoping that things would go well for all of us. Subconsciously, I knew that anything was possible with my mother, so I always braced myself for an unnecessary explosion. She greeted us warmly and seemed genuinely happy we were there so she could show off her family. I began to breathe a sigh of relief after the first 24 hours still not sure if it was safe to let my guard down. On the second day of our stay, I made contact with another brother who resided in the same parish and his response to my call was immediate and he arrived at the house in quick time to make that long-overdue connection. I had not told my mom about this visit, so when he arrived at the door, it was very interesting to see her reaction. He picked me up in his arms, just like my older brother had done, and held me up like I was a long lost doll. He said he had "waited for years for that moment". This demonstrative behavior was unusual for me as I was not accustomed to being greeted in such an affectionate manner, especially by someone who was a stranger to me. Here seemed another person (then a stranger) on the planet who longed to see, to feel, and to embrace me in such a loving manner. It was surreal and it was so pure. This was not like the embrace in a romantic relationship. It was much deeper, from within the soul.

I formally introduced my brother to my mom, but I believe she already knew who he was as he had by now become a public persona in the nation. I could tell she felt blindsided that she was not told any of this was going to happen. She had no idea I had found out about my adoption or that I had already met family members. I could tell that no amount of scholastic achievement had prepared her for this moment. She was always the one person in the room who was the smartest, most educated, and in control of the conversations and now at this moment she had no words. There was a look of fear in her eyes as if she had been betrayed. For a moment I asked myself if I should have done this differently. Should I have told her in advance? I finally stopped trying to rationalize a situation where this unbelievable secret was kept from me all those years. It was their secret. Why should I now have felt responsible for her emotions?

My brother stayed for a short while but was on a mission to introduce me to my biological mother, Nettie. I was very nervous about this meeting but curious at the same time to meet the woman who had given birth to me. It was like watching a movie in slow motion on a television network. We left the house that same afternoon and chatted while driving to the residence, as he prepared me for the introduction. We entered the small residence and there were several people around to whom I was introduced – including more brothers. Their faces were a blur and my recollection of that moment is still a blur. I was taken into a room to have a private meeting with Nettie. She was very pensive and said she wondered if that day would ever come that she would see me again. There were no tears, but Nettie wanted to ask my forgiveness for giving me away. She explained that it was not intended to be a long-term situation, but she was going through a period where she found herself in a relationship in which she had no control. She explained that my adopted mother saw me and asked if she could care for me. She must have known of Nettie's circumstance but Nettie willingly agreed to the proposition as an escape from her reality. I was only three years old at the time and I have no recollection of living anywhere but with the parents with whom I grew to know.

These are the thoughts of one of my brothers: -

"For as long as I can remember, my mother (Antoinette – Nettie) would always talk about her childhood experiences and reflect on the circumstances of her life, revealing the many episodes of growing up in Westmoreland. As a single parent caring for three young children in rural Jamaica during the 1950s, which typified the lives of thousands of Jamaican women who were deprived of proper education, she lacked the much-needed support and wherewithal to provide for their young ones. She formed relationships that eventually deteriorated but produced three children at the time. The outcome forced her to remain resolute in her determination that none of her children would endure a fate similar to hers.

While living in the rural parish of Westmoreland she had only obtained a primary school education and the economic opportunities were non-existent to survive. In the travails of her storytelling, my mother would speak of buying her a new dress, to bathing her and attaching matching ribbons to the freshly combed hair. She talked about her pride in walking her through the community, the joy in taking her to infant school, the delight in her appearance, and the obvious prospect she showed in her early years for academic success. We could hear her carefully nourishing the promise and possibility that Peggy showed. This was her constant refrain as she maintained that twinkle in her eye.

She confided in Mrs. McDonald, the principal of the local primary school, about her hardship and her desire to temporarily relocate to Kingston to be better able to provide for her children. She recalled on several occasions how much she dreaded the idea. By then, Mrs. McDonald had taken a keen interest in Peggy who was always admired by the local folk. She was noticed.

Nettie decided to have Mrs. McDonald care for Peggy while she placed the other two children in the care of relatives. Over time, Mrs. McDonald requested to legally adopt Peggy.

Nettie spoke frequently, reflectively, and soberly, perhaps trying to offer some kind of justification, if not endorsement, for her decision to grant the request for adoption. It was as though she needed to state her case with self-righteous justification, and that she owed Peggy a chance to make for a better life. It took several years however for her to come to grips with her decision. The German writer, Johann Wolfgang Von Goethe, suggested that one would have to look an individual the way she could be so that she would become what she should be.

My mother had an insatiable desire to learn everything she could about Peggy but it was only after Mrs. McDonald's death we discovered there was a condition for the adoption of Peggy. It was agreed that there would be the minimum if any contact between biological mother and daughter. That my mother honored the "agreement" under the weight of an enduring burden and guilt reflects the purity of innocence and moral courage. As it turned out, there would be no contact.

Before meeting Peggy, I had formulated an impression of my sister as self-assured and confident based on her middle-class upbringing and the social standing of Mrs. McDonald. While the circumstances of our upbringing were quite different, I was however confident that being my mother's child, a certain element of noblesse oblige would be evident. My mother's reflection about Peggy was that she would have been bright, articulate, and well-spoken – traits evident in the personality and character of Mrs. McDonald. I would often wonder what she would be like.

Well, the wait was finally over when the eldest sibling engineered the re-union with our sister. I remembered it as a joyful day, to finally meet her. The resemblance to my mother was striking, with her face chiseled in perfect unison, high cheekbones, the same dreamy eyes, tone, texture, and complexion. She wore an air of sophistication but as I was soon to find out, was never affectedly or irritatingly grand or given to self-importance. She was charming, to say the least, and I became relaxed in her company right away, feeling her genuine warmth, even as I sensed a deep and stirring thoughtfulness. She was exactly what I would want my big sister to be, to show off to the world. The memory of that day – seeing her the first time, standing poised and confident, and freely sharing her thoughts – was magical. The sister I met seemed ambitious, focused and I loved her immediately. My mother's prayers had been answered".

During my first meeting with Nettie, she couldn't resist repeating over and over how sorry she was for not being there for me. It wasn't the ideal time to explain the emotional details surrounding the adoption and the aftermath. I am not sure what could have made the occasion different, but it was awkward for me. The conversation was strained; everyone was looking for a reaction and I was not comfortable probing for answers or to make her more fragile than she already appeared. There was not enough time to talk about her other two children she left behind to be cared for by others. I cannot imagine what her life was like, but on meeting her, I sensed she was a kind, gentle soft-spoken person who could have been easily manipulated by cunning, crafty, self-serving individuals. She received help from other family members but still struggled to make the right decisions for herself and she felt lost, helpless, and alone. I met other brothers who were present during that brief visit, who lived with Nettie for the greater part of their lives. I have learned that the other siblings had a very hard life with their father so while I was given up for adoption and supposedly having a better life, they lived in fear and trembling in their home. Nettie lived with her common-law husband who seemed to have operated like a drill sergeant, delivering punishment that was brutal and extreme. Their life was tough.

I wasn't sure what emotions I should have had at that time with this revelation. Confusion or uncertainty? There were so many unanswered questions. There had been so much drama already that I had to process but I was also preparing for my return Venetia's house after this visit. My brother made his departure quickly as we suspected that the emotional tension would have been high, and we were right. My husband and children were left behind as I wandered off on my adventure. Venetia was very emotional when I returned and nervously asked where I had been, although her intuition had the answer. She then posed an absurd question as to why I had not told her I had been in contact with the family and that I had made arrangements to meet Nettie. She had figured out what the mission was and so the atmosphere had changed from happy to see you, to why are you deceiving me. I confronted her about *her* secret and she stuttered through an incoherent response as she was caught off guard, not having had time to develop one that was plausible and intellectual. She couldn't explain why I wasn't told and of course, she couldn't blame my dad because after all, she was the academic one in the family with all the answers. I deduced at the time that because of the rocky relationship she and I had had over the years, she felt that I would have deserted her and moved on to develop a more cohesive relationship with my other family members. I tried to assure her that she was the only mother I had ever known and although the secret was now out, I could not have abandoned her to cleave to other family members. Why couldn't we share? Her insecurity and vulnerability became pronounced at this moment, as it was obvious that she had nurtured so many people in her lifetime and they all abandoned her because of her harsh and aggressive personality. I was the only was stayed the course.

On the flip side to this situation, I had a new family who felt I should have done more to develop my relationship, with Nettie especially. There were always innuendos to that effect, but I was in recovery mode trying to process the emotions of the discovery. The family had no idea what my life had been like and the maze I had to fight my way through to reach the other side. I had by now had several disappointments of my own; I had rejection, abandonment, and now this just compounded those emotions. I had endured feelings of not being loved, not being appreciated, of not being recognized for my abilities, of not being accepted for who I was. Now there was the added pressure on me to reach out to get to know and to love a previously unknown circle of people. It was like having an out-of-body experience. Who am I?

I had hoped during this trip that a good bond would have been created between my husband and my brother but that was not meant to be. They both had opposing political views concerning a regional political situation in Cuba at the time and unfortunately, the possibility of friendship was shattered at that moment. Intellectual egos were at stake and I was tossed in the midst of it. My brother had invested time in the local and regional political arena, interacted with the members of the government in Cuba, was a speechwriter for Michael Manley, the former Prime Minister of Jamaica so I had hoped my husband would concede, but that was not meant to be.

While on this trip, we were invited to the home of Leon, the family friend I had had my own "Me Too" experience with, several years previously. There were only two people at this reception who knew of the situation and that was he and I. I went out of curiosity, to see how he would have reacted to my family and especially to me. We arrived and were warmly received, had a wonderful meal and the gentleman was just as charming and the perfect host as usual. His wife remained oblivious to his antics and I was told that he continued with his behavior of indiscretion with a few young women who also rejected his advances. There was never any apology for his behavior, as I believe he thought he was entitled and he would not have been exposed or penalized. It was incredible to me that someone could be so callous, showing no remorse. One of William Shakespeare's famous verses was, "The evil that men do lives after them, the good is oft interred with their bones". Unfortunately, generations of these predators could suffer the consequences of these irresponsible behavior patterns.

We returned home to Canada and I had a lot to ponder regarding my roots and wondered what the future had in store for us as a family. Would my life have been any different? Would it change the relationship with my husband now that we both shared in this revelation together? Would there have been any empathy towards my emotional state as I processed things? I desperately needed trust and transparency in any relationship, especially at that time in my life. I needed to feel safe and secure with those around me. What I failed to realize was that my source should have been God alone and not that of another human being, who was just as broken as I was. My expectations were flawed and unrealistic. If I knew then that God was the only one who could validate my existence, who could establish my purpose, who knew the plans He had for me and would bring them to fruition, I would have known that my latter days would be better. If I knew that, then I would have had no fear. There are so many what-ifs in our lives, but we fail to realize that there are lessons to be learned when we go through the fire and the rain so we can become polished and made whole.

To keep myself entertained, I befriended a few tennis players and that gave me great joy to be able to challenge myself once more. I could take out any frustration on the one thing I felt I had control over at the time – the tennis ball. Exercising was always an important factor for me and it was great to be able to enjoy this activity, even in the dead of winter. I also enjoyed engaging in one on one meetings with people who wanted to share their stories, whether they were joyful or painful ones. I was a very good listener, and so it was easy for people to share with me and I felt satisfied that on many occasions, I was able to allay their fears and bring hope to situations. I wish I had had similar mentors to help me work through my stuff when I had needed help.

There are many fond memories of living in Canada. The country had earned the reputation of being one of the cleanest yet coldest countries and the city of Ottawa certainly represented that classification. The sanitation services were outstanding unlike that of NYC. The snow on the streets was removed overnight; traffic was not inhibited, there were very few disruptions to one's daily routine because of the weather conditions, there were lots of outdoor activities year-round and people were generally kind and friendly. The public buses were clean and well maintained, they ran on schedule making trips in and out of the city quite easy which encouraged commuters to use public transportation rather than driving into the city. This beautiful city which boasts four seasons although I suffered through those long, cold winters, will always be one of our favorite residences as a family, especially because one of our children was born there.

There was some trepidation with the idea of moving to Barbados as I would not have had close relatives and friends to lend the support I would need. I had no clue what was in store for me but it was important to trust God and the process.

Chapter Four

Barbados

When our family took a trip to Barbados in the summer of 1983, we were in the company of a large contingent of Barbadians going home for their annual holidays. I can remember hearing conversations about the small islands in the Caribbean but I never studied nor paid any specific attention to them including Barbados. Visiting the island allowed me to gain great respect and understanding for the small nation, of its people, the economy, and most importantly, the culture. We would be moving there permanently the following year and that would eventually become my new address. It was imperative that I grasped all that I could to be able to enjoy this new environment and what it would mean to me as a foreigner. The education was quick and the adaptation had to be equally quick. My discoveries came in interesting ways, but like it or not this nation would be adopting my children and me, a place we would call home, a place where many prayers would be answered.

Introduction to Barbados

The island of Barbados is the most eastern of the Caribbean islands measuring, 21 miles long by 14 miles wide at the widest point. It is geologically unique because it came into existence because of two landmasses merging due to a volcanic eruption causing the accumulation of coral. Archaeologists reported that the early settlers were Amerindians who arrived from Venezuela. They were adventurers who travelled from Alaska, through Canada and further south, thrived on agriculture and grew produce such as cotton, guavas, corn, peanuts, and papayas, to name a few.

These Arawaks were successful explorers who chose to reside on the island until they were later challenged by the fierce Carib Indians who were taller, sharp bowmen, were cannibals who used poisonous arrows to capture and destroy their enemy. The Caribs had inhabited other neighboring islands as well such as Dominica and St. Vincent and the Grenadines.

The next arrivals to the island were the Portuguese who were en route to Brazil. They decided to name the island *Los Barbados* because of the large, bearded fig trees that were very prominent on the island. It was the arrival of the English who would have a long-lasting impact on the island eventually establishing the Westminster system of governance still operating within that framework to this day. When they arrived and claimed the island in the year 1627, they would settle there with a few slaves to farm the land. Once they had settled comfortably, they began creating an economic system that benefited their homeland for centuries to come. In fact, the system made the British Empire very prosperous while it stymied any type of indigenous economic growth or development. The plantations were established to produce tobacco, cotton, and of course later sugarcane, with a deeply rooted enslaved system. It was after a few natural disasters that the island finally recovered and the slaves continued to farm various crops.

There was a small Jewish presence that settled on the island in the 1600s, both in Bridgetown to the south and Speightstown to the north. Their knowledge in trade and commerce helped to rejuvenate the local economy and they applied their expertise to engage in the production and cultivation of the sugar cane industry with new technological methods. With the input from those Jewish settlers in the 1660s and 70s sugarcane became one of the country's highest currency earners, a position that continued for several decades. The majority of the natives originated from West Africa as slaves, to work on the plantations, while the whites and mixed races either came as the colonizers, indentured slaves, or merchants. Some political prisoners seeking religious asylum also formed part of the early population of the island.

Once slavery was abolished in 1863, some newly freed blacks had both the courage and intelligence to know that they could be truly free and empowered by becoming educated. They took advantage of the educational system which became available to them and some made the ambitious decision not to work in the fields, while others remained working the land.

Barbados was established as a colony under the British Empire until 1966 when they sought political independence from their European colonizers. The Rt. Honorable Errol Walton Barrow, Barbados' "Father of Independence" would be one of the formidable leaders who contributed to its newfound independence while maintaining ties with the British monarch, represented on the island by a Governor General.

One important discovery I made much later was that between 1881 and 1937 the Barbados Railway progressed from an idea to a fully operating mode of transportation, initially servicing the areas from the capital Bridgetown to Tree Houses in the parish of St. Philip. There was a steep incline the train had to maneuver, carrying sugarcane and passengers who at times were asked to disembark and help push sections up the hill. Several strict rules were governing the operation of the service but the attendants complied to ensure its success.

The Crop Over Festival was one of the historically entrenched hang-overs from the colonial period which was celebrated at the end of the sugarcane season. It was referred to as "harvest home" indicating that the months of plowing and planting of the sugarcane had now been harvested, and it was time to celebrate. This traditional harvest festival, having had its early beginnings on the sugar plantation, began as early as 1687 featuring singing, dancing, music with instruments like shak-shak, banjo, guitar, triangle, and fiddle. In addition to the musical side, there were traditions like climbing the grease pole, feasting, and drinking competitions. There was also the burning of an effigy called Mr. Harding, which represented difficult times and the hope for better days. The festival was disbanded for a while and revived in 1974 by the Barbados Tourist Board in collaboration with the entertainment community. It has evolved and continues to become a springboard for phenomenal creative talent, a festival that attracts the attention of international revelers, celebrities, and the media. Barbados would come alive in every way possible during this season. Although not the largest carnival in the Caribbean, it is unique in its ability to send a message to the world that the island has numerous packages to offer and this summer event offers a few weeks of Caribbean rhythms, food, and cultural explosion. Visitors have the opportunity to enjoy some pudding and souse and sip on the Banks Beer or Mount Gay Rum.

The Crop Over festival begins in May and culminates on the first Monday in August referred to as the Grand Kadooment festival, a public holiday. The specific genre of music is calypso which was generated in another Caribbean island, Trinidad and Tobago. The music is played on single musical instruments or full orchestras depending on the desired effect. Metal drums, called steelpans are cut and the tops hammered into shapes producing a high pitch, melodious sound, quite different from other musical instruments. The composers write lyrics based on topical issues, political satire, and other cultural issues that the average person would be talking about in the rum shops, the hair salons, or other gatherings. The music is constantly evolving and lends to young and mature talent filling the local airwaves with beats that are popular among all demographics around the region.

The festival was in full swing when we arrived on the island and I had never experienced an event like that before. I was never interested in participating in such cultural activities in New York or Ottawa where many from the West Indian diaspora marked them as compulsory, annual events. I learned very quickly that this was also a competition to select the best single or group in various categories of music and costume design. The calypsonians had built a loyal fan base who had memorized the lyrics and at each gathering, there would be a sing-a-long. The judges comprised locals who were experienced musicians or entertainers themselves, who were charged with the responsibility of crowning the best in each category, once he or she satisfied the criteria set by their governing body. Radio air time certainly contributed to the appeal and popularity of the songs. Some of the lyrics were very risqué but most of the patrons were satisfied with the creativity of the artists. Barbadians (Bajans) are not as vocal publicly as Jamaicans are known to be, but will express their opinion vehemently among friends, in lunchrooms, hallways, byways, driveways, and among family. Through their music, however, they can give a voice to the many issues they are passionate about.

During the several events leading up to the finale, locals and visitors spent hours critiquing the quality of the songs and everyone by now has become an expert in calypso music appreciation. There were many moods, an abundance of food, drinks, laughter, and building of relationships. The Barbadians from the diaspora, who planned their annual holiday well in advance, were referred to as the Bajan Yankee, the British Bajan, the Canadian Bajan claiming that "this is we culture". Visitors would have been seduced by the Tourism advertisements and Bajan acquaintances, to come and celebrate with the locals and so they too flooded the shores, to enjoy the spectacle of what was Crop Over. The island has been known to be a safe destination, so it was easy to attract visitors and celebrities who desired the slow pace and easy lifestyle that the island offers.

The day of Grand Kadooment is a public holiday and all the months of designing and manufacturing of the costumes and floats are now on display for all the world to see. The costume designers worked hard at conceptualizing the costumes and floats ensuring that they had adequate time to develop an excellent product. Their displays were themed and they all strived to achieve a greater impact than the previous year.

The revelers would have selected the groups (or bands) they wished to join based on the personalities, style of the costumes, affiliations, and cost. Some people would spend weeks in the gym preparing their bodies for the grueling time of partying in the heat in barely-nothing costumes. There were huge sums of money spent to join certain bands and they were required to assemble at the starting point as early as 5 am. The expression "jumping in the band" was coined to highlight the high energy movement of street dancing. Their costumes included waistbands with flasks of liquid to keep them hydrated en route and several groups had choreographed formations for the revelers to appeal to the judges.

The event started at the national stadium where a selection of qualified judges would rate the costumes and performers before they began their trek through the streets, winding their way along byways. As I stood on the sidewalk, I gazed at the revellers some of whom were intoxicated by the intensity of the heat, the pulsating sounds of the music while sipping on the beverage in their pouches.

The beat of the music and chatter of the crowds seemed to command them to finish the course. As an observer, one could feel the excitement as the bands went by and as this was the climax of the event, could easily have become infused with the joy and laughter of it all but from a distance. The kaleidoscope of colorful costumes that took hours to be created and the floats that took months to be designed and built would soon be on full display heading to the final destination.

This festival was a much different experience from what I was exposed to as a child. There were smiles, joy, laughter on the faces of these people who seemed genuinely happy. In comparison, the Hosay festival which I shared earlier was intense and there was no laughter, no visible joy to indicate they were having a good time. From the eyes of a child, it appeared to be a sad occasion back then. To support those gathered to celebrate the Grand Kadooment event, food and drink stalls were set up along the roadside while the local television station broadcasted several hours of the parade from various locations along the way to appeal to the wider audience of local and international viewers.

The parade could take as much as 10 hours from start to finish and bands were judged based on originality, theme, creativity, choreography, colors, uniformity, and cohesion through the stadium. There were also the wayside judges who were very vocal about their opinions. The costume designers were greatly influenced by designers from carnivals in other countries like Trinidad & Tobago, and Rio de Janeiro, adding their creativity to the designs, incorporating some of the cultural history of the island. The curious bystanders peered through the crowds to see if they recognized church folks, politicians, their neighbors, their children, work colleagues, local or any visiting celebrities.

By early afternoon the bands were in the final leg of the trip and one would observe the skimpy costumes becoming skimpier a result of the heat and sweat and I am sure many costumes fell apart. The vigorous gyrations, sweat, and drinks were by now out of control. If there was a drizzle of rain it was welcomed to cool things down but it would affect the condition of some of the very fragile/flimsy costumes. Those conditions, however, would not have dampened the spirits of the revellers and may even have had added to the pleasure of playing mass.

With aching feet and hoarse voices, they finally assembled to share drinks and food. Some continued with feeble gyrating of their bodies, still wedged onto each other, sharing their laughter, sweat, and body odor. The young, old, middle-aged, children, politicians, Christians and non-Christians were all one on this occasion. The only criteria to "jump in a band" was one's ability to pay the fees as required and withstand the intense heat. Some groups chose to have professional, choreographed segments, so rehearsals were necessary.

In addition to the celebrities who clamber to the shores of Barbados, the island was catapulted into worldwide fame by Robyn Rihanna Fenty, a native of the island. She is a style icon, successful businesswoman, songwriter, singer and an actress who has defied the odds and proven that if you go after your dreams and are prepared to work hard, anything is possible. Rihanna is admired for her devotion to her nation and carries the flag with dignity and grace.

I have written extensively about the festival in Barbados because that was the first cultural experience I had and learned more over time about the development and execution of the event. I have lived much longer in Barbados than any other territory so there was more to share about my life there. Things returned to normal on the island very quickly once the carnival was over so as a family, we began to explore the unique places of interest as recommended by friends. As I interacted with a few of the residents, I remembered the advice I received from some Bajan women I met overseas that I was to be very careful as the local women were very unhappy with their men marrying "foreign" women. It was recommended that I remain somewhat aloof as a way of protecting myself, my marriage, and of course my family as a whole. "They will not support you or your position", I was told. It seemed odd that these were women of Bajan heritage who had migrated to other countries but seemed well versed about the nature of the women who resided on the island. How does one react to that when you are in a foreign country with no extended family of your own to stand with you when the going gets tough? That advice remained in the recesses of my mind, always sensitive to my encounters while living every day merrily enjoying my little family.

There were two families with whom my family and I bonded fairly quickly and their care of us was invaluable and there are only fond memories as I cherish every effort they made to love us unconditionally. These were two of the most sincere friends I could ever have asked for. They were all accomplished in their own right and stood shoulder to shoulder with me throughout my journey, never judging me, but always welcomed me with open arms. I was introduced to a host of activities by a new friend Roseanne, so I attended my first fashion show at the Sandy Lane Hotel, joined the original Kiwanian Club of Barbados and eventually served on the board of the American Women's Club, the Barbados chapter.

I was wooed by the island known famously for its white sandy beaches, good infrastructure, good roads, and excellent water supply due to the coral stone foundation, but there was anxiety about relocating to the Caribbean. I still considered myself a city girl, who liked the accessibility to everything and anything night and day as I had grown accustomed to that lifestyle, but that was about to change. I now had a young family and needed to stop looking back but to acclimatize myself to some new conditions. I had to adjust to the fact that supermarkets and shops were closed early weekdays, 1pm on Saturdays, and closed on Sundays. This proved quite a challenge for me initially and forced me to plan my activities in keeping with the times that services were available to us. We managed well in a small apartment hotel and relished every opportunity to sit on the shores of the magnificent beaches of the south coast watching the waves gently caress the coastline. With little buckets, shovels, and sunblock in hand, this became a part of our daily routine.

The children were happy to be anywhere their parents were and we easily made friends with our neighbors. Our living quarters were very small but adequate and provided all the facilities we needed, including access to the restaurant located on the premises. I felt safe and secure in my marriage then, while we both were readjusting to island living as we had both lived in North America for many years. There were several months of waiting for our personal effects to arrive from our overseas assignment, but we enjoyed not having to deal with the changing seasons from Winter to Spring to Summer to Fall.

With time we were offered a house that was just suitable for our needs, close to public transportation with a nursery and school for the children nearby. Quickly I began the process of arranging our furniture to recreate a comfortable environment for us to settle. A large part of island living is realizing that your life could be an open book. I was by no means used to neighbors watching my every move, peeking through the louvers of their windows, not only to see who came and went but so much more. It felt so intrusive as if my privacy was under siege. I can remember I was out one day and a neighbor could give me a full description of the person who stopped by, how often they turned up, the type of vehicle, the color, registration number, sex of the person, and the time they visited. That was such a shock to me coming from a big city where people hardly spoke to you unless you spoke first. Island living brought a new set of rules and expectations. I could understand if this was done for security reasons, but this was not about security, this was "community awareness".

I didn't work for the first few months on the island so I would fill my days starting with a gym I discovered around the corner with a spa, and go for extended walks. It wasn't long before I met an American woman who was married to a very successful Barbadian man and we quickly developed a friendship as we had a common interest and that allowed me the opportunity to play lawn tennis. I looked forward to those moments when I could engage in one of my favorite outdoor activities. There was no better time for me than being on the tennis court.

A short while after we were settled, I heard a knock on my front door. It happened to be a woman from my country who had been residing on the island for many years. Can you imagine making a lifetime friend all because of some cardboard boxes? She was introduced as Martha and stopped by because she saw these large boxes in the garage and she wanted them as she was moving house. That short encounter fostered a very close, lifetime friendship. I had never had a friend as fierce and determined as she was to stand up, stand firm, and support me as she did. Through personal experience, she developed a passion to care for women whom she felt were disenfranchised and she had no qualms about making her feelings and presence felt. She stood up for her rights and the rights of others whenever she suspected rights were being violated. She was determined to be the best, to have the best, and made no apologies for it. She was a good example of how one should live their best life.

Martha and I went everywhere together during the day which gave people the impression that we were sisters. We didn't look alike by any means but had a great rapport. She kept diapers and food at her home for my son and always had many meals to entertain us. I took advantage of the fact that she was passionate about cooking and was an excellent cook who could whip up a meal from scratch in a moment, but I must admit I learned nothing from her in that regard. She was extremely generous and loved to entertain her friends and they loved to be entertained by her. It was so special to have a friend with whom we could freely share our childhood experiences and have a laugh or two.

For all those years, she never knew that painful part of my childhood even though she did meet my mother on one occasion. It was still that part of my life I was uncomfortable sharing. The idea of adoption made me feel inadequate, a failure, unworthy to some degree and so it never entered the conversation. The bond that developed with Martha was like that of a sister. She loved me and I treasured her as a friend and a confidante. She took great interest in showing me the island, where to shop, things to do, and how to remain sane. She was privy to the experiences of some women from other countries who had struggled with being accepted in Barbadian society by the local women. Their perception and conversation were that we had "come to take away the best local men; the crème de la crème" they said. It was never our intention to handpick a specific group of men to target and capture their hearts, however, in many situations, there seemed to be a deliberate attempt to undermine some of those marriages. The situations ultimately became unhealthy for everyone including those outside the marriage. Quite a few marriages were destroyed as a result to the point where some were told, "You could go back to where you came from." Thank goodness this did not apply to all foreign marriages, but just a handful that I became aware of quite early.

During this time of adjustment, a mutual friend introduced me to a lovely American woman whose husband was a local diplomat. Their home base was in Barbados but he was assigned to a high profile overseas posting representing his nation. Once he retired, they returned home to what was to become a life of peace and calm. His wife loved to cook and was regularly hosting lunches, brunches, afternoon teas, and dinners. She reminded me so much of my mother who also had a zeal for entertaining her friends and associates frequently. As I watched the lady prepare her table, I could see the passion she had for people, reminiscent of the joy in our home when our tables were also set with the finest crockery, flatware, tablecloth, napkins, and flowers to entertain the elite.

I felt very sad for her when her husband passed away because she had also migrated from the US and while not a Bajan opted to remain on the island after his death. For all the entertaining she did there was only one family who took any interest in her well-being. Very few others took time to visit her or extend an invitation to entertain her in any way. This behavior pattern was all too familiar to me. There were so many memories/similarities of experiences that my mother endured when all the high-profile people she would have entertained suddenly became too busy with their own lives to share a few moments with her when she craved that companionship during the latter days of her life.

Life for me was simple in those days; taking care of the children and window shopping with my new BFF (Best Friend Forever). I was used to having my own money which gave me a sense of financial independence, so I felt it was time to earn an income for myself and so the search began for employment. I very quickly found a part-time job at the local hospital which allowed me another taste of the Bajan culture.

I still spent time relying on external sources for guidance and mentoring, until one day I had the sense that the Lord was saying to me, "Why are you seeking answers from third parties when you could come directly to me?" Some may not understand what that means but it was a profound statement to me. It was an eye-opener to come to grips with the fact that I was straddling the fence with what I believed. I wasn't trusting that God's divine providence was already responding to my needs and I needed to exercise the faith of a mustard seed. At various times in my life, I realized that God was just waiting for me to put away childish things and seek Him for the answers I was in search of.

How often do we seek answers from persons who quite often are not equipped to guide us? We classify them as older and wiser or have had similar experiences so they would have an idea of how to get us out the rut we are in. The truth is the only person who has the answers is the Lord Jesus Christ and unless He gives his prophet a word in season for you, trust Him and Him alone. He says in his word, "I will never leave you nor forsake you." The Bible also says, "Blessed is the man that walketh not in the counsel of the ungodly, nor standeth in the way of sinners, nor sitteth in the seat of the scornful, but his delight is in the Lord and in Him should he meditate day and night". Who are you standing or sitting with? Who do you trust in this season? Who is your counsellor? Who is whispering in your ear?

For a very long time, I was socialized to believe that church was compulsory on Sundays to sing songs to the Lord, repeat some scripted prayers, give an offering, take communion, and leave. For me, there was little or no sense of God's presence or evidence of any transformation taking place in my mind and spirit to bring about any change in my behavior or circumstance. I had the perception that people were hypocrites going to church and sharing in communion when they didn't even like each other. It was just hard to accept that people's lives were being impacted positively. Nevertheless, I continued to go as a matter of routine. I also did what I thought was the right thing to do by having my children attend confirmation classes and eventually got confirmed in the Anglican Church. This was my attempt to try to inject some measure of spirituality into my household and satisfy a need to be connected to God.

My need to find my worth drew me in search of God. How do I find Him and if I did what do I say to Him? How will He speak to me? Will I hear him when He speaks? There was that part of me that was sensitive to a "knowing" that I couldn't explain, that yes, He existed but in what form? I visited a few churches during this season when I was invited by acquaintances. My children became disillusioned with the church and found it boring so it became challenging as they got older to get them to go. As I continued my search, I became aware through testimonies of people that God was able to perform miracles whether we believed He could or not. People were delivered from drug use, healed of critical illnesses, marriages restored, spared job losses, healed emotionally from rejection, and abandonment to live wholesome lives.

One pastor I met along the way and with whom I have the utmost respect, made a statement one morning that had a tremendous impact on me. He referenced our ability to choose the direction our lives would take. He said that you are not responsible for who your parents are, where you grew up, who your siblings are, where you went to school nor the neighborhood you were brought in. You are responsible however for where you are now and where you are going in the future. You have no idea how much that meant to me and that was the beginning of a paradigm shift in my mind. I had no choice about my situation, but I could choose how I dealt with events and how I moved forward. I could ask myself what were the positive things I learned over time or keep looking back at hurt, despair, and pain. I knew I could affect someone else's life in a meaningful way by just listening to their heart and trying to touch their soul with words of hope, kindness, sensitivity, and Godly love.

In March 1985, the year after we arrived on the island, the country was plunged into a state of mourning when the Rt. Hon. Tom Adams, the Prime Minister at the time, died. He was the son of the Premier of Barbados, Sir Grantley Adams, and was educated at Oxford University before rising to the leadership position of the country, an office he held for nine years. As Prime Minister, his influence politically, regionally, and internationally was well established but on a social level, he was very known to be charismatic and acquired a reputation with the ladies. Following his death, it was publicly reported that he died of a heart attack at his official residence, Ilaro Court, becoming the first Prime Minister to die in office. My early memory of this Prime Minister was how charming he was when I met him at a function in the USA.

I surprised myself by my emotional reaction to the news as I mourned with the people of my newly adopted nation. My friend, Martha was a personal friend of the Prime Minister and I watched as she agonized over the loss while I could only empathize with her as she bore the pain. Questions as to how he died and why so soon were the subject of conversations for several months. The rumor mills ran deep with speculation, but there was only a coroner's report which could not be challenged. A new Prime Minister was quickly installed and it was on to the business of running the government as usual.

The continued search for Spiritual grounding

I decided that it was time to plug into a church where I could be discipled and mentored into greater spiritual awareness. The Anglican church was not satisfying the unquenchable longing and it was clear that neither were earthly possessions and human interactions. There are numerous denominations in existence, but one of the groups I was not considering was the Pentecostal church. As a child I can remember driving past many of those churches and couldn't understand why the parishioners were so loud, needed to be banging on tambourines, shouting "Hallelujah" and "Amen!". I was invited from time to time to a few but here again was a struggle to understand why the worship sessions were so long, lasting 45 minutes or more. Once the worship was over, there were greetings, announcements before the message/sermons were delivered which constituted another 45 minutes or more. One could have spent three hours at church and after some consideration decided I would arrive close to the end of worship session.

I paused at one particular assembly where I found Pastor Eliseus, a man of God, and an excellent teacher. He brought the scriptures to life, keeping it simple, clear, and easy to understand. He shared his life story from time to time so the audience could appreciate the human side of the life of a pastor, reinforcing the fact that pastors are people too. His transparency was refreshing as he too had struggled through his childhood and had to go through counselling and deliverance, to become whole. His journey could be duplicated many times over by many people hearing his message to demonstrate how early childhood experiences can affect one's life many for years. The reality is that God had a plan for him, pursued him, and brought him out of that dark place, cleaned him up, and set his feet on solid ground. God accepted him when he said yes and as he submitted his life to Christ, he would become the effective teacher of the gospel he was created to be. Men and women from around the world have had the benefit of his teaching and have come to know Jesus in a meaningful way. His transparency and knowledge of the scriptures affected my decision to make a change in my own life. I slowly and finally began to understand what the Christian walk was all about. There was a transformation about to take place.

We have no idea what some people in our sphere of influence have endured with so many untold stories. Have you ever had an impression of a person and when you hear his/her story, you were forced to see him/her in a whole new light? Quite often we measure individuals based on the way they appear, or comments from third parties who may or may not be speaking the truth, but sharing their perceptions, void of facts. We take that information, develop an opinion, and often reproduce the story with slight exaggerations here and there. Character assassinations are commonplace and only when the truth is exposed can some people's lives be fully restored if they had been the target of malicious criticism. Don't judge me unless you have walked in my shoes, is an expression we have heard.

It became evident that the modus operandi of some local men was beginning to influence and seriously affect my marriage. They began asking questions like, "Does your wife have to go everywhere with you?" Many of them were already divorced, separated, or living in unhappy and unhealthy relationships while simultaneously exploring other avenues for entertainment. It didn't take a long time for the negative words to penetrate the confines of my situation and for their destructive agenda to become a reality. Of course, there must be willing participants in these cases and slowly, communication broke down and the stability of the home became compromised. Despite my woes, I made every effort and remained determined to do my part to invest in my marriage.

I discovered in the meanwhile that some women were comfortable with their living conditions as long as their husbands took care of the household and paid the bills, giving them a false sense of safety and security. They kept a tunnel vision by turning a blind eye to their husbands' lifestyle of infidelity and promiscuity. There were reports of some, whose husbands stayed away for days, happily wandering with whomever they pleased abandoning their families announcing that it was all business-related. I would have been privy to conversations as a child about several cases that caused tremendous heartache, pain, and the breakdown of family units. In recent times I have heard the expression that who you will become in five years is based on the people you hang out with and the books you read. It is incumbent upon both men and women to determine the kind of future they desired for themselves, their spouses, and their children.

Many still have not learned that lesson and instead of trying to emulate people with successful marriages, actively engage in ways to satisfy their reckless desires. There are many lessons to be learned from those who are determined to stand up and be counted as change agents.

Those partners who are bold and intentional about loving and respecting their partners publicly and privately are far more attractive than the others. In the book of Proverbs, the admonition is, "guarding your body for your wife and not allowing the lust of the flesh to lure you into promiscuous behavior". Some are led by the lust of the flesh, follow the fashion of others, taste the forbidden fruit, adopt the precept that if they cheat and not be discovered, they can continue the practice.

As a child, I overheard adult conversations of some marriages that suffered significantly when wives made huge sacrifices to support their husband's professional and political ambition and once success was achieved, the women were no longer relevant. They had outgrown the women who could no longer stimulate their intellect, behaved disrespectfully towards them causing some to become mentally and emotionally distressed. The breakdown was debilitating for several of these women, several of whom never recovered from the anxiety and fear of the unknown. Their reality had shifted in a way they could not have anticipated. Children in these broken relationships are often the ones most affected by the breakdown in the fabric of such family circles. These were scenarios that were discussed as far back as I can remember.

The matter of tertiary education was a big talking point in certain circles in the Caribbean. Where did I fit on the grid when my university studies were incomplete by the time I relocated to the Caribbean? I was indecisive regarding the direction I would follow to further my education, but completed courses in subjects that I had a keen interest in, like Studies in Prose Writing, Biology, Spanish Immersion, Psychology, and Microbiology. As I learned more about human behavior, I became fascinated with the work conducted in the laboratories, exploring the properties of DNA, RNA, chromosomes, and more. There is so much discussion today on the testing of DNA to determine the risk of genetic diseases, to forensic identification of bodies for court cases, discovering genetic family relationships, and has allowed for breakthroughs in cold, criminal cases and racial profiling. Several persons are curious about their roots and are willing to be tested to discover who their ancestors are. DNA is found in white blood cells, semen, hair roots, body tissue, saliva, and perspiration but sterile conditions are mandatory to ensure accuracy from samples taken for DNA testing.

Separate and apart from the genetic makeup of individuals, there were other influences, that affected one's acceptance in certain positions in the local community. Your status was determined by which elite high schools you were a graduate of; were you a high-income earner, a graduate of a tertiary institution, lived in a neighborhood with luxury homes, drove a high-end automobile, or related to one of the wealthy established families on the island?

Migrating to Barbados exposed the fact that I fitted into none of those categories listed and to compound the narrative, I was a foreigner. I had entered into a marriage agreement without discussing expectations of the union, so we never really talked about what a future would look like. We were not unique in that sense as many couples don't ask the important questions before marriage, like; what we hoped to achieve in the future; where would the children be educated; our spiritual needs; would we purchase a home; how would we handle our finances, would we consider having more kids and so on. There was no such conversation for us, but none of that seemed a consideration at the time as we just let life evolve, while we settled into what appeared to be our rightful place.

I was getting older and had spent enough years psycho-analyzing myself and the time had come when I needed to get serious about my future. I was desperate to be more productive and I made a bold step to cry out to the Lord with a very simple prayer: "Lord, I am not sure what to do with my life, what to do next, where to go as there had to be something better for me on this planet. I need you to guide me as to the next phase of my journey. If I am to stay on this beautiful island, I need to have a meaningful job, not just for the sake of working but one that would become my career. I give you permission Lord to rearrange my life and circumstance." I went on to say, "Lord just establish me where you choose. I will hear other voices/people offering advice, but I ask you to move me; set me up". This was a simple act of blind faith to a God who is more than able even when I didn't fully understand the magnitude and power of who He was. It was such a simple prayer from the heart that some religious folk would have scoffed at, but He answers the simplest prayers, as I was about to find out. For those who believe that prayers have to be long and super-spiritual, that is not the case as God wants to hear your heart and not some superficial babble. He certainly heard and responded to mine, time and time again.

I continued to positioned myself to be ready for whatever was to come as God directed my path. I was no longer willing to spend several more years trying to figure it all out and with two small children, it wasn't any easier as it was no longer about just about me. Barbados was still an unfamiliar territory and the USA had been home long enough for me to be comfortable there, but transitioning with two small kids was a disconcerting thought. I just had to sit and wait on the Lord to organize and establish my footsteps. I occasionally had these little conversations with God as though I was talking to a friend but there were times when I would prefer the advice from a friend which seemed more logical or even pay attention to the enemy whispering in my ear. I continued with my daily routine caring for my family, knowing that I had no control over what would happen next.

Answers to simple prayers demonstrate how valuable we are to God and how much He cares about everything that concerns us. Life seems so complicated sometimes but when one is in the valley trying to determine which way to go be assured that God is trying to get your attention. How often do we hear or say, it's the devil creating havoc in our lives and that's why certain events took place? Consider this, that there are times when God is trying to get us to acknowledge His presence and His desire to get to know us and us Him. We can become hysterical about situations when we have no answers, but God who is omnipotent has the answers. Sometimes God also changes your partner so you can become His partner and He will reward you with the better life He has carved just for you. I have no regrets and bear no animosity towards my situation because God knew it would happen, brought me out on the other side and I am now able to empower some who may not have had the opportunity to be free.

Venetia in Barbados

My mom decided to visit us and we were very pleased to have her join us as this was her first visit to Barbados. I can remember distinctly the moment she arrived in my home, her first words were, "You should have studied interior decorating." Really? Her brief visit was uneventful this time and the children took great pleasure in enjoying time with their grandmother. We did the normal sightseeing trips to places of interest and I could breathe a sigh of relief when she left that there was no major drama to contend with.

My mom returned home and continued to enjoy her retirement and social life. The farm was sold by now so that lifted a huge burden for everyday activities. The years rolled on very quickly and she gradually developed a few medical issues that are synonymous with the elderly. Her particular challenge was that she was soon diagnosed with glaucoma. We had no idea of the rapid deterioration of the disease for a long time as she had made several attempts to have treatment through one source or the other. Her doctors conducted as much research as they could and eventually one suggested the use of medical marijuana (1996) to reduce the pressure in the eyes. As a last resort, however, she tried the laser treatment but sadly her condition was too advanced and the surgery proved to be unsuccessful.

I began receiving frequent phone calls from my mother which was very unusual. There was an urgency in her voice that she needed to see me as soon as possible so I decided to pack my bags and visit her. I was quite shocked to see that her vision was so severely impaired and she was unable to find her way around her townhouse. I couldn't fathom how she coped all this time living alone in this residence. To see this very successful woman reduced to becoming an individual who was completely dependent, incapable of taking care of her basic day-to-day needs without stumbling, was heart-breaking.

My trip was planned to spend four days with her, assess the situation, and while I was there to engage in one of my favorite activities - cleaning and redecorating her home. So much of her personal belongings had been stolen from her home that I was alarmed. When I approached the second bedroom, I noticed an item protruding from under the bed. I instantly realized it was the top shelf of a large metal trunk she had used years previously for traveling. I became very curious and pulled it out to find eight packages, very tightly taped, very lightweight, and neatly stacked and stuffed under the bed. I had no clue what they were initially, so I hurried downstairs to find out from my mom what exactly they were. Her vision was so impaired by now that she was unable to see but could only stroke each one trying to figure it out herself.

I needed to find out what these mystery packages were. My thoughts were racing by now as I suspected that they were marijuana packages someone had stored in her home. Funny thing is that there was no smell for one to make a connection. There were a few people who visited her from time to time and someone was using the opportunity, knowing how badly her vision was impaired, to store the bundles in her home. I had my suspicion but couldn't prove anything. I made a call to a friend who advised that he would "handle it". It was suggested not to contact the police as it was felt that mom would not have been able to explain the situation.

Following that harrowing experience, I realized that it wasn't safe for her to remain in the house on her own so we devised a plan for her to relocate to Barbados. It was a discussion we had on previous occasions, however, she had to decide when she was ready. By now she had isolated herself from everyone else. I needed to be careful not to appear to be manipulating her but the situation was dire. It didn't take a long time for her to accept that she couldn't manage on her own, that her house-help had stolen so much of her personal effects that she really couldn't manage. Once the decision was made, the transition was very smooth. I felt that with age she would have mellowed, become more reserved, and far easier to communicate with. I looked forward to finally being able to create that bond that was missing for a lifetime and my children would have shared precious moments with the only grandmother they knew.

On her arrival she was escorted in her newly constructed apartment, the first thing she exclaimed was, "This apartment is way too small. Where am I going to do my exercises?" Well, no surprises there!!! I made every effort to put things in place to make her as comfortable as possible. I increased the hours of the housekeeper to take care of her while I was at work and the children were at school, retained Eric, a very trustworthy taxi driver who was completely dedicated to taking her wherever she needed to go. He was the best; loyal, attentive, caring, and honest. He chauffeured her to the hairdresser and church, the two most important activities for her. The housekeeper took her for walks every day until she complained that she was not "seeing" anything new even-though the fact is she couldn't see much. It wasn't enough that she was being well looked after, she demanded much more. I thought it was all falling into place despite her incessant grumbling. I was the only one in the family who was brave enough to take on the responsibility of caring for her as everyone else had virtually abandoned her, even her closest family members. No one else was willing to cope with her excessive, unrealistic demands. I had hoped with household help and the kids' things would change.

One day I arrived home earlier than expected, just in time to hear my mom telling my housekeeper all of my intimate, personal business, including the fact that she adopted me as a child. This was just another occasion where my mother had crossed the line and she knew it. The shame of her actions caused her to stay hidden in her apartment for the next three days. I had to process this situation for a while, trying to fathom if she had regrets about the adoption, was it the result of the early onset of dementia, or both. I was not impressed. I have had to forgive my mother over the years but never dared to broach the subject to get clarity on the adoption process. I believe that it was a subject she was uncomfortable talking to me about and having kept it a secret for so many years, it became even harder for her.

Her vision continued to deteriorate as glaucoma had become more and more impaired. She asked that her table lamps were upgraded to have brighter lights so we got gooseneck lamps with 100-watt bulbs. It was like daylight in the apartment. She often mentioned to my friends who visited her from time to time that I left her in the dark quite often. She gave everyone the impression that she was not well cared for and complained endlessly about her treatment. She often commented on the state of her vision and that there was nothing else that could have been done to reverse the situation in the Caribbean so she would attempt to get further treatment in the US. With one last desperate attempt for improvement and after many consultations with specialists in the US, she came up with a plan.

Several months after making these new arrangements and altering my routine to accommodate my mother, she got up one day and decided she wanted to move to the US to spend time with a niece who resided in NYC. Without the consent that this lady was willing to be her guardian for a while, she insisted on making her way there. She made her arrangements and off she went to the USA. She was even more excessive in her demands as she got older and expected to have things done her way and, in her time, whether it was convenient for you or not. Before we were fully aware of what was happening, she had made arrangements to check herself into a nursing home and returned to Jamaica. We were all puzzled that she had contacts who could organize the move and accommodations so quickly. The arrangements were settled unknown to her family and off she went to her new place of abode.

It wasn't long before I got a familiar phone call one day again asking me to come to see her in Jamaica. It was difficult not to respond when one gets a call like that as you can't tell what is happening at the other end of the line. I decided on this occasion to take my daughter with me. One of my brothers kindly escorted us to the residence and we were very thankful to have had the company. When we arrived, we just could not imagine the deplorable conditions under which she lived and to discover that her fee more than likely covered the running cost for the entire facility.

How could an accomplished woman like this end up in a facility like that? My brother graciously and patiently helped to search diligently for a new facility to have her transferred to while I had only three days to make this happen. After much resistance both from the owner of the facility and my very stubborn mother, the move took place. It was always with fear and trepidation that I answered the phone from a particular area code, as I wasn't sure what to expect. My phone rang late the night she arrived at the new facility and I could hear my mother demanding to be returned to the previous location. I had to be the adult and insist she settled in which she did. A couple of years later, she was transferred yet again to another facility which turned out to be more accommodating.

***

Sandy Lane Hotel – a Five Star Five Diamond property.

I went about my daily routine with no focus on what seemed like a simple request I had made to God months before. I was so confident that He would work things out and I left it all in His capable hands. A few months later, I was invited to be interviewed for a job at the most prestigious hotel on the island and it was imperative I made a good impression.

The History of the hotel

A British politician named Ronald Tree visited the island and fell in love with it. He very quickly became obsessed with the idea of designing a playground for his friends to play in Barbados. Once the required documentation with the local authorities was completed and he was given permission to construct a new road so that the hotel could be situated along the beachfront, he assembled his team with the architect Robertson Ward and construction began in 1958. The hotel welcomed its first guests in February 1961 operating as a guest house for Ronald Tree's friends to play, eventually developing an inventory of 52 rooms and a nine-hole golf course. It became an exclusive hideaway for the rich and famous who were able to spend time in very private quarters and bask in the cool Caribbean water of the west coast of the island. The staff was very disciplined and well trained to be discreet.

In 1967 the British hotel chain, Trust-house Forte, headed by Lord Charles Forte, acquired the property and it became one of their five-star properties and considered one of the best in the Caribbean, and has maintained that reputation. The property increased the number of rooms to 120, with a swimming pool, tennis courts, and a fully operational water sports facility. In 1996 there was a hostile take-over as the Granada group offered the shareholders a very high rate which the majority accepted, and in quick time the hotel was taken over.

The hotel did not, however, fit the business profile of the new conglomerate and before long, several properties within the group were put up for sale of which Sandy Lane was one. The shareholders of the company were very excited about the takeover as their pay-out was fairly lucrative. A group of wealthy Irishmen acquired the property for an undisclosed amount of money and proceeded to demolish the building in 1998. The plan was to have it rebuilt within 18 months, but the reality was that it took 3 ½ years to rebuild, and soon after became the best five-star diamond hotel in the Caribbean with two Tom Fazio designed golf courses and a world-class spa. It then was established as the most distinguished address in the Caribbean. The new hotel was recreated on the same footprint as the original hotel much to the delight of the returning guests and friends of the hotel.

I had no idea in those days how valuable it would have been to research the company before going for an interview, but I was desperate and I had prayed for employment so the least I could do was to dress for success. I can remember wearing a white linen dress with buttons cascading down the front, red pumps, and carrying my statement Gucci handbag. I walked in the room and made every effort to exude as much confidence as I could muster while sharing honestly with the personnel team that I had no experience working in a hotel. I had no idea of the intricacies of running that type of operation from what was visible from the front office to what took place behind the scenes. I made a good enough impression that I was called back for a second interview and was immediately offered a job. I was scared about the future once I left that interview. I remember my friend Martha celebrating with me but deep inside I worried about whether or not I could settle in this job. It was a new area for me and I needed to create a balance into this new environment, with new people, a new job description, time away from my children, and working through a marriage. There were very high standards set and technical tasks I had no previous experience in but knew this had to be the opportunity God had released for me. The working hours were at times challenging, with changing shifts, working weekends, and Public Holidays. There were many questions I asked myself at the end of the first interview but had to convince my interviewers and myself that I was the right person for the job.

I was petrified the first day on the job but bonded quickly with other staff members who were also starting for the first time. As part of the orientation, we toured this marvellous facility, learning about its history before becoming immersed in the very demanding Front Office training sessions. The trainer was very well versed in her subject matter and there was great camaraderie that developed with the new team. I consider myself a visionary, creator, problem solver, and found the paperwork quite mundane but with a three-month probationary period it was imperative newcomers proved their ability to comply with the specific standard operating procedures of the company.

The challenges began on my second day when my first supervisor who had been at the hotel for 25 years or more, made her presence felt. She was a middle-aged woman, very well dressed, coiffed hair, a slender frame, and a fierce personality. There was no room in her world for creativity especially from a newcomer whom she felt may upstage her. There were so many ideas I had, to be more productive, save energy, store information, but she was not interested, instead, she kept a little black book in which she recorded errors and reprimanded her team openly, forcefully, and regularly.

I can remember praying from the moment I left home until I placed my handbag under my desk at work, asking the Lord to teach me the rudiments of my assignments so I could be successful. Looking back, I don't even think I understood the power of those prayers and how much God loved me. I didn't have the depth of knowledge about God, but I knew for sure that He responded to my simple prayers regarding everything I asked of Him, after all, He was an all-seeing, all-knowing God who would never leave me nor forsake me. Three months after I started the job my supervisor was made redundant. What? After 25 years? Just like that? The entire staff was shocked at such an abrupt termination. Her assistant became my supervisor and that was the most dramatic change the department had seen. The environment became civil and the team became more cohesive, supportive of each other and great working relationships were formed. I knew at that moment I was on my way to developing a career.

Several members of staff had good connections with the repeat guests and were passionate about offering good service. Some of those who made a significant difference were Michelle Babb, Frankie Browne, Michael Forde, Archer the beach attendant, and Eric Mapp (there was one Countess who referred to him as Mr. Mop). Then there was one of the most recognized team members, George Forte. George began as a laborer who worked on the foundation of the building of the hotel but eventually graduated to become the first Public Relations Manager of the hotel. Guests assumed with a name Forte he was a family member of the owners of the hotel and seemed in shock when this very distinguished, charismatic black man appeared in his well-tailored suit accentuated by a complimentary pocket square. George in his inimitable style would set them at ease right away while trying to hold back the big grin he wanted to display. There was no other member of the team who had the knowledge George had of the history of the island, the culture, the hotel, the surrounding areas and the gossip. He was a master of his craft and I learned a tremendous amount from him. His mantra was, "We are a can-do hotel", so we could satisfy any request.

Within a short time at the hotel, the hotel's General Manager changed from a Portuguese manager to an Englishman named Pierre Vacher (PV). This was the beginning of many changes to come for me at the hotel. PV spent a few months assessing improvements he thought necessary for the running of the hotel and within a short space of time approached me to make an offer. He recognized my ability to communicate with people at all levels of the social strata and how relaxed and comfortable I made them. I soon transferred from the front desk to a new position that he created for me. The hand of God was motioning me into my destiny in response to my prayer request and was the catalyst in shaping my future. PV was very caring and considerate to me and would often ask how he could help me improve in my job. I had never had anyone that interested in my success before, so this was a new and welcomed experience.

One day PV called me to his office and suggested a new role called Concierge which I was unfamiliar with. I had not paid much attention to hotels I had visited previously and there was no such position at any hotel on the island. I was flattered that he had a plan for my upward mobility but I proceeded to investigate what was the function of a Concierge. The feedback was hilarious: its literal translation was that of a French janitor, holder of the keys, caretaker of an apartment building, or small hotel. PV probably chuckled at my naïveté; however, he went on to explain that it was a very prestigious position in the five-star hotels in the UK and Europe. In those countries, there were no opportunities where one could apply for that position so he suggested that it was a special offer I should not refuse. After much deliberation, he convinced me to accept the role for which he thought I was well suited. He also explained that in the UK, it was a position exclusively offered to males, and candidates had to be recommended by another well-respected Concierge. They were known to earn very good incomes with the added benefits of access to luxury hotels, high-end restaurants, theaters, and to all the popular venues frequented by international celebrities and wealthy business people. I trusted PV enough to be my guide and slowly gained the confidence to follow his lead to take a leap of faith. He was a good mentor to me and we had a great working relationship. It was rumored that I was his favorite but I believe he saw my passion for people and desire to make a difference. The mark of a good leader is the ability to see the potential in an individual and help them to flourish and he was just that. His counselling and coaching changed my life, creating pivotal moments in time that allowed me to peel the layers off what had been some dire circumstances.

Once I accepted the challenge to start the necessary training for the role, arrangements were quickly made for my flight to the UK. The trip was all-inclusive with provisions made for airfare, transportation, accommodation, meals, uniforms, and a stipend. This was going to be my first trip to the UK and there were the expected anxious moments but I hoped the transition would have been easy and I would fit in well.

I arrived at Gatwick Airport in London and had to connect to a train that would take me to the seaside resort of Torquay in Devon, a two-and-a-half-hour ride away. It was daylight when I arrived, so I was able to see much of the beautiful countryside. Torquay developed the nickname, the English Rivera, due to the reasonable weather they boast in the summer months. Over the years its tourism market developed and became a hub for foreign students to learn English. The main street was strewn with pubs, ice-cream parlors, art galleries, many restaurants, sidewalk cafés, and even when the temperature was chilly in the mid-60s, the locals could be seen sporting their skimpy bikinis on the beach.

My training began at the luxurious 19th century Victorian Hotel, **The Imperial Hotel**. The hotel boasted an impressive sea-view of the area and the beautiful South Devon coastline. It is a historic property with all the rooms featuring the same breath-taking sea-views while hosting various leisure activities to entertain their guests. When the guests arrived in the afternoon, they were ushered into the lounge to partake of the traditional English afternoon tea, served daily including freshly baked scones, with clotted cream accompanied by varying flavors of jams and jellies.

The hotel offered 152 rooms and luxury suites spread over seven floors but the heart of the hotel was the restaurant with a panoramic view of Torquay. The challenge for the restaurant staff was to accommodate all the requests from diners who wished to be seated to get the best view. The hotel was decorated with heavily brocaded drapes to help keep the heat in the rooms and velvet-upholstered chairs throughout. There was a well-stocked flower room with a variety of beautiful, fresh flowers that were delivered to the hotel daily to support the enormous centerpiece arrangements situated in the lobby and throughout the public areas. The petite female florist who used her creative ideas to design masterpieces could often be seen climbing a ladder to get to the top of some of the arrangements to add the finishing touches. Her workshop was stationed within the hotel, so she was also able to satisfy any guest requests to have flowers sent to their suite or have gifts delivered to others. It was a very thriving and rewarding business.

My first day on the job proved to be very interesting. None of the guests had seen a woman acting in the role of Concierge before and a black one at that!!!! That was unheard of. I was constantly bombarded with questions like, "Who are you?" and "Where are you from? What language do you speak? How long will you be here?" It was fascinating to see the reactions. Daily, I had to explain that I was being trained to be the first Concierge for the world-renowned, Five-Star hotel owned by the hotel magnate, Lord Charles Forte. I shared that the Sandy Lane Hotel was located in Barbados for those who knew the Caribbean. My trainer was very efficient and well respected by the guests and suppliers, but I recognized very early that I had to put some boundaries in place to safeguard my integrity.

The hotel employed a very interesting personality named **George.** He was a retired professional dancer; was given complimentary accommodation within the hotel and had all the benefits the visiting guests were entitled to. He was an absolute delight to speak with.

There were three other members of staff from my hotel who were assigned to this hotel in various roles while I was there. The team consisted of two cooks, Connie and Heather, and Frankie a Food and Beverage supervisor. This group had arrived before I did and were settled in their accommodation across the street from the hotel. They anxiously awaited my arrival so we could reconnect. On my arrival, I was immediately escorted to my room which was not within the staff quarters but on the hotel compound. Before I settled in, I gazed out the window to see a view of tons of garbage piled high in bins that had not been cleared for a few days. I was horrified at the thought that my room view would be that of garbage for an entire month or more. I believed it was most unacceptable and so I returned to the lobby with my request to change rooms. The front desk staff went scrambling to find the General Manager which seemed to take a while. Of course, they became curious to know who I was and why I thought I was so special not wanting to accept this free accommodation. While they figured out the next move, I met my group, and off we went into the town, enjoyed some of the best ice-cream, and wandered around the town for a little while, debating what the outcome of my request would be. We nervously made our way back and amid the chatter knew it would have caused unnecessary attention among the local staff. I had already made it clear that I was not willing to stay in that accommodation and prepared to return home if they couldn't resolve the matter to my satisfaction. I was very bold and determined to fight for what I felt was fair. At this moment, I was comparing the conditions established for visiting staff at our hotel in Barbados and so I felt we deserved to be treated in a similar fashion.

After they searched their inventory to find a room I could occupy for my entire stay, I settled into my new room. It still was not the greatest but the fact that I was assertive and a change was made was satisfying to me. My team was pleased that I insisted on a change and I believe they were proud that I stood firm and it had a positive outcome. I appreciated the friendship I developed with them during that period.

The shock factor of my presence continued as long as I remained at the front desk of the hotel. The guests arrived in Rolls Royces and Bentleys of all colors and models - gold, silver, black, white, and so on. These guests wore the finest jewellery and of course all haute couture designer wear. I can imagine the questions they asked about me when not within earshot. The ones who were brave enough to ask, I would share about my hotel and invite them to visit Barbados.

One evening **George** invited me to join him for dinner in the restaurant to see the role he performed on a nightly basis. I graciously accepted his invitation but could not have anticipated what would have occurred later. The furnishings were very formal with more heavily brocaded drapes with large tassels and seats upholstered with dark velvet, printed fabric. The sea-view was spectacular and guests who had made advance requests to have sea-view tables were happily seated in their locations. There were quite often little incidents the Restaurant Manager was confronted with by guests who demanded to be seated at a table with a view, forcing them to use all the negotiating skills they had to pacify the situation.

I had to ensure I was immaculately dressed to join George for dinner as I was well aware, I would be scrutinized by all. There was no one of my complexion staying in the hotel except for the waiting staff. I silently thanked my mother for my etiquette training so I did not embarrass myself dining in the presence of such an opulent atmosphere.

George and I had a lovely meal and the staff couldn't have been kinder and I believe my group was very proud to know that I was representing them, but they were also very nervous for me as we all knew this position was not normal. After dinner, we went to this very large ballroom with just a few couples who had already assembled in anticipation of the entertainment to follow. There was music for dancing already filling the airwaves so I took a seat off to the side as I watched as George methodically escorted one lady at a time to the dance floor and gently guided her into a waltz. Several of these guests visited the hotel exclusively to enjoy these moments with George while their husbands, sipped their drink of choice and watched. Once George had made the rounds, he turned to me and said, "It's our turn. Let's show them how it's done". As romantic as that sounded, I had not danced a waltz for a long time so I shuddered at the thought of embarrassing myself and not living up to the expectation that black people have rhythm. It didn't take long, however, to fall in step with George and because he was an experienced dancer and teacher, I glided across the floor with ease, much to the delight of the small audience present. I would have loved to dance every night while I was there, but that would have been a breach of the hotel protocol.

I started the next day with a little pep in my step, only to be summoned to the General Manager's office as soon as I arrived at my station. I was ushered in and could hardly have sat down in his very ostentatious office when he fielded his first question. He demanded to know who had permitted me to dine in the restaurant. I found it odd that he posed the question to me rather than to George. I explained that George extended the invitation as he thought it could be viewed as a part of my training to add a unique form of entertainment for their guests. The General Manager told me in a very controlled tone that I was not allowed to dine in the restaurant and to ensure there was no repeat performance. There was no explanation as to why - it was just the rule. Was it racism at play? Was it because of my position or my color, one may ask? What if I was paying for the experience would the outcome have been different? Later in the day George humbly apologized explaining that he didn't realize he was violating the rules. I continued my duties in a very professional manner and remained polite as always to the GM when he was in my presence. It wasn't clear if there were complaints raised by the resident guests or just the General Manager's prejudice. I never got any answers while I was there but my relationship remained cordial with everyone I came in contact with.

I wanted some adventure while I was in Torquay so I dragged my teammate Heather to go on a ferry trip to Jersey in the Channel Islands. The novice I was; I didn't think of doing enough research before we booked. We just wanted to see another town/city while we were there. We boarded the vessel in the evening only to discover that a rugby team was also on board. They drank and sung throughout the entire journey which must have been 9-10 hours of sailing into pitch blackness. There were no views, no landscape, just pure darkness, with a twinkle of lights here and there off in the distance. We finally arrived on the island, had a quick tour of the quaint little city, visited some of the landmarks, and had just enough time to head back for our return journey that day. That was not the adventure we had hoped for but would consider returning at a later date for a proper tour.

I left the Imperial Hotel fully equipped to start my new job and knew there would be a few hurdles to overcome as I had inherited a team of men of varying ages who had been working in their respective jobs for more than a decade and had become quite set in their ways. To be productive, I needed to work in a disciplined, organized environment, and now armed with some new ideas, I was going to rebuild my team. I was energized but had to win the respect of this team and assure them that we were striving together to be the best that we could be. Sandy Lane was one of eight luxury hotels operating under the umbrella of an international Forte Hotel brand and therefore we had to bring our A-game to compete worldwide.

In those days, we didn't consider ourselves competing on a local or even a regional level.

The hotel closed its doors for several months for extensive renovations and during that time it provided an opportunity for me to travel on behalf of the hotel for further exposure. It was mid-summer and I was excited about the benefits of exploring another exclusive luxury hotel. I had a very comfortable flight with very little sleep on British Airways and arrived at Gatwick airport around 6 am. I had the pleasure of being met by a couple who were frequent guests of the Sandy Lane with whom I had developed a friendship. They insisted on meeting me on arrival, a gesture I greatly appreciated, as there was going to be a long layover before my connecting flight. I was taken to a wonderful restaurant near the airport which had a vast selection of breakfast items at their buffet station, but unfortunately, I couldn't enjoy the meal as I was overcome with sleep. After I struggled through a few items on the menu, I was taken on a brief tour before visiting the couple's very modest home in a quaint area of London. By now my eyelids were getting heavier and soon had to succumb to taking a nap. The couple was very understanding and ensured I was awake early enough to make the connecting flight to Calgary, Sardinia. They offered to take me back to the airport that afternoon, demonstrating the fact that despite our perceived differences, kindness does matter.

There were amazing opportunities for me to visit luxury hotels in the United Kingdom, Germany, and the United States of America on behalf of my company, where I met many more kind and generous people, leaving long-lasting memories. I will feature my trip to **Sardinia** as one of the highlights of my career. Once the flight left London, I flew to Calgary, the capital city located in the south end of the island, arriving late evening. The Forte Hotel Village was owned and managed by the same Forte Hotel group that owned the Sandy Lane Hotel. The property had 900 rooms in total which included villas and two small hotels. The hotel hosted international visitors, many of whom did not speak the Italian language so it was interesting to see how they were able to interact with the staff, most of whom did not speak English.

My first impression was that it was the most extraordinary location I had ever seen. The staff was super-efficient, very disciplined, well trained, and worked extremely hard. It was summer when I arrived there and the weather was hotter than what I was accustomed to in Barbados, but no one complained. They wore very simple but elegant uniforms and I was impressed with their physique and they all maintained a low body weight. Everywhere you looked you only saw striking features, chiselled cheekbones, well-arched eyebrows, jet black hair, they were tanned and all had welcoming smiles to enhance their impressive images. The staff knew how to hustle to get the job done and no one was caught slacking in their responsibilities.

The hours of work were quite different from what I was accustomed to, but one adapted quickly. The hours of work were 8 am to 1 pm followed by a four-hour siesta in the afternoon when all services stopped and then everyone took a nap. The guests would have been briefed on arrival so they would be prepared for the break. Siestas are part of the culture in that region and seemed luxurious to me initially, but when I observed the demand to provide the services for hundreds of people on a twenty-four-hour cycle seven days per week, I too was happy to participate in the exercise. Work resumed at 5 pm and continued until the last guest went to bed. Dinner was served to staff in the staff dining room and they were not permitted to dine with the guests nor in the restaurants.

The grounds were extensive and cars were not allowed on the property as transportation was limited strictly to bicycles. Fitness was encouraged and even though their eating pattern did not represent a healthy lifestyle, the majority of people were trim with no visible trace of excess body fat. They ate a lot of freshly made bread, pasta, pizza, shrimp, and tomatoes. A custom I observed was the dipping of the pieces of bread in a good quality olive oil unlike our habit in the Caribbean of applying butter to our bread. They had no qualms about eating late at night or going to the pizzeria off-property at 1 a.m. and ordering large slices of pizzas with various toppings. They enjoyed a good bottle of vintage wine with their meal and sipped it slowly to help relax their aching bodies in preparation for a good night's sleep. The next day I was fascinated to watch the staff convert an outdoor space into a restaurant to feed hundreds of people at one sitting. It appeared to mimic the changing of backdrops on a movie set with all the players knowing exactly what their roles were and executing them in record time. There was no stumbling into one another as though their actions were well choreographed and they had lots of practice.

I was invited to get some exercise by walking during one of the afternoon siestas and I gladly accepted. Dressed in what I thought was the proper gear I headed off only to have a surprise in store. The woman who invited me turned up in a swimsuit and was barefoot. I wasn't fazed so off we went. To my surprise almost all the women laying there, were topless. It was quite a new sighting for me to see the women exposed, as though they had no care in the world. We walked for about one hour before returning to the villa to be greeted by sore muscles that had clearly been ignored for a while. My body ached for several days and I intentionally tried to avoid climbing stairs, until the pain subsided somewhat. Needless to say, I chose not to venture out for any long beach walks for the duration of my time there. I was amused at the thought of the likely reaction if a lady walked on the beach in a traditional one-piece bathing suit. She may have drawn more attention and seemed out of place. Bear in mind, I grew up in a Caribbean culture where we tend to be much more conservative in our style of dress. Fascinating as it was, it was equally delightful to see and sense the freedom they exhibited, to be uninhibited: just lying there or sauntering on to the shore or wading in the water and letting it all "hang out". No one seemed to notice or care!!! It is, in fact, illegal to be topless on any beach or in any public arena in Barbados. How fascinating cultures can be, so different which can lead to either reckless abandonment or overly careful deportment.

There were nine restaurants on the premises from which the guests could choose to dine, ranging from the traditional Italian meals to the fish-and-chips offers to appeal to the British guests, to the coffee shops that served freshly brewed gourmet-style coffees, pizza parlor, bars that served premium drinks and specialty wines, the ice-cream parlor, a few fine-dining restaurants, a bistro and so much more. Every palate could have been satisfied on the premises which was good for business and it helped that there was little competition on the outskirts of the property.

The village was designed for families of all ages so the activities were geared to entertain everyone and arrangements were easily made at the activities desk. The children's activity center was managed by an Italian team, but there was always often a challenge when the English-speaking children visited the center as the majority of the staff only spoke Italian. I mentioned this to the General Manager one day that there was this "problem" in that area and I was happy to assist. He kindly informed me that they don't have problems there, they only have solutions. He promptly dispatched another bilingual member of the team, to manage the children's center for that period. He politely told me to mind my own business without saying it in so many words. I was always brave enough to share an opinion or observation which came naturally to me, but he probably thought I was highlighting a flaw in his operation. I deduced that he was a perfectionist and how dare I expose that loophole. There was a daily learning curve. There was great emphasis on discovering and catering to everyone's needs to ensure all the guests were satisfied at the end of their stay and desirous of not only returning to the village but recommending it to friends and associates for future holidays. It was extremely safe for families as the children could roam the property without fear of injury or kidnapping which was a huge concern for people in Sardinia. The team had mastered the art of creating a space for pleasure, fun, and family. For me, it felt like an atmosphere that needed to be replicated around the globe.

I kept very active during my tenure at the Forte Village especially after meeting members of the resident band. It was a small group of four, three Italian males and the lead singer an American girl. They played all genres of music much to the delight of the many nationalities represented in their audience. There was a tennis player within the group and I was thrilled especially when I discovered the gentleman was quite gifted and we played well together, way into the early morning many times. It was much cooler then and it allowed me to unwind after a long day and I got the physical exercise I needed to compensate for all the bread and pasta I had consumed. I was a long way from home yet I felt I had adopted a new lifestyle within a very short period.

My first safari tour around the island in one of the open jeeps included other visitors from the village and a few residents on the island. It was very rugged terrain and this open jeep offered a bumpy ride careening down the road to the point where at times I thought I was going to be catapulted over the edge. There was no air-conditioning so it meant enduring the sensation of hot sand brushing against your face. It was quite scary at times and even though you were required to wear seatbelts, you were forced to hang on for dear life. The passengers on board this trip ranged in age and nationality so it was interesting as they were all curious as to my origin. Most black people in this region were considered immigrants from one of the African countries, so to mention the Caribbean invoked a different conversation. Most knew very little of the position of Barbados or the Caribbean on a globe and while a few had a vague idea, others assumed Barbados was in Jamaica.

A week before I was due to leave the village, I was invited to the home of one of the staff members of the hotel. The family consisted of a mother, two brothers, and this young lady. At dinner that evening it was apparent that everyone at the table spoke Italian except for my host who spoke English, and myself. By now I still understood only a few words but was lost throughout most of the conversation. She attempted to translate but it was like rapid fire trying to keep up as her family just rattled on almost "disrespectfully" entertaining themselves.

Her two brothers were extremely handsome and very polite while they made every effort to make me feel comfortable, still speaking in their native language. The meal was very simple and consisted of the most succulent red tomato wedges, jumbo prawns served on a large platter, fresh rolls, and bottles of chilled red wine. It was fun to see the family dig in with their hands, picking the prawns up one at a time, biting the heads off and eating the shrimp in its entirety. There was no wastage at that table. The interaction between them was special and the respect they had for each other was refreshing. On the way back to the village we stopped at the regular pizza parlor at about 10 pm and there were several members of the staff sitting in their usual spots in front of large pizzas with lots of toppings, eating to their heart's content well into the night. It was wonderful to see such joy and experience the culture and make new friends and also seeing how much they enjoyed each other's company. To stay awake throughout the day the staff was allowed to enjoy freshly brewed coffee from any of the coffee shops at no charge.

My Tour Guide in Sardinia

My tour guide Turid had visited Sandy Lane Hotel and was a keen golfer. She had a wide circle of friends mostly from the ex-pat community in Barbados whom she entertained and they reciprocated equally. We developed a very good friendship and on my first trip to Sardinia, she extended an invitation I could not refuse. She happened to own a small apartment in **Porto Cervo** a small township in **Sardinia** and I had the privilege of spending a weekend there. It was situated right on the water's edge overlooking several million-dollar yachts and positioned above a row of exclusive designer shops. These establishments served as showrooms, with just a limited number of retail shops that catered to walk-in customers. As I sat gazing over this expanse of wealth on display, I enjoyed some chunky pieces of freshly baked bread with gouda and Jarlsberg cheese, sipping a glass of Moet & Chandon champagne followed by a glass of vintage Merlot later in the evening with dinner. I could have pinched myself … how did I get here???

On my first day out to explore the area, I enjoyed riding around **Porto Cervo** in my friend's Volkswagen Beatle convertible. What a great experience it was seeing homes that not everyone was privileged to view, walking through incredible landscapes, nursing that one glass of white wine and posing next to a bright yellow Lamborghini at the entrance to **The Costa Esmeralda Hotel** pretending it was my vehicle for the day. What could be better? The hotel was spectacular and the top suite cost US$1000 per night which I thought was outrageous at the time. The building was crescent-shaped with a marina in the center of the crescent showcasing the exclusive, very expensive yachts which were anchored there. I was invited for lunch at the all-you-can-eat buffet spread which seemed to be a mile long, as far as one's eyes could see. How do you choose from the display of goodies? The golf course at the hotel was much different from the ones I had seen in the Caribbean, with no trees, just shrubs that had been planted to enhance the landscape. Here I was feeling very much like a princess being chauffeur-driven around this well-manicured property.

My time in Sardinia was like being on the set of a made for television movie. The places I was able to visit and the people I met along the way were so unexpected that I had to save bits of memorabilia as a reminder of many special moments in time. I was very impressed with the island to see how the wealthy lived. There were so many coves or inlets with million-dollar yachts anchored offshore and property lines for homes were defined by walls that were 10-12ft high with electronic gates, cameras, and alarm systems installed as a deterrent to kidnappers. There was a security presence to the entrance to the many developments to ensure that only the persons allowed to enter within a small radius of the properties once granted permission by the owners. I was able to visit one of those properties that overlooked a spectacular view of the coastline. It housed an Olympic size swimming pool, large gazebo, outdoor grill pit, and a landscape of cactus-type plants with edible flowers due to the low level of rainfall. The earth was just arid land so the limited variation of vegetation had to be ideal to withstand those conditions. Drinking water from the taps was prohibited so residents only used water from filtration systems.

I had an opportunity to dine at a historic, exclusive restaurant named Pacifico Rosemary, which was privately owned at the time and labeled as one of the more expensive restaurants in Porto Cervo. It was known as a destination for the jet set and the crème de la crème of society. On entering the restaurant, you would walk along the corridor to see the chefs at the stove whipping up some delightful dishes for the rich and famous guests. There were walls of photographs of some of the famous people who had visited and many were noted as repeat guests. The restaurant is perched on the edge of a cliff and it was alleged that the photographer who took the famous photograph of Princess Diana wearing her swimsuit, captured the shot from that location with a telescopic lens.

My dearest friend at the time, who allowed me this amazing opportunity to visit these sights as we drove around the rather rugged landscape, was one of the ways God demonstrated how His creation had no boundaries and though we are different in make up and culture, we all desire the same things. We all want to be loved and appreciated. Those are memories that have been etched in my mind to this day. Turid has remained a friend for life and even though we don't see each other often we know that the bond of friendship remains strong. There is an expression that people come into your life for a season; some seasons are short and some are for life. I could not have had this opportunity to visit these locations without her desire to show me one of her many homes. She grew up very privileged as the daughter of a very wealthy, successful European businessman and she inherited great wealth on his passing. The humility she exhibited not only to me but to all those she met, reminds me that yes, we can love one another with no strings attached.

This friendship is one I have learned so many lessons from. It is one that opened up a new world for me by showing me how to appreciate people who have had different lifestyles and cultures from those I was familiar with. In fact, it is through friendships like this that you learn freedom, truth, and openness. It is through these cross-cultural experiences that one values your history and culture. There are those around us who need to be set free from the mind-set that everyone is against them and that the racial divide is such that hatred is easier than making the effort to love. When we are willing to be vulnerable, share our testimonies so our listeners understand that we have all gone through some not so happy times, then they will realize we are not alone on this journey. Throughout life, we will encounter some impossible situations and we will wonder if we will get through them, and we will. We just need to be determined to press on, stay focused, stay plugged in to God's plan for us and He will see us through. This exposure helped me to understand the expectation of tourists from other destinations when they visited the Sandy Lane Hotel.

There were new things in store when I returned home and with the support of the General Manager, small steps were taken to bring about the changes I desired to make. Our team was determined to set the standard for others to follow and that we did, starting with a simple exercise of the meet-and-greet service at our Grantley Adams International Airport. This practice was later adopted by several companies to fast- track the clients through the airport. The idea of going on holiday to a foreign country and feeling secure that you will be met and escorted from the airport to your hotel must be very reassuring. The pampering for each family began immediately.

My position as The Concierge, placed me squarely in the lobby of the hotel allowing me to easily welcome everyone who entered the lobby. The visitors to the hotel consisted of locals who could afford to pay the high prices for accommodation and services, but the sighting of international celebrities raised the bar for us as we were on the frontline. They came from all areas; film actors, musicians, athletes, the food industry, successful business tycoons, politicians, and many other affluent people some of whom we may not have been familiar with. Some of these visitors stayed in the hotel, while others preferred the solitude of a private villa on the estate located nearby.

Several of the American ones were easily identified unlike most from the European countries. One vivid memory I have was the day I was sitting at my desk in the lobby and glanced in the direction of the boutiques to see an amazing bronze statue of a man standing, gazing in the show window of a store. He wore tiny olive green swim-trunks and the evening sun created a silhouette as airbrushed for in a magazine. The gentleman started to head in my direction and my heart skipped a beat. Was that happening? As he approached I realized that I knew who he was but could not remember his name. I had never seen a bronze body so chiseled in my life. When he got to my desk I said, "I know who you are. I saw you perform in Sophisticated Ladies on Broadway and your name is ????" I was stalling for time, hoping I would remember, but still no recall. He was so impressed that I saw him perform live on Broadway he gave me the biggest grin. He said. "Yes, I am **Gregory Hines**." "That's it," I said. As if he would have given me an incorrect name. I cannot remember the rest of the conversation or what his request was but that was enough for me. He was known as a suave singer, actor, choreographer, and one of the most accomplished tap dancers in the world back in his day. This would explain the frame and posture of his body, a result of all those years of hard work in training for his performances. Gregory began tapping at age two and became semi-professional at age five. He was handed the baton to dance first from his musical father and later from the great Sammy Davis Jr. He loved Barbados and could be seen in local restaurants enjoying meals and always willing to greet the locals.

Non- residents were not allowed to use the facility including the beach chairs unless they were granted permission by the management of the hotel. This policy was designed to safeguard the privacy of the clients as there were often paparazzi who tried to force their way on the property to be first in line to get the next scoop for some international tabloid. There are no private beaches on the island so anyone can walk along the shore in front of the hotel, but only the resident guests and those with reservations were and still are allowed the use of the facility. A couple of many the non-residents requesting permission were Julian Lennon, the son of the music icon John Lennon, as well as the rock star, Mick Jagger.

It was interesting to see what people valued. The ladies wore the finest most exquisite pieces of jewelry to dinner. They would make their selection from the hotel safe before dinner, returning the items to their safety deposit boxes immediately after. The extravagance was obvious when one guest arrived on the island in her private jet and checked in with 25 pieces of luggage for a two-week stay. Once she was settled in, she realized that she had left her jewelry case at home in Europe so she immediately dispatched her pilot to return home to retrieve it. Such is the life of the rich and famous.

There were numerous stories of extravagance which you can well imagine was "foreign" to the majority of us. There was the couple who arrived with their newborn and nanny. That was not an unusual occurrence, however, the following year she arrived with her second child, two nannies, and a chef. She was granted permission for her chef to be allowed access in the kitchen to provide meals for her family. The vast wealth and luxury were both synonymous with Sandy Lane.

In those days, the celebrity sightings were endless and exciting. Names that were known across the world, brought faces that would become familiar to us at Sandy Lane Hotel. A few of the other celebrities visiting were Lena Horne, Stevie Wonder, Her Majesty Queen Elizabeth11, and Prince Andrew, David Dinkins, a former mayor of New York, an avid tennis player, Rowan Atkinson (Mr. Bean, the British actor), Michael Keaton (American actor – the first Batman), Roberta Flack, Ruby Dee and her husband, Ossie Davis (American film actors), Maestro Luciano Pavarotti, Kirk Douglas, the American actor who arrived in his black leather pants and leather jacket, the Forte Family, Michael Winner, Joan Collins, Fidel Castro, Earl Greaves of Black Enterprise Magazine, Sir Jeff Boycott and Sir Gary Sobers, the island's coveted world-renowned cricketer and the island's only living national hero.

Some of these guests left more of an impression than others. I was truly impressed when I saw Ruby Dee and Ossie Davis dining in a public restaurant, holding hands, and praying before they started their meal. This was a public display of their faith, honoring and praising God, not an act I had seen by any public figure before. Of all the celebrities I met, one of the most humble was Jimmy Connors, a champion tennis player whom I had admired and recognized right away. He was extremely polite and always made his requests with, "Please and thank you". There were many other sports personalities including Virginia Wade, Bjorn Borg, Billie Jean King, and several others mostly from the UK and Europe.

Another memorable occasion happened when it was announced that **Her Majesty Queen Elizabeth II** would be visiting Barbados as one of the Commonwealth countries. The government wanted to ensure she received a royal welcome and that the island was well presented for her visit. The government agencies responsible for the island beautification were dispatched to prepare the route she would travel. School children in uniform were invited to line the route in certain locations and many adults were also keen to get a close view of Her Majesty, so they joined the lines along the highways to give her a rousing Barbadian welcome. Several service groups participated, including the service clubs, Girl Guides, Boy Scouts, the Royal Barbados Police Force, The Barbados Defense Force, and any other national group with a uniform. She was scheduled to have lunch at our hotel with a select few locals and members of the Diplomatic Corp. who had been chosen to be presented to her as is the British Protocol. You never offered your hand to the Queen but you accept hers if she offers it. In preparation for her arrival, the hotel team ensured the staff who would be attending to her was immaculately dressed and service in the restaurant was white gloves only. There were clusters of people straining over the hedges and ledges to get a glimpse of royalty with special mention of the operator of the water sports facility who chose to be dressed in her vintage swimsuit and broad hat. Fortunately, her vantage point was obstructed and out of sight of the visiting guests.

The police outriders entered the front gate just ahead of the white Sandy Lane Rolls Royce. Several other police motorcyclists were accompanying the entourage while Her Majesty Queen Elizabeth 11 was accompanied by her attendants as well as a representative from the British Consulate on the island. The Queen's representative on the island was the Hon. Dame Nita Barrow, the first female Governor General for the island. The Governor General herself was quite a well-respected figure in Barbados, a woman who was revered locally as she came from a political family known to have done well for Barbados as a country and society. They were welcomed by the General Manager of the hotel and they were walked very slowly towards the restaurant so they could absorb the picturesque setting that the hotel is renowned for.

Her Royal Highness is quite a diminutive frame, wearing her usual ensemble to include hat and gloves. She is about 5'4" tall, very dainty, and commands the attention of those around. The team would have been briefed by the local British foreign office regarding the protocol for this special visit. The lunch menu meal would have been approved and modified by her chief executives and had to be served on time as protocol dictated. The selection consisted of bite-size pieces ideally suited for her palate. It was also noted that once Her Majesty the Queen stops eating everyone stops eating, so knives and forks down on cue. If you eat slowly you could be in trouble. We had the pleasure of welcoming another member of the royal family years later when Prince Edward graced us with his presence. On this occasion, he was introduced to the management team of the hotel before enjoying the vista of the hotel. His visit was much more low key than the visit of his mother, but just as significant to our island.

Hotel guests have a range of demands when visiting hotels around the world and some are determined to have any service they wish regardless of any rules that may be enforced. An interesting thing happened on our beach one day when a well-known American singer decided she wanted to have her hair braided. She went along the beach to find a stylist who was skilled in creating intricate hairstyles. Hair braiders were required by law to be licensed operators once in the public domain, but this lady chose one who was not licensed. The security guard on beach duty approached the singer and advised her that she was not allowed to have her hair braided by that individual who did not have the proper documentation. Without skipping a beat, the lady curtly responded, "Do you know who I am?" The guard very cheekily said, "I don't care if you are Diana Ross!!!" This was not Diana Ross and I think the singer was insulted that she was not recognized and addressed by her proper name. She stormed away from the beach to seek services elsewhere. The rich and famous are very comfortable holidaying in Barbados as the locals are known to be very discreet, respect the visitors' privacy, not bombarding them for autographs or photographs. This confrontation by the security guard with this well known American singer who was a frequent visitor to the island was not the norm, but thankfully there were no repercussions.

There was the annual visit of one of Britain's infamous food critics, Michael Winner. Many establishments in the UK shuddered at the thought of his visits and waited in anticipation of his comments on the location, chefs, the quality of the food, the service, and the cost of the meals. Even though several of the restaurants had received the prestigious Michelin Star awards, no one was spared the wrath of his criticism. At the hotel, everyone was on high alert from the moment he arrived on the island.

Each time Mr. Winner visited the island he arrived on the Concord flight from Gatwick airport landing in Barbados at 8:30 am on a Saturday morning in December. He was the first one off the aircraft as he travelled with very little luggage. He insisted that the white Rolls Royce owned by the Sandy Lane Hotel was awaiting his arrival. To arrive on the island on the Concord indicated that you were someone wealthy and important. It was a major coup for the Government of Barbados to have been awarded the luxury of being a host destination for this flight and something the Barbadians celebrated proudly. There were many demands made to satisfy Mr. Winner, and the staff made every effort to accommodate them. He insisted on registering in his suite, He demanded to have the newest mini-moke, (an open-top, open-sided jeep), ready for his use on his arrival and of course the staff delivered. His first order of business was to change into casual wear, grab towels for himself and his traveling companion, and armed with a bottle of vintage champagne, hopped into his mini-moke, and took off.

Everyone at the hotel was vigilant, making every attempt to avoid him so they were not the target of one of his vicious comments in his next article. He had no qualms about naming people and to be specific about their shortcomings more often than their accomplishments. Once he discovered this gem of the Caribbean, he couldn't resist booking well in advance for future visits. There was always a buzz around the hotel as the staff wanted to know, "Is he coming this year, after the critique last year?" This food critic was robust in stature and who wanted to enjoy the best life had to offer so he had a bevy of the ladies whom he entertained over time. They all seemed mesmerized by his charismatic personality. I can remember one actress who felt the need to please him in a moment and she hopped on top of the reception desk full of glee just to make a scene for him, much to his amusement. He giggled throughout her little performance. The housekeeping, restaurant, and beach teams were the ones most often in the firing line so certain things had to remain constant, like the location of his suite, the table in the restaurant, and that no one was placed close to him on the beach. It has been said that any publicity is good so those familiar with his annual visits would eagerly search for the newspaper articles soon after he arrived at the hotel. Although he was critical of some areas of the management of the hotel, his comments challenged the team to ensure that quality products and services were of supreme importance.

There were some guests I found fascinating. One such person was **The Maestro, Luciano Pavarotti**. On his first visit to the island, he was greeted on the tarmac at the airport by a member of the hotel staff. With permission from the Airport personnel, the hotel's Rolls Royce was allowed to park at the bottom of the stairs of the aircraft so there was no distance for him to walk. He made his way down the stairs, sat briefly on his portable stool before he climbed into the back seat of the car. I was privileged to be assigned to greet Mr. Pavarotti in the lobby of the hotel and many members of staff left their posts to catch a glimpse of this superstar. As we walked across the lobby en route to the penthouse suite all the guests on the top terrace and in the adjacent areas broke out into applause, shouting, "Maestro! Maestro!". We made our way along the long narrow corridor when suddenly he commented, "I feel like I am going back to the airport". We both chuckled as we entered the elevator to the top floor of that block of buildings. When we arrived at a well-appointed, very private location with a breath-taking view of the Caribbean Sea, he declared that he was not staying in that suite. He thanked us for the consideration for his privacy but he needed to be on the ground floor so he could open his door and walk right out to the beach. It would have been less hassle, moreover this allowed him to go as frequently as he wished.

The very professional team hustled to make the adjustments to accommodate this very special guest as well as his staff traveling with him. The Maestro had specific needs regarding his bed, the refrigerator size, a table on the patio covered by a tent where he could dine privately, a table top stove where he could cook the pasta he brought with him, and a dedicated butler. All the stops were shifted to ensure his comfort. His fridge was stocked with items he brought, like chocolates, bread and pasta and he had a daily delivery of platters of fresh fruit which his butler handled with ease. The hotel chef was honored to prepare meals as he requested and not necessarily just items on the menu. The Maestro enjoyed cooking and oftentimes prepared meals for himself and the Sandy Lane Hotel catered to every luxurious need Mr. Pavarotti required.

The UK tabloids discovered he was at the hotel and as much as the hotel security tried to shield him, the paparazzi were always close by. Before long there was an article published that, "Pavarotti was having a whale of a time in Barbados". He was a genius and it was hurtful for a performer who had shared his musical talent and given so much joy to the world. The Maestro was a gentle giant. We were all disappointed but it was out of our control.

During that visit, he was introduced to a young Bajan lad who was about 17 years old at the time, and very quickly he trusted this youngster to be his butler and cater to his every need. The young man worked long hours during the visits and The Maestro was so impressed with him that he offered him a job to travel the world with him. It had to be a very difficult decision to make but the youngster turned the opportunity down, much to the surprise and horror of others who wished they had been given that offer.

When my young son, Sacha David graduated from Class One in primary school, he surprised me by performing a solo at the school event. I had no idea he had such a voice (took after his father) and the biggest surprise was that he sang a song made famous by the Maestro. During his visit, the Maestro kindly agreed to meet my son, an opportunity of a lifetime. My son and his best friend arrived at the designated time and the conversation started with the cordial hellos. The Maestro then asked the boys their names, but they were so completely star-struck that all they could utter was, "babababa". They couldn't even remember their names! It was a funny but memorable moment. The Maestro was warm and welcoming recognizing their fright and nervousness upon meeting a celebrity for the first time. He flashed that beautiful smile without trying to force it or pretend and kindly offered to be photographed with the boys.

On one of his visits to the island, The Maestro offered to do a single performance on the majestic polo field, within a few miles from the hotel, which was transformed into an open-air theatre. The excitement filled the air as lovers of classical music from around the Caribbean flooded the island so they could witness one of the greatest performers of all time, up close and personal. The Maestro did not disappoint his fans and we would bask in that memory for months to come. He continued to visit the hotel for many years and the staff always had the distinct pleasure of caring for his every wish.

There were many wonderful stories of clandestine activities with some guests. There was a very handsome gentleman, who seemed obsessed with tanning and so he spent many hours in the sun developing his bronze image. Every afternoon after lunch, he would leave the hotel he would go for his "walk". The beach attendants were well tuned in to all the action and soon discovered that his mistress was staying at a hotel nearby, so he would make his daily visits. Then we had another who was vacationing with his girlfriend and on the day she was due to leave, someone must have tipped her off to stay another week. I am not sure if she was told why but she decided to extend her stay another week which put the gentleman in a panic as another lady was arriving on that same flight in the afternoon. We had to intercept lady number 2 at the airport and check her into another hotel until the original girlfriend left. A situation like this puts the staff in a precarious position to ensure confidentiality, but thankfully they were professional enough to do the right thing while covering up for the wrong thing.

The visit **of President Fidel Castro** was one of pure anticipation and excitement. The security forces were at work, checking every nook and cranny, weeks before his arrival to ensure his safety. This gentleman represented the Cuban communist revolutionary and lived in constant fear that the US government was plotting to assassinate him, so the local security force took all precautions necessary to endure that didn't happen on their territory. An entire block of rooms in the hotel was selected by the security forces for the exclusive use of the President's entourage. The hotel staff assigned to his block had to be vetted and no other staff allowed in the area. Before the Cuban delegation arrived at the hotel there were several Cuban security personnel seen hiding in the bushes and trees with their small black attaché cases. This seemed comical at the time as though a set was being prepared for an espionage thriller. The police outriders entered the main gate and almost immediately President Castro got out of the vehicle, choosing to walk from the entrance to the lobby. He was very approachable and without hesitation stopped along the way to greet the gardeners. He had a very large entourage who was loyal and committed to his safety.

Once the President and his entourage were settled into their accommodation, they proceeded to order room service meals and the main choice took us all by surprise as they delighted in ordering dozens of hamburgers, a popular American staple. President Castro had the image of a true statesman. He wore his traditional military green uniform, carried a very erect posture, made eye contact with those he met, and exhibited all the characteristics of a charismatic leader. He seemed very comfortable roaming around the premises and didn't allow himself to be confined just to his quarters as he trusted his security team. There must have been a sigh of relief from both nations when President Castro left the island free of any security breaches.

It was indeed a privilege to have had the opportunity to meet this cadre of human beings who had accomplished so much in their lifetime and yet we may never know what obstacles they had to overcome to reach their goals. We may never know who or what their influences were, how they were able to circumvent the incessant chatter of naysayers, and how they were able to stay focused on their short term and long term goals. There are so many questions one could ask of these successful people, but we all have a personal tale to tell as our journeys continue.

One of my responsibilities at the hotel and also one of my most satisfying activities was planning and managing nuptials. Organizational and creative skills are paramount to execute events at this luxury level. I grew very fond of one couple in particular who contacted me concerning arrangements for their upcoming nuptials. This fairy tale romance was really special. She was an air hostess and on one of her flights, a passenger who was traveling for business discreetly expressed an interest in her. The strict policy of the airlines was mandated that the staff was not allowed to fraternize with the passengers so the possibility of any contact seemed daunting. This knight in shining armor was determined to pursue this princess, donned his 'Sherlock Holmes' hat to locate her, and he did. A story made for the movies.

Their wedding was the first high profile function I had planned and certainly the most elaborate but I enjoyed every moment of it. The ceremony was due to take place at one of the historical churches on the platinum coast of the island about 10 minutes' drive from the hotel. The legal paperwork was being processed while the team contracted the best florist on the island to manage all the floral requirements including huge pedestals of flowers and bouquets for the church and reception areas. The bride wanted a very simple bouquet so that was easy. The scale with which the church was decorated with flowers was certainly impactful. The ceremony was short and to the point followed by the photographer seizing the moment to capture the best lighting as the sun was setting. Following the ceremony, there was a hustle to transfer all the pedestals and bouquets back to the hotel to decorate the area for the pre-dinner cocktail reception before the guests returned to the hotel. The time spent with the photographer allowed us the grace period to recreate a beautiful ambiance in another location. The staff was diligent as well as excited to make this occasion special so we all scampered around like big elves at Christmas.

As a wedding present, the bride received a huge gift from her husband which came as a total surprise to her. The love they had for each other was very evident and time proved that this was true, pure, and tender. With her years of experience as an air hostess, she developed a love for flying, so encouraged by her husband she acquired her pilot's license. He generously presented her with her own private helicopter, designed a landing strip on their property so she would have easy access to fly whenever she desired under favorable weather conditions. What I loved most about this family was that their wealth didn't define the way they treated me, the way they treated the staff, the way they treated their designated taxi-driver and so the respect was reciprocated by all of us. They have over the years continually demonstrated that we can love and care for one another at all levels of the socio-economic spectrum and color is not part of the equation. Their children have grown to be very respectful and that is a testimony to the example set by their parents.

It is a fact that there is so much emphasis on race and color and yet we neglect to identify many families across the divide who care about each other, respect each other, support each other, and have not allowed these social imbalances to influence their relationships. May it continue to be so.

There were many high profile personalities from around the world always visible at the hotel over time. Some we discovered their fame after they arrived and other guests in the hotel would identify who they were, especially the European celebs. When I first met Lena Horne, an American icon, she arrived one afternoon accessorized with the large, cream floppy hat and the largest sunglasses available, a feeble attempt at a disguise. I approached her and said, "Welcome to Sandy Lane, Ms. Horne." She was so shocked that someone on this little island recognized her. I went on to say that I had seen her perform on Broadway when she did her solo act, *Lena*. She was very impressed. I can imagine she was probably trying to figure how, on a small island like this, someone would have seen her on Broadway. Her beauty had not faded in any way and she remained very elegant and very accommodating, I thought.

Two celebrities visited one summer David Denkins and Ossie Davis during the Crop Over Festival and decided they wanted to experience what our carnival was all about, having seen carnivals all over the world. It had rained very heavily that day so the bands and revellers were soaked, as were the other spectators on the side line. The gentlemen had a lot to report on their return.

Lord and Lady Forte, the founders of the Forte Hotel group of which Sandy Lane Hotel was a part, were an extremely charming couple and he especially personified what being a gentleman meant. He and his wife visited the hotel annually and the teams had the utmost respect for them both. Lord Forte's smile was visible from one hundred yards away. He greeted you with a friendly, warm gaze like a friend, genuinely happy to see you. His wife was very dainty and regal in her attire and her graceful manner modelled true femininity of a high standard. They had a love affair with this hotel and I believe considered it their pride and joy. The Forte children visited often in the company of their parents and were all very gracious in the way they treated the staff. There were specific arrangements made for the Fortes before their arrival, and every detail was carefully put in place weeks in advance. Lord Forte played golf every day and had his designated caddie who escorted him around the course. There was a tangible tenderness between himself and his wife.

One of my favorite guests was a British couple and their family, **Lord and Lady Rayne**, and their children. I was to discover after many visits to the hotel that Lord Rayne was born of a Jewish family. His father was a garment manufacturer and they lived in a very modest home in London when Lord Rayne was a child. Lord Rayne grew up to become successful in his own right and after many years, created and funded influential charitable institutions, including teaching hospitals, under his foundation. In 2007, Lord Rayne's foundation founded the hand-in-hand school, a bilingual school located in Jerusalem to teach Arabs and Jews alongside each other.

Preparing for the arrival of the Rayne family was always exciting for me. There were specific instructions such as details on type and placement of flowers in their suite, dinner reservations in restaurants within and outside the hotel, activities for the children, tee times for golf, and reconfirmation of first-class seats for the return journey. It was such a pleasure catering to this family because as wealthy as they were, humility was in their DNA. They exhibited respect for everyone they encountered and seemed to always enjoy each other's company.

There was a strict dress code in the hotel and blue jeans were not allowed in the public areas after 7 pm. If the Rayne family chose to dine out one night it was not unusual to see Lord Rayne arrive in the lobby wearing blue jeans and a short-sleeved shirt with the sleeves folded. He was comfortable in his skin and didn't need to show off or prove anything to anyone.

Then there was a British gentleman who had a very successful glass business in the UK. He jokingly made a statement to some folks that if he won the UK lottery, he was bringing 10 friends on the Concorde to stay at the world-renowned Sandy Lane Hotel where all the celebrities go. As mentioned previously, the Concorde, a British-French turbojet-powered, supersonic passenger jetliner was the most sought after mode of transportation for the rich and famous to the island as it took 3½ hours flying time. The aircraft was operated solely by British Airways and during Christmas week, one could see three such planes on the tarmac in Barbados. The airfares were exorbitant but the idea of being able to have breakfast in the UK and lunch in Barbados was very appealing.

It so happened that the gentleman got his wish, won millions of pounds in the UK lottery, and did just what he said he would do, arriving bright and early one Saturday morning on the Concorde with his friends. He had not anticipated however that the UK press was also coming along for the ride. The visit made headlines in the UK press and there were photographs of his group splashed all over the tabloids with the most unflattering comments about their attire and that they did not belong in such a prestigious hotel. They were considered lower class citizens and they didn't and couldn't fit in. The press described their clothes as polyester garments, scoffed at their excessive jewelry and tattoos, and argued that they did not represent the rich and the famous.

The struggle to enjoy a holiday became real for this gentleman and after a few days in the hotel, he decided he had enough of the slanderous comments made about him as they photographed every move he made. Within five days of his arrival, he decided he had enough. I had to go into a clandestine operation mode, making contacts with airline personnel to get him off the island secretly. Having developed a good working relationship with airline staff, they facilitated the process to ensure a seamless, clandestine departure. On the day of his departure, his luggage was taken to the airport before he departed from the hotel, he settled his account in his room and he was ushered through a side door in the event just in case a photographer as lurking in the wings. He also very kindly settled the accommodation for his friends as he was their host and they remained in the hotel until their designated time of departure from the island. This was one of the many lessons on how to respect people, manage my expectations, have set standards, and to be kind everyone regardless of their status. I felt empathy for this man as he only wanted to celebrate his winning with his buddies and enjoy a life of luxury for the first time.

Promotions don't always come easy but thankfully, I worked with General Managers who trusted my judgment and as one would say confidently. "If you think it will work Blackman, then do it." With that vote of confidence, I was able to tackle new assignments that did advance the hotel experience for the guests. I knew I had found my niche and that caring for people was what I did best. My teams over the years were very faithful and we became "family". The bond that developed between us was more than just a manager and her staff, empowering them to be the best that they could be. As my General Managers PV and RRW imparted in me, I was compelled to pay it forward. I arranged counselling sessions and encouraged team members to stay the course even when things seemed impossible. I can remember one team member threatening to quit because he had been verbally, publicly abused by one of the line managers. I had to encourage him not to walk away from his job until he found another since he had a family who depended on him. It was always my mission to help guide those who were disenfranchised. He stayed the course and eventually found a more lucrative livelihood.

I had never worked with so many women in an organization before and found it difficult to understand why women sometimes pitted themselves against each other rather than support each other. It's bad enough that there is an obvious male dominance at the upper echelon of most businesses, however, there seemed to be obvious confrontations between women in the workplace. Friends of mine would share stories of women fighting hard to gain recognition, some took advantage of their superior positions to laud their authority over others they determined were not their equals and then some intentionally sabotaged others out of jealousy. I have always believed that women are equally gifted and in some cases more talented than their male counterparts in the workplace, but unfortunately some women have not matured enough to care for each other in a holistic way.

⚜

Celebrity Weddings

We were asked to host a few celebrity weddings for OK and Hello magazines during my time at the hotel. The publisher of the magazine sent their teams of photographers to the hotel for a site visit before the couples' arrival so they could set the stage for the production. There was a great interest in one such couple in the UK so there was no room for error so every detail had to be researched and executed to perfection. For example, the table settings had to be right with the correct wine glasses, wrinkle-free tablecloths; correct furnishings; to be mindful of casting shadows, reflections, hence the correct lighting, to measure the intensity of the sun; complimentary floral arrangements; the best time of day, discreetly displayed props and so on. This exercise was all new to me but I was absorbing it all with great interest.

There will always be dream killers in your life and you must be sure to recognize them. I can remember being told by someone concerning one of the photo shoots, "You will never capture the cover of the Hello magazine". Note to self: when someone says you can't, work twice as hard to succeed. That comment fuelled me to work even harder to ensure the photographer had everything he needed to get the best shots, selected the most photogenic staff and that all the surrounding areas were well-manicured and up to the required standard.

I was completely exhausted after a gruelling week of coordinating my first photo shoot but felt gratified that I had given it my all. The photographer returned to the UK to do the editing with the expectation that he would meet the deadline for the next edition of the magazine. There was a very tight window of opportunity but he was determined to make it. The process was extraordinary and exhilarating. Some of the requests meant sourcing props from locations around the island, redeploying staff from their regular duties to be involved in segments but in the end, the hard work paid off. We were most elated when we were told that not only were we featured on the cover of the magazine, we were also featured on 10 pages inside. It was time to celebrate.

How do you top that and do the impossible? We were approached and accepted the offer to do another photo shoot due to the success of the first one. The photographer requested to photograph a celebrity couple on the lower level or the Starlight Terrace of the hotel. The scene was set that they would be seated in a horse-drawn carriage at a specific time of day and there should be no guests in the immediate area. The request seemed impossible as access to the location was not straightforward, but I was determined to make that happen. I had to find a well maintained horse-drawn carriage on the island and I enlisted the help of some contacts who not only delivered but gave me all the assistance I needed to place it in the desired location. After hours of negotiating through narrow passages guiding the horse, who was not impressed, on the sand, they slowly entered the terraced area into the location. Unauthorized photographs were not allowed so we solicited the corporation of the resident guests and most of them complied. While I managed the surrounding area, I noticed a man on the upper-level patio, whom I recognized as a "resident guest", taking photographs. I discovered that he was a member of the UK paparazzi fraternity, who cleverly booked into the hotel as a normal paying guest for the same period to upstage the magazine. I went over to him, grabbed his camera, and demanded he take the film out. I was undeterred at the moment and completely committed to fulfilling the request of the client. Many of the hotel guests recognized the wedding couple as the groom was a famous English athlete and so they were happy to be witnesses to the event.

There was a wonderful little story of a well-known supermodel who arrived for a private photoshoot arranged by her agent for a major magazine. She only needed to be on the island for three days, so she arrived with her crew; make-up artist, stylist, and photographer. The background was to be on one of the remote beaches on the very rustic southeast coast of the island. The staff was dispatched to take refreshments to the site for the visitors. Much to their shock, the model stripped to her birthday suit as she changed clothes with no care in the world that these foreign eyes were gawking at her frame. Needless to say, those guys could not contain their excitement at the free show and remained mesmerized for days as the chatter continued.

⚜

There was a lot of activity on Christmas eve in the hotel. The bellmen performed the role of elves distributing gifts to all the guests in residence that night. The gifts were beautifully wrapped, tagged with the names of the guests, room numbers assigned and off they went to place the gifts in the rooms. Christmas day the arrival of Santa Claus was another major event that the guests looked forward to every year. The arrival was a secret that could not be shared with even the staff until "D-day". So many creative ideas were birthed with Santa arriving from submarine emerging with seven staff members dressed as Santa Claus; Mr. and Mrs. Santa Claus arriving in a sleigh; on a kayak; by speed boat or jet ski. The children of all ages were eager to be photographed with Santa and to receive a gift on the beach. The final Christmas before the hotel closure and before the major reconstruction, there was the most spectacular event, never before attempted on the island. Santa arrived by parachute. British Airways kindly offered to sponsor the arrival of a professional parachutist who would be the actor for the moment. The guests assembled on the beach in anticipation of Santa's arrival. One could overhear the questions, the guessing games, and the bets of people who were on a need-to-know basis, trying to bribe anyone they could, to figure out how Santa would be arriving. At five minutes to noon, the anticipation came to a crescendo when there was a sighting way up in the sky of a small aircraft approaching the west coast and circling for a brief spell. At the stroke of midday, the aircraft came lower towards the hotel and in a flash, someone jumped from the plane. This parachutist jumped from that small plane, several feet above the ground. He had already determined the exact spot he would land on the beach and we all watched in pure amazement as he navigated through the trees and landed on the exact spot he had marked. The beachfront has several mature, flourishing mahogany trees that form a crest along the beachfront, but he managed not to fall within the branches of any of them. There was much howling, whistling, and cheering after such a successful feat. He was greeted very affectionately by the guests and I am sure offered drinks to calm everyone's nerves. The guests would soon after be contemplating lunch, but the buzz surrounding the event was similar to a wrap at the end of a movie production. I believe the adults enjoyed the exercise more than the children who were keener on getting presents.

⁂

Once the Christmas festivities were over, the gifts, the hangovers, and the partying, my responsibilities quickly switched to arrange the New Years' Eve celebrations.

One of the most magical and completely exciting times for Sandy Lane Hotel was planning the activities for New Year's Eve. It was tiring because of the level of detail and design necessary to get the hotel ready for this occasion but the adrenaline fueled everyone to succeed. The designers were brought in to decorate the restaurants and public area, the bands were selected and rehearsed, the balloons that would fall at midnight were put in place and you prayed that they would release at midnight. Extra staff were employed, the cases of wine and champagne selected and delivered, all the food and beverage requirements were processed and stored. The housekeeping was on the alert for the influx of clientele and was well aware that the demands placed on them would be significant. The beach staff prepared themselves for the disagreements with guests selecting the specific spot on the beach they wanted to sit regardless of who was there first. The reservations department had to ensure that all the rooms assigned were in agreement with the travel agents, tour operators, and the individual guests. The pressure was on to deliver at the highest level of service in the midst of what could have been chaos if people were not informed and equipped. The staff grew excited as the night approached - some not as much concerned about the hard work, but the anticipation of the tips they expected to receive at the end of the night. Extra security was arranged, the noisemakers were placed on the tables along with the celebratory hats, cases of champagne chilled, menus tried and tested…and all systems ready to go. It would soon be show time.

Some guests arrived early to have cocktails in the lounge before being seated in their restaurant of choice. The gowns the ladies wore were regal and I would guess were more than likely custom designed or selected by their stylists. I can remember one such lady who was staying at one of the private homes on the Sandy Lane estate arrived at the lobby driven by her husband. When she alighted the car, she wore a dress that had a full-bodied skirt with a large bow that projected from the waist quite away off her body. I could only assume that it would be comfortable enough for her to sit in the restaurant for those long hours. The bellman loved to see this couple arrive because her husband was extremely generous and always tipped the bellman $100USD, just to valet park his car in the parking lot close by. It became a jockeying for position to see who would be the lucky beneficiary of this gift. They would each place themselves in a strategic place for his return.

This was a night when you would see the effects of alcohol on the human mind. There were occasions where some gentlemen never made it to their beds that night and were seen in the bar area at 6 am the next morning still fully dressed in their tuxedos. Some youngsters did not have permission to drink but would sneak sips from their parents' glasses and end up falling asleep in the lounge only to be rescued or rudely awakened by the staff early the next morning.

Those nights were the most expensive to host and extremely busy. After dinner the guests would gather on the Starlight Terrace, which as the name connotes, open to the stars, where they would dance to the Caribbean beat of one of the best local bands. The MC would announce to the audience that they were approaching midnight and to prepare for the countdown. This prompted the guests who were not on the dance floor to get into position to embrace their loved one and the New Year. At one minute to midnight the countdown started and "Happy New Year" followed by an elaborate fireworks display.

On New Year's Day, we hosted a Caribbean carnival. The creative idea was conceptualized by a former member of the team and the onus was now to improve and add an element of surprise each year for the guests. There were extremely talented entertainment producers on the island who helped in the design development, installation of props, and to be on hand to direct the events of the morning to bring a cultural, Caribbean element to the week of entertainment. Placement of the props for the event began as early as 6 am and having left work at 4 am from the New Year's Eve celebration, I was responsible to ensure the carnival organizers operated on schedule. The festivities were always well received by the guests and so the challenge was to create a bigger, better event the following year. I thoroughly enjoyed using my creative edge and working closely with the experts in the field to bring a new theme each year to our luxurious hotel. There were so many repeat guests who confirmed their reservations a year in advance so it was incumbent on us to keep striving to improve our offering of food, music, and entertainment, Caribbean style. Year after year the team delivered opportunities for lasting memories for the guests.

⚜

Several job attachments took place within the Forte Hotel group which the staff on both continents welcomed. During the very busy winter months in Barbados, there was an exchange of staff from the Forte Village to the Sandy Lane Hotel and the exchange in the summer from Barbados to Sardinia. There was great camaraderie that developed between this unlikely group of individuals from different cultures. The fondness for the island and its people especially the local women who flocked to the beach when the foreigners came, would inspire the Italian teams to return year after year.

There were more good times than bad during my tenure at Sandy Lane hotel. I learned a lot about the tourism industry, I met some very successful professionals, forged some good friendships, loved and respected so many people at varying socio-economic levels, earned an income to support my family and have so many memories, too numerous to mention.

There were many opportunities to stray from my moral values but the spirit residing within me made me pause, time and time again, to identify what my purpose was and that is just what kept me from becoming a happy wanderer and focused on doing the right thing even when I wanted to do the wrong thing. The Apostle Paul says in the Bible, "when I want to do the right thing, I sometimes do the wrong thing".

I have reflected over time about the friendship with my friend Turid with whom I toured in Sardinia and when the time was right to share a little of our history, I realized that there were so many similarities between us with the feelings of rejection as children. Her father had not been very kind to her and she often felt like an outcast even though she seemed to have it all. She grew up very privileged and yet we had similar struggles. It was yet another light bulb moment for me to acknowledge that we all desire to love and be loved which is innate and not an emotion that is taught in the educational system. It doesn't matter if you are rich or poor, ugly or beautiful, educated with multiple degrees, we all want the same thing, to be embraced, and to be valued. To be treasured by another human being is a plus, but to know that the one true lover of your soul is God who will never leave you nor forsake you, that's a deep and unconditional must-have.

⁂

There is a funny story of an incident that occurred on my 50th birthday. I arranged to host a cocktail party at a Turid's house with just a few close friends. There was a butler serving, the champagne flowed, we danced, we laughed, I cut the cake with my young son and we all had a great time. Later that night a few of us went to a local club to continue the celebration before returning to my friend's house to help with the cleanup. There were just 4 of us at the house by now and while my hostess went off to bed, I continued to clean the dishes, etc. A few minutes into this exercise, I noticed from my peripheral view that someone was approaching me. When I looked it was a young man (an uninvited son of a very wealthy family who showed up with one of my guests) stripping his clothes; first, his belt, then his pants, then his shirt and he was now in his briefs. I was stunned. He then proceeded to approach me in the kitchen while trying to remove his underwear. I was so shocked that all I could do was to yell at him like a mother to a child, "Get back in there and put your clothes on!". He very sheepishly returned to the living room, flopped on the couch, and fell asleep instantly. That was a picture I replayed many times over. What was that chap thinking?!

⚜

There have been a few historical events that captured the world during my lifetime which I will share.

1990 -
NELSON MANDELA

Nelson Mandela was born in Mveso to the Thembu Royal family in South Africa. He studied law at two universities, Fort Hare and Witwatersrand before working as a lawyer in Johannesburg. He was appointed president of the ANC's Transvaal branch and rose to prominence in other campaigns before multiple arrests due to sabotage campaigns against the government and conspiring to overthrow them. He was sentenced to life in prison in the Rivonia trial, served 27 years both in the Robben Island and Pollsmoor prisons. Mandela was released in 1990 by President de Klerk after both men agreed to end the apartheid regime in 1994. Mandela was inaugurated as president until 1999. A staunch advocate for democracy and social justice, he won the coveted Nobel Peace Prize in 1993. Among his people, President Mandela was referred to by his clan name, Madiba, meaning Father of the Nation. The entire world watched the live broadcast of his funeral when he was laid to rest.

1997-
DIANA, PRINCESS OF WALES

The world was introduced to Lady Diana Spencer in 1981 when she became engaged to the Prince of Wales. At the age of 20 the entire world, approximately 750 million people were transfixed watching her walk down the aisle to be married to Prince Charles. She was resplendent in a one of a kind gown with a white train that seemed endless, flowing down the red-carpeted of St. Paul's cathedral.

We were up at the crack of dawn, called our friends to make sure they were awake, coffee, and snacks in hand so we didn't miss one moment of this fairy tale. There were no bathroom breaks allowed so plans were in place. Years later we were introduced to her sons William and Harry but much to the horror of her fans, the fairy tale exploded and the couple divorced. Never before had the royal family faced this dilemma. No one could have prepared the world for the shaking to take place in 1997 when a car accident in France ended the life of the worlds' Princess. Her funeral was broadcast live around the world and the tributes continued for weeks and months after.

2001 -
911 – WORLD TRADE CENTRE – NEW YORK CITY

On Tuesday, September 11th, 2011, I was on my way to have a small medical procedure at the local hospital, but when I got there it was postponed. On my way out I received a phone call from a friend who told me to turn on my television. There was pandemonium in the US as a series of four coordinated terrorist attacks had been launched. An American Airline and a United Airline plane had crashed into the north and south towers of the World Trade Building in NYC and within an hour and a half, a 110-story building collapsed into rubble. A third plane American Airline plane crashed into the side of the Pentagon in Washington D.C. and another United plane crashed into a field in Pennsylvania.

The catastrophic event changed the world. Approximately 2,996 died, 6000 were injured and that number increased with time with at least 10 billion dollars in infrastructure and property damage. Intelligence sources identified Osama Bin Laden as the mastermind and an international manhunt resulted in identifying his hideout and he was killed in 2011.

2008 and 2013 -
BARACK OBAMA

Mr. OBAMA was born in Hawaii two years after the territory was included as the 50th state to join the states in the union of the USA. His parents were an interracial couple with his father of African descent and his mother was a white American. He was raised both in the US and in Indonesia. Mr. Obama attended Harvard Law School, becoming the first black President of the Harvard Law Review before becoming a Civil Rights attorney. He gained notoriety when he delivered the keynote address at the Democratic National Convention in 2004, won the election as the first African American President in the USA in 2008, and re-elected in 2013. He gained a Nobel Peace Prize in 2009 for his efforts to strengthen international diplomacy and cooperation between people. His election and inauguration to the highest office in the USA was another event that caused the world to stand still and recognize that things were changing. It gave black people hope for the impossible when he chanted his inclusive slogan, "Yes we can".

⁂

CREATE IN ME A CLEAN HEART, O LORD AND RENEW A RIGHT SPIRIT IN ME - Ps 51 vs.10

One balmy summer evening I was awakened to the knowledge that I was truly loved throughout my entire life. I finally understood what it meant to fall in love. You see I fell in love but it was with Jesus. I gained a new confidence in myself and was not as concerned about dressing to impress but more focused on the needs of others that were in a lesser position than I was. I was never a woman of great means but knew I always had enough to share with someone else. That summer as I lay on my pillow, I had a moment when it occurred to me that when I rest on my pillow, I sleep, I hope for things, dream, talk to God, ask Him for stuff, give thanks, cry, laugh at my jokes, reflect on my day, on my relationships, on my financial situation, on my accomplishments, on my failures, just stuff. My thoughts would roam free on those pillows.

At that moment there was an epiphany, what some of the millennials would call a heavenly download. My heart struck a chord with heaven and the 'Pillow Talk Prayer Time' idea was conceptualized. As the excitement grew in my mind I shared the idea with a few close friends who immediately caught the vision, of resting on pillows in a quiet place. We agreed it was necessary to put action to the idea and so our ministry was established where we spent countless hours laying on the floor on our pillows worshiping the King of Kings and the Lord of Lords; just crying out to the Lord and entering into His gates with praise and thanksgiving. There were many, many late nights and prophetic words were spoken which we recorded. As women, we were fuelled to pray for, care for, encourage, offer spiritual and financial assistance to women in need. For us, prayer was the most important and only weapon we could use to get the necessary breakthrough. God is knocking, He is waiting, He is longing for all of us to come to Him. Will you say "Yes!!!"?

Pillow Talk gave me focus and as I continued the discovery of my purpose, my passion, my strength and just let God lead. I had a reality check that I had ignored people with debilitating issues when I was younger, feeling that it is not my business to interfere, but the Holy Bible says that we are our brother's keeper. Our lives have become so busy and we have become so self-centered and inwardly focused, that we miss opportunities to give a helping hand to others. Someone prayed for us, gave us an opportunity, said yes you can, said they would take a chance on you, so it's your turn to take a chance on someone else. It is your responsibility to reach out and touch someone. Their very existence could depend on it. Through the Pillow Talk Prayer Time Charity, we have been able to support women in covering their rent, some medical expenses, education, and other needs through prayer while loving them through the process.

As my understanding of God grew, I desired to be intentional in my walk and to be one of His authentic representatives, so some lifestyle changes had to be made. Several years post-marriage, I became involved in a unique relationship that lasted many years. It seemed an unlikely match to some, but my close confidants understood and supported me wholeheartedly. They were happy that I was happy and became my biggest cheerleaders. It felt as though I had found a soul mate, someone who cared for me with no hidden agenda and no unrealistic expectations, and the feeling was mutual. My role was to help make him a better version of himself and to help build his confidence to achieve the success I knew he was capable of. Several factors were not in our favor and time was one, so the painful separation began, opening old wounds. I was transitioning to a new place spiritually without recognizing it and as a result, certain things lost their appeal. When God wants your attention, He will pull you away from the familiar, comfortable place so you can direct your gaze on Him. It took many years to glean how God was making changes for both of us and I am grateful and have no regrets to have had that experience. To be torn from a relationship that seemed authentic, from someone who supported my passion for life and the future, who had the heart to be always present was difficult and yet it was all part of God's plan to restructure my life for His purpose. It took time to regain that peace and joy we all long for, but time does heal.

The journey has not been easy and at times you can't always verbalize your actions to those around you, but you have to be true to yourself and follow the path that has been designed just for you. There was a renewed birth, an awakening, a new zest for life, and others. My creativity evolved exponentially and I was creating spaces I didn't know were possible. I would often be asked, "how were you able to accomplish so much alone?" I had figured out by now that the gifts and ideas were not generated by me, but God-breathed. I had to learn the importance of forgiving quickly so ill feelings did not fester and cause long term diseases. I learned in that season that all those experiences from childhood were designed to prepare me for a life I could not have imagined. To help others overcome what may seem like insurmountable obstacles is truly a favor-filled life.

I have lived a life often feeling intimidated, fought off a rapist, almost died in childbirth, called disparaging names, but I am an overcomer and a survivor and I am still here to talk about it. I have made so many wrong turns thinking I was strong enough and could do my own thing. My new reality will not allow me to blame my parents for my life story and the many twists and turns I endured, as they did the best they could with the knowledge they had. Realistically speaking, there is no manuscript as to how to master the art of parenting. My parents had their struggles, their insecurities, their emotional baggage, so they needed as much nurturing as I did.

God made me into a strong, black woman to fight and overcome many battles and I thank Him for placing those in my life who were part of the journey - the good and the bad. To the adults who didn't validate me as a child, to my fellow students who didn't think I would achieve much in life, for the guys who passed this way but once, to the co-workers who showed their colors, to my staff and friends, I wish them all the best life has to offer and trust that they too will have the same awakening I did with God.

My tenure at the Sandy Lane Hotel ended when the hotel was acquired by new owners who opted to demolish and rebuild a world-class resort on the original footprint of the property. I was fortunate to spend the next two years at a premier golf resort where I gained new skills in real estate and property management. I have always been successful in gaining employment in luxury properties, so my next job was at a Relais and Chateaux hotel on the island. This small boutique hotel replicated an English country home where all the rooms were positioned in a crescent shape with a well-manicured garden in the center. The Godsals who developed the property were longtime friends of one of the owners of the Sandy Lane Hotel, and as they both shared a love for the island, its location, the weather, the people - they created a little haven for themselves.

Customer service has always been my forte so when I was offered this new job, I was pleased to have the opportunity to once again interact with hotel guests regularly. During the first couple of years however, I became disappointed that I was not allowed to contribute more to the operation when I was, as usual, bursting with ideas. On my way to work one afternoon, I sensed in my spirit that the Lord was telling me that if I stopped complaining and started thanking Him for the job, things would change. Have you ever suddenly had a strange thought and you couldn't explain the source? I responded however from that moment by each morning, thanking the Lord for my job and became excited and expectant that every day was going to be a good day. My entire attitude changed. It was another paradigm shift to remind myself that if I trusted and had faith in God, that something good would happen. Within four weeks of this revolutionary way of constantly giving thanks, I received a promotion I was not expecting.

During this season, a wonderful friendship developed with a young woman I worked with at that hotel. I recognized quite early that she was not achieving all God had intended for her, so I encouraged her to consider other options for her life. She became excited that someone was taking notice and empowering to achieve more. I am extremely proud to see how she blossomed and bloomed into a strong woman of faith. She was unfairly treated, endured much pain, was damaged emotionally by others, but God had a bigger, better plan for her and no weapon that was raised against her could prosper. She was able to rise above the victim mentality and has achieved a great measure of success both academically, relationally, and spiritually. This truly was a demonstration of God's mercy and grace.

Everyone has battled with something and most of us wear masks so others won't see the pain or stress we endure, so we laugh it off and often numb the pain by entering unhealthy relationships. While hoping for relief we are challenged by the notion that it is too uncomfortable to share our deep-seated pain, because of guilt, shame, fear of exposure, and that people will think less of us. Who can we trust with such sensitive, personal information?

I can remember a young man named Anthony who was born with severe disabilities and he thought people didn't like him because of his visible scars. I tried to comfort him by explaining that a lot of people had scars that are invisible to the naked eye and many of them suffer in silence. The fact that they are not outwardly visible did not make their scars any less painful, maybe even more so. It is so easy to adopt a façade to camouflage the hurt. If one can get the help they need to peel off the layers of those masks, slowly they could become eagles and soar or butterflies finding the nectar to pollinate other flowers.

My fervent prayer was for God to open my spiritual eyes and reveal to me the needs in others and the ability to make a difference. It was a long time before I became comfortable with my spiritual gifts and why I always knew I was different, but I could not explain it.

Chapter Five

The spiritual side of life

There were seeds of virtue planted as a little girl during those early morning devotions which never died but took several years to germinate. The manifestation of the metamorphosis destined to take place was evident as I was continuously, subconsciously searching for God while He was relentless in His desire to connect with me. There seemed to be a growing sense of urgency to satisfy the constant tug in my mind and in my spirit that I could no longer ignore. I knew I needed something more, but what? I thought that by visiting a few churches at some point, I would finally get some answers.

I became excited when I heard a well-known hotelier address a small group at my hotel, and his message stimulated my interest, so I invited him to meet with my team. We arranged to have lunch in the hotel restaurant and he was presented himself as noble, knowledgeable, confident, and articulate in his delivery, reassuring us that there was value and potential in each one of us. He was emphatic in stating that we were all created equal in God's sight, a phrase many would have heard previously but not internalized. Most of the men on my team grew up without positive male role models; some never knew their fathers and others had not developed wholesome relationships with the ones they knew. For some, there were uncles, grandfathers who stepped in to create a sense of balance, but some were exposed to promiscuous, decadent lifestyles and that's all they knew. There were very few who had meaningful relationships with their dads and they just did the best they could. I was so pleased to have had the opportunity to provide this session for the team and it was evident that they were all affected emotionally. Time did not permit a lengthy question and answer session, but on a personal level, I wanted to know more.

I extended an invitation to the gentleman and his wife to continue the conversation, so a group was formed to meet in my home. I wanted to share this experience with a group of women who I thought could benefit from this teaching. What should have been a single session became weekly Wednesday night sessions focused on what it meant to have a relationship with God. Most of us were all novices, so the gentleman, ably assisted by his wife, guided us through the scriptures. We lacked the confidence or so we thought the competence, to openly bring petitions to the Lord. It was very refreshing and my curiosity was even more piqued to know more of the God I had been praying to all those years. We learned about biblical principles and Kingdom lifestyle and eventually in our own simple yet passionate way, we gained the confidence to pray for our immediate desires: for jobs and better jobs, to acquire our own homes and one lady wanted "out" of her marriage. We believed God heard and would answer our prayers so we encouraged each other while we waited. By the end of the first year, all the prayers were answered, much to our delight. The principle of praying alone is admirable but it is equally important as the scripture instructs us to come into agreement in God's name with someone of like mind and purpose and His presence is guaranteed.

It became increasingly difficult to encourage my children to go to church as they were bored but I dare say I was not firm enough to insist that they attend and so the more they resisted, I eventually stopped pushing. My quest continued as God was wooing me and He was not about to let me nose dive over another cliff as His plans for me would be completed in the fullness of time. I visited different churches but gradually I developed an interest in the charismatic or Pentecostal churches. As I shared previously, I could not understand their style of worship, dancing in church accompanied by live bands, loud preaching, shouting amen, hand-clapping, and praising God with hands raised. Why the drama, I thought.

There was always the hope of finding one that would fulfil my spiritual needs so I continued the search. Eventually, I found one that I was becoming comfortable with, but again the long worship sessions were challenging for me. I enjoyed the teaching so I decided that I would arrive at the church just about when I thought the worship session would be over and this way I would miss most of it. I was being strategic, I thought, but who could be strategic with God? The messages the pastor delivered were very clear and very relevant to everyday life with practical applications one could ascribe to their daily routine. He provided bullet point flyers with the related scriptures so one could read on their own to seek clarification in the quiet of their own space. I used those pages as my daily devotions for several months as my desires were activated with each passing moment to increase my knowledge. I was eager to learn about God and became a God chaser.

The vicissitudes of life can have varying results on an individual's wellbeing and how one navigates the events will determine their success or failure. I made every effort to visit this church as often as I could but had not quite settled at this stage. This did not diminish the zeal or the motivation to keep studying the word of God. Unexpectedly a Canadian neighbor of mine invited me to visit her church which met on Saturday evenings. This church began when a young local missionary, who was the son of an elite local family made a dramatic decision to start an assembly. He had just returned from a life-changing event in the US where revival was taking place and he wanted to discover more of God's purpose. He was radical in his intention to share the gospel and partnered with his cousin to host regular meetings in her living room. It wasn't long before the word spread and others caught the vision, expressed an interest in becoming part of this intimate gathering soon to be registered as The Living Room Church.

What kind of church was that? I questioned, that would meet on Saturday evenings and it was not the Seventh Day Adventist? I was very skeptical at first, but I thought the meeting time would have been ideal for me as I could rest on Sunday mornings and not have to feel guilty about not attending an assembly. The first opportunity I got, I visited the church with her and was very warmly received. I noticed almost immediately the disparity in the racial composition but was not deterred as I was socialized with multi-racial families. To illustrate the point, I was exposed to a diverse mix in our immediate community but also my mother's best friend from university was a petite Jewish woman standing tall at about 5' named Ruth Goldberg. Both women maintained a wonderful, long-lasting friendship throughout and she enjoyed many visits to our home. There was a lot of commonality with my Mom and Ruth although they grew up under such different circumstances. They both were subject to discrimination on campus and I can only speculate that a special bond was created as they compared notes of their encounters. Ruth freely shared about her family so there were times we felt as though we were transported into another time zone, listening to episodes of trauma her family suffered. She was charming, had very strong family values and we loved the peaceful and calm atmosphere she invoked by her mere presence. Ruth always came bearing gifts so Ulit and I would eagerly await her arrival. My mom's demeanor when Ruth was around being far different from what we had grown accustomed to. She seemed much more composed, light-hearted, and gentle during those visits.

I felt very comfortable at this church on my first few visits and decided I would fellowship there for a while. On one of my early visits to this church, I saw a young boy named Simon, who was about 12 years old at the time and who had his hands raised worshiping God in such a sincere way. I was mesmerized by this as I had never seen a child so passionate about praise and worship and so were some of the other youngsters in attendance, all appeared hungry for the things of God. With time, I became a member of the church and grew in my knowledge of Kingdom principles. I reflected on the many times my mother sent me passages of scriptures in the mail and she would scribble all over the Bible. I had been given several copies of the Holy Bible which moved from one bookshelf to another, collecting dust for many years. All this was her attempt to help me develop some spiritual growth.

I finally got a teaching Bible that made the information much clearer than other Bibles I had seen so I became immersed in reading and gaining understanding along the way. There were several groups at this church that would meet in homes during the week (cell groups they were called) and I was invited to one such group in the home of total strangers, but again I was very warmly received. This was in the home of a white local family and the composition of the group was predominantly white, with just two of us black attendees. Did it make a difference? Not at all. We developed a special love for each other and still today I consider them a part of my extended family. They really cared for all the members and had a genuine desire to bring hope and comfort to those in need. They never wavered in their commitment to serve others, while remaining pure in heart and living a very humble lifestyle. They proved themselves to be transparent and God has truly blessed them as they poured into the lives of others. They knew how to demonstrate what it means to be your brothers' keeper. One evening I had an urgent plumbing issue which I was unable to solve so I called my cell group leader who immediately jumped into his truck and raced over to my house with tools in hand. He turned the water off, called the hardware store to advise we had an emergency and he was on his way to get the required part. He managed to coerce them to remain open a few minutes longer until we got there. He and I jumped into his truck, turned up the worship music and we sang at the top of our lungs all the way up the highway. Once we had the part in hand we returned home where he did the repair at no cost. What an opportunity to see the heart and experience the true love of a friend who was not of my race, not a native of my homeland, but someone God handpicked to walk this journey with me. We should never be willing to discard the possibility of sharing meaningful friendships with people of all races, color, creed, or nationalities. This type of bonding is what God desires for His people, to love one another as we love ourselves. Building authentic relationships is not that difficult.

As I delved into the scriptures I seemed to have been on a mission to test His Word, but He always showed up and I would be in awe. I remember one instance where I had read a passage of scripture about the "planting of a fleece" (Judges 6 vs. 40) or getting a sign from God and was eager to do a test. A few nights later I was dining alone in the restaurant at work when I looked up to the sky and saw a very small but bright light. With my cheeky self, I said to the Lord, "I am planting a fleece Lord as your word says." Whatever was my heart's desire at the time I asked the Lord to let that star fall so I would know He was paying attention to my prayer. Of course while sitting there, waiting, I couldn't blink for fear I may have missed this falling star. It didn't matter that my food was getting cold I just kept my eyes fixed on that star. After a while, I noticed that the "star" was moving forward. To my dismay, I suddenly realized it was not a star after all, but a small plane awaiting a signal to approach the airport. I quickly reversed my request and thanked the Lord for not answering that prayer which would have been a calamity and one story I needed to recover from. There was movement but not the way I expected it.

I was fervent in my search for answers but what I valued most in those days was being able to interact with persons who were just as eager to know more about God and His purpose. My group leaders were always available to explain anything I didn't quite understand so there were many mornings I couldn't wait for the breaking of dawn to call them with a revelation I had. Those were exciting times for me. Each day brought a new revelation as I became more sensitive to the things of God through visions and dreams which were coming alive. I was finally beginning to understand that God has given us all gifts and talents which should be used for His honor and glory. How often we tap ourselves on the shoulder and declare to ourselves that we are so clever, so creative, so intelligent, not accepting the fact that these are attributes given to us by God. He made us in His image and therefore we should represent Him with righteousness, grace and humility.

God wants so much to bless us but there are conditions to achieve all He has in store for us. For example, He has said that we must be born again to enter into His kingdom. What does that mean? It means to repent of our sins and accept Jesus as Lord and Saviour of our lives; an act that can only be done by faith. It's by faith that we believe. It is by His spirit we are led. If you ask God to show up, He will. He waits patiently for us to acknowledge Him and He will not force himself on us at any time. The funny thing is, even if we don't really understand or believe, when there is a crisis and we call out the name of Jesus, He dispatches his angels immediately to take charge of the situation. Sadly, once the problem is solved, we move on to the next adventure and quickly forget about God's mercy and grace, not caring to engage in any conversation about Him.

God had created a circle of persons to embrace and support me in this foreign country as I had no family of my own to lean on and had to bear the responsibility of two small children whom I cherished and they were both mine to have and to hold. In the scripture, it clearly states that God looks after the orphans, widows, and foreigners. He says in Jeremiah 22: "Do no wrong or violence to the alien, fatherless or the widow." Even without knowing this passage then, my faith was tested and strengthened as I realized, that I often had no answers but God was setting the wheels in motion for me. I was forced to make critical decisions in foreign countries that would alter the trajectory of my life for years to come.

Here is one of the many prophetic words I have received over the years delivered by Jimmy and Waverley Kellett.

"God is putting you higher on the watchman wall in intercession. You will have an aerial vision and an underground vision.

The Lord is going to give you precise things to begin to intercede and He is going to show you strongholds and the names of the strongholds. God is going to begin to have you pull them down.

You are going to intercede for people as God shows you and to intercede for ministries and you are going to see things solidify.

The Lord says, daughter, I have called you as a watchman on my wall. I am putting you up on my wall in your place. There are those around about you who say she is not this and she is not that, but the Lord says, "Touch not my anointed."

The Lord says that even as a small child you were very mindful of Him. You knew when you wanted something you knew who to go to get it.

The Lord says when you hit your knees the enemy runs because the enemy knows that when you hit your knees, things are going to be done.

I see you as a mover and shaker says the Lord. You are going to pray and things will move out the way and begin to shake.

The Lord says, "Daughter I put in you, the heart of an intercessor and the heart of a watchman."

The Lord says, "You are going to fill.…. I see you are going into travail - really pounding the gates of hell." And the Lord says, "Daughter, even your own family is going to line up with the word of God."

The Lord says every word, curse, ever spoken over you is null and void says the Lord. The Lord says, "Get ready – the dreams are coming; prophetic dreams." Your dreams are going to be elevated, says the Lord.

You will take a stand - even as an intercessor and a watchman in your dreams.

The Lord says those family members that you have prayed for, that others have given up on, the Lord says, "This is the season. I'm bringing them in."

And the Lord says that you have prayed and you have prayed and you have prayed and you have not seen a lot of results, but the Lord says you are going to begin to see the fruit of your labor".

I had become resilient by then and more determined as a young woman to be successful. I had had many failures in my life but I knew in my heart and soul that there was more I could do so I was forced to press into God for guidance. I am reminded of the scripture, "Can anything good come out of Nazareth?". **(John 1 vs. 46).** Yes, it can and yes it did!! The Lord reminds me to call on Him and He will answer, knock and the door will be opened. There was just so much to learn and keep learning about the faithfulness and grace of God.

There were those moments when I would discover a worship song that captured my emotions and unleashed a love for God I didn't know was possible. How could I have missed the signs and signals of the Omnipresent, Omnipotent God I had come to know in that passionate way before? I suddenly felt safe, secure, gaining confidence that, I can do all things through Christ who strengthens me. Writing this book is a major accomplishment. I can imagine my peers from school who were much more accomplished than I was, had no idea any of this could be remotely considered a part of my future. They would have witnessed a young miss struggle with poor grades and rapidly falling into a state of low self-esteem. There were those high achievers for whom much was expected and most of them did not disappoint. The rebellious spirit in me caused great pain and disappointment but God allowed me to make my mistakes and learn from them. We are all created equal in God's sight, with different skill sets, in His image, unique in many ways and our fingerprints are a testament to that fact. When we get to that place of maturity to acknowledge the contribution we can make, we no longer focus on characteristics like our height, skin tone, the texture of our hair - whether straight or kinky, academic ability, socio-economic background, and potential, but the tremendous value we can bring to each other. We speak different languages, adapt to specific cultural norms, and based on our unique gifts we influence, and are influenced differently. God makes no mistakes so when you look in the mirror, see God's masterpiece. We will have obstacles daily, but how we react is a choice. Do I say, "Yes I can and will get through it? This too will pass" or do I say, "Oh no, not again, why me." If we didn't have challenges to overcome, why would we need God? May I remind you that God is our creator. My success is not a result of my ability to perform in my own strength but what was planted inside me at birth forcing me by God's grace to leap over major hurdles to secure my place under His watchful eye.

On this journey, I still felt it necessary to figure things out, so one evening at the end of one of the church services I attended, I made a decision to respond to a passage of scripture I had read which stated that we should test God with the little things and watch what He will do. I took the word literally and wrote a cheque for a significant amount and dropped it in the offering basket. No one knew what I had done, just God and I. Three days later I got a call from the car dealership to inform me that someone had deposited a cheque for my car payment for five times the amount I had dropped in the basket. Some may say that was a coincidence, but I choose to believe that God was showing up and showing off His power and His might.

We can't see God in human form so we are scared to put our trust in the unknown. Trust means to rely on, count on, be sure of, and to be confident in. We trust a chair that when we sit, it will bear our weight and not break into pieces so, in the same way, we know that trusting in God takes a measure of faith. I awake with such joy in my heart and reflect with great humility knowing that God was my compass all these years. There must be something special He expects of me and one passage of scripture states that, to whom much is given much is expected so I continue to strive to be the best I can be and to have a positive effect on the lives of those in my sphere of influence.

I have realized that my early beginnings have prepared me to be the compassionate woman I am today and so I wish to leave a legacy for my children and the women, and young men whose lives I have impacted. What is your legacy? What will people say about you when you are gone? Would you have left a positive impact on peoples' lives? There have been multiple manuscripts written on human behavior, but there is so much to learn directly from the bible, the word of God. Once we ask God to come into our hearts, change us from the inside, trust me, He will show up. God's love is explosive and He creates a safe haven for us. He helps us attain characteristics: to be fun-loving, modest, purposeful, humble, positive leaders, and how to be kind to one another. There will always be traits that are not trending, but our role is not to fit into the wiles of the world but to play our part in establishing God's Kingdom.

Recognize then that He is always watching our every move and quite often He must cringe at the things we do and say. We all fall short and I have had to repent daily for my thoughts or the curt response when I lose patience, but we have an advocate who groans for us to the Father. As we confess our sins, God is willing and ready to forgive us and so we must forgive others who have trampled on our emotions and robbed us of our joy and peace. We must, however, ensure that we guard our hearts and not give anyone the power to control our minds and distort our senses.

There is the story in the Bible about the 10 lepers who were cleansed and only one returned to say, "Thank you." Jesus responded to that by saying, "Were there not ten cleansed, so where are the nine?" Let us hasten to thank God for the many blessings and protection we receive every day. We are not aware and could not begin to imagine all the dangers that we have circumvented unknowingly each day because God placed His charge to protect us. I am still in transition to a place of complete restoration while working hard to become all that God has designed me to be; to be a loving, caring, tender-hearted, compassionate, and to be a wise human being. It's not an easy position to be in when people you come in contact with don't understand your motivation for saying or doing things, especially when you are genuine in your efforts. Having had a past that left so many questions in my mind, I oftentimes have to re-evaluate those in my circle to ensure that I bring value to them and them to me. There are times when I have had to walk away from some relationships to stay grounded in what is right for me and you should do likewise.

My one desire is to be an authentic representative of Jesus Christ. I spent many years living with layers of masks because I wasn't sure how I would be treated if people knew the real me. Would they love me anyway? Would they see an adult who had endured much, had insecurities she couldn't share, or someone who loved deeply and needed those close to be honest and faithful? I didn't handle infidelity well. It was a violation of my person because I gave my all to my relationships. I wanted to feel safe in my own space and not broken as I did as a child and yet I wasn't that lucky. Lies and deceit are normal in many households, but I simply refused to accept it, as I felt I deserved better. I didn't feel as accomplished as some, but I knew all along that there was so much untapped potential inside of me yet to be discovered.

God allows us to have these experiences to build character, to draw us closer to Him, and to fulfill His purpose on this earth. When we realize our life is not our own and we can humble ourselves and repent before the Lord, we can freely let God reign in us. His plans are better than our plans anyway as He says in His word, for us to prosper and to be in good health. This story has caught many by surprise as my journey unfolds as an encourager, a dreamer, a new author, a visionary, a mother, a friend, a woman of prayer, a woman of purpose on a mission, and most significantly a woman of God.

Leaving the safety of my home in the Caribbean to be thrust into the vast communities of New York City at such a young age was an exciting, yet scary adventure. I look back at how God manoeuvred my path, allowing for peaks and valleys, through the good, the bad, and the ugly and interrupted the daily routines when He needed to get me back on track. I did not walk that path alone, but He carried me through like the footsteps in the sand. Who could have imagined a little girl from a rural town in a small island in the Caribbean could be in the presence of royalty, international stars, making arrangements for superstars from various industries, high profile travel agencies, and journalists from international travel magazines? Amid all the glitz and glamour, I remained grounded to see the need and cared for those, especially women who have struggled emotionally, financially, and spiritually. I was given an opportunity for a better life and it was and is incumbent upon me to help someone else to have a chance. If not me, then who? We can all help someone in small meaningful ways. What's your excuse?

A scripture that speaks volumes is, "Blessed is the man that walketh not in the counsel of the ungodly, nor standeth in the way of sinners, nor sitteth in the seat of the scornful, but his delight is in the law of the Lord and in His law does he meditate day and night...Psalm 1. Meditate with me on this scripture. It has been an amazing journey and I thank God every day for allowing me the privilege of calling him, Father, and Friend.

As you thumb through the pages, I believe that God will release the gifts and talents He has placed inside every one of you. You may believe that you are an ordinary person but trust that God is going to do some extraordinary things through you. Release and live your best life. Your latter days can be better than your former days, if only you have faith and believe.

We too shall rise – Monique 2013

We too shall rise from pressure and pain but believe for the relief.

We too shall rise from a defensive position and move into the offensive.

We too shall rise from gossip and slander to speak in truth.

We too shall rise from the negative and plow forward in the positive.

We too shall rise from financial and emotional challenges to reap the prosperity promised.

We too shall rise from physical and mental stress to give thanks in the good times and bad.

We too shall rise from broken relationships and be open to love again.

We too shall rise from lack and walk in overflow.

We too shall rise from discrimination and embrace inclusion as God breathed.

We too shall rise from doubt and unbelief to believe the word of God.

We too shall rise from despair, and lack, to discipleship, abundance and grace.

We too shall rise from the ashes of rejection and forge a new path of acceptance.

We too shall rise from guilt and shame to walk in forgiveness.

We too shall rise from niggling physical pain that maturity brings, and focus on God's plan for us to prosper and be in good health.

We too shall rise from unhealthy eating habits and acquire the taste for healthy food.

We too shall rise from wheelchairs and crutches and take up our beds to walk in the power and strength of our Lord Jesus Christ.

We too shall rise from dependency on another human being and cast our cares upon God alone.

We too shall rise from indecent behavior and language but walk and operate in Kingdom principles.

We too shall rise from mental battles and know that we do not fight against flesh and blood but against principalities and powers of darkness, so let the heavenly angels fight the battles.

We too shall rise from our disappointments and trust that God is taking us to a higher place with Him.

We too shall rise from constant complaining and know that God's purpose will be established.

We too shall rise from the tail to the head, from the back to the front.

We too shall rise from humility to be exalted.

We too shall rise from the lower seats to the high heavenly places.

We too shall rise by God's grace and mercy.

Jesus conquered death, hell and the grave and in three days He rose.

We too shall rise.

Will you join me and rise?

❧

One of my prayer partner sisters whom I treasure wrote:

"For those God foreknew, He also predestined to be conformed to the image of His son that He might be the firstborn among many brothers and sisters. And those He predestined, He also called, those He called; He also justified; those He justified, He also glorified." (Romans 8:29). This scripture demonstrates clearly that it was God who determined the exact time when each one of us would be born, who our parents would be, and where we would live to advance His Kingdom

A relationship was nurtured with Monique and me for well over twenty years. As time and seasons passed, we have laughed, sighed, cried, moaned, and groaned over life's fractures. Our regular convocations over spiritual and life matters have repaired broken relationships, marriages, healed the sick, interceded and travailed for nations - taking back kingdoms from the enemy, birthing, and establishing the Kingdom of God. That is the type of quality friendship and association that cherish with her.

I protect our friendship in a very serious way because as women and especially "God-fearing Women", we need each other and "must have each other's back". She has had my back from the beginning, whether it was meeting a "felt-need", holding each other's hand in the doctor's office, not being ashamed or afraid to share personal information (similar to the relationship with David and Jonathan). I rest in the knowledge and confidence that there is no greater privilege in our relationship than the fact that we trust and honor each other and have grown and matured in every way.

I believe the most vital and important fact for me where our friendship is concerned is her relentless fervor and desire for the things about the "Kingdom of God"; whether it is taking care of the needs of the disenfranchised, the poor, the alien, the fatherless, the widow. She has always championed the "under-dog". This love and compassion for these embody the heartbeat of Jesus Christ our Saviour and nothing surpasses that. I call her life "The Purpose Driven Life".

⁖

Another dear prayer sister Joan wrote:

I met Monica 10 years ago at a Life Group/Bible study where we were both members. She soon became my friend, confidante and counselor.

She keeps her knees on the ground and her face towards heaven. She has held my hand and prayed me through many a crisis as a true prayer warrior and intercessor. These thoughts were underscored by many persons who have crossed her path. She is blessed with many gifts but most significantly of discernment and design. My late husband would have agreed with me with these sentiments expressed.

Chapter Six

Returning to my roots

Road trip

My sister Ulit and I did an important road trip from Kingston several years ago to retrace our roots, starting very early in the morning and stopping at little roadside restaurants along the way. I had to get my fix of more chicken patties and freshly baked coco bread directly from the oven. Several workers were lining up as early as 7:00 am to partake of the traditional breakfast menus which consisted of hot porridge, ackee and saltfish, green bananas, breadfruit, fried dumplings, callaloo, and saltfish.

We travelled on a new highway that was unfamiliar to me as I could remember trips on steep winding roads that took at least five and a half hours from our home in the country to the capital city. This improved roadway reduced the travel time significantly but at the end of this new stretch of "barber greene", the asphalt surface, the road changed dramatically and the potholes seemed like rugged craters, waiting to puncture unsuspecting tires and chassis.

We arrived at Paul Island early afternoon and it looked just as I had remembered it with a few changes. The exterior of the primary school looked the same, the interior was the same and there were just a few new buildings on the grounds. The house I grew up in was demolished and replaced by a solid concrete structure designated as a community center. There was no more wooden house with a wraparound veranda, no gardens, no fruit trees, no chicken run, no dogs, and no familiar smells. It was all gone, but the memories still lingered.

The same Indian family that had lived next door in mud huts had now constructed a modest but well designed concrete house for the family to occupy. We went to visit those neighbors and I was pleasantly surprised to meet one of the occupants who was my contemporary. She was a retired teacher and she remembered me immediately, reminding me of climbing through the fence to enjoy their authentic meals of rice and dahl and how I tried to mimic them by using my fingers to eat.

There was a very bright, good looking Indian boy (an Omar Sharif look-a-like) who lived on the other corner and everyone expected him to succeed academically so when he won a scholarship to a boarding school, I went with my mom to see him registered at the school. She was committed to the success of her students and this was one example of that passion. This young man did not disappoint and went on to achieve a successful career as expected.

While we were retracing our roots, the same young man invited us to participate in a Town Hall meeting where he was petitioning the government to rename the primary school after Venetia as a tribute to her achievements. The speakers were very complementary and spoke about how important it was to leave a good legacy for one's family and community which they felt she had done and she should be recognized in a significant way. It was so odd to be in the company of these people, several of who remembered me and knew my story, but I only had a vague recollection of names I would have heard. They made me feel very welcome and were pleased that I had "come back to my roots". They had big plans for the advancement of the school and the wider community with an emphasis on the exposure for the students to technology. It was a mammoth task to undertake but this was their first step.

We thanked them for their invitation and their efforts to recognize our mother and joined in the mix and mingle where refreshments were served as well as allowing us the opportunity to interact with some of the old-timers. There were wonderful stories of what life was like back then and I gleaned once more a little glimpse of the history of the area and the people. There was a special moment when I was introduced to Ulit's brother Neville and was surprised to learn that they had maintained a friendship and were active in each other's lives over the years. Unlike my situation, I had heard the name Hopeton but had no idea he was my biological brother.

After the function, en route to Grange Hill, I observed only minor changes to the infrastructure in Paul Island. The little Post Office was no longer there, there were a few more shops and there were many more houses situated along the main road. As we approached Grange Hill, I was very disappointed to see that the cottage where we lived was abandoned and dilapidated, the carport in shambles, no gardens, no fruit trees, and a broken gate barely hanging on to the support posts at the entrance.

By now several families had migrated to the UK, USA, and Canada, but there were remnants of families I knew still residing there who welcomed the barrels of supplies they received from the migrants oversees. The little town was just as busy with people hustling through the main streets on foot and on bicycles. Memories of political meetings came flooding back, with the late nights and loud music. The movie theatre was closed, but most other businesses were still operating by the Chinese families, a few of whom had now married outside their race.

I wanted to experience a church service so we attended the Anglican church service one Sunday morning. We arrived early and speaking of nostalgia, we sat in the same pew we did as children. The choir of older ladies proceeded down the aisle and the acting priest in charge conducted the service. I realized very quickly that I was "inappropriately dressed" in my short, sleeveless dress while the congregants wore long sleeves and a few in hats. There were no more than 25 people in attendance half of whom were youngsters. The pastor was passionate in her delivery but seemed a little distracted by our presence. We introduced ourselves at the end and several people were familiar and had vivid memories of our mother. We needed to visit another godmother who was then 102 years old, the widow of the Dispenser. She was amazingly coherent, still on occasion played the pipe organ at the church, and was a phenomenon to her doctors. She took no medication, did not need reading or distance glasses and her memory surpassed that of people half her age.

Paul Island has held bitter/sweet memories for me because this was the beginning of a journey I could not have imagined. It seemed like such a sleepy village where time stood still but so much remained the same. The roads were just as rugged as I remembered and the people I met were shy about approaching me but seemed genuine in sharing their memories. It was good to go back and reflect on my humble beginnings and it keeps me grounded in the true essence of life and how privileged I am. If God had not kept me close to His bosom, I don't know where would I be.

Ulit and I reflected on the days of early morning cold showers, the cocks crowing in the wee hours, eating roasted corn on the side of the road, and "going to town" late evenings with our nanny, which was a favorite pastime of ours. We walked the streets of the capital city of Savanna-la-Mar as part of the retracing of our roots and many people recognized Miss Ulit or Mrs. Wright depending on the situation as she spent most of her life working in the area and some seemed surprised when I was introduced as her sister.

This trip lasted only one week during which time I was spoilt by my sister and it was a wonderful time of bonding as it the first time we have been together for so many days since I was 18. She demonstrated true love by pampering me and providing me with my favorite dishes and beverages and there was nothing I could have wanted that she would not have offered. On our return journey to Kingston, we had to make one last stop to indulge in some of my favourite things; deep-fried, crispy escoveitch red snapper served with a generous helping of bammy (cassava bread), garnished with onions and slices of scotch bonnet pepper on the side. We watched in awe as the vendors flipped their spatulas turning the fish as though they were preforming for an audience. As is customary, they prepared this delicious treat in huge pots of hot oil set on some flaming hot coals. We placed our order and continued on our journey.

We drove through a beachfront village called Bluefields where time stood still. This was one of many locations we visited for a quick dip in the ocean as children. The rocky, sandy patches of beach still featured the large tree trunks that had become more pronounced over the years as erosion peeled away along the roadside. There were only a few locals visible who stopped to stare at the intruders spying on them. The beachfront was crowded with grapes trees, making it more secluded and difficult to see the beauty of the crystal clear water in the distance. I was told that during high tide it was not unusual for the sea water to cascade on to the road.

We travelled very slowly along the country road to capture as much of the landscape as we could just so I could rediscover any significant memories of this journey of long ago. I spent the last few days of this trip with one of my brothers and his family, filling my mind with the true essence of family, what we had in common and what were the differences we still needed to overcome. There were traces of an unmistakable bloodline that could not be denied. This road trip allowed me time to process the full circle of events that encapsulated my journey and to remind me of how fragile life can be.

Epilogue

We may have met at various stages in my life and you may wonder about my many names. I have been called, Peggy, Monica, Monique, Mons, and Mom. I was born Monica Hew, became Monica McDonald, Monica DaCosta, and then Monica Blackman. Peggy was a name that should have been placed on my birth certificate, but my dad neglected to add it. That is all part of this extraordinary journey I have been navigating for a lifetime. We have heard the expression that we should be mindful of how we live from the time of our birth to our death and that the dash in-between is significant. It is important to remember it doesn't matter where you started, but it matters what your current position is and where you aspire to be, so make every moment count. Let your light so shine before men that they may see your good works and glorify your Father which is in heaven. Call Him by name, "Abba, Father".

The events shared in this story are purely my understanding of what was happening at various stages of my life. There is one thing I know for sure and it is that although some people were not legally **Adopted in the Natural** as I was, there are many who have been loved, raised, nurtured, influenced and hurt by relatives, family, friends, household help, neighbors and even strangers. If that is you, I am sure you have many stories of your own and I implore you to share. To be **Adopted in the Spiritual** is all one could ask for because God is always fighting for you and pushing back the darkness so you can see the light and be that light to others.

I believe in you and pray that this chronicle of events as simple as it may appear, will inspire you to bring the healing, the hope, the victory, the joy and peace you long for, realizing that you are not alone. Someone else has overcome your battles and much more. The fact is that the battle belongs to the Lord so rest in that assurance that He will see you through. Walk into victory from a place of victory. You are more than a conqueror.

As this story comes to an end, I decree and declare that you will have the courage to allow God to take control of your life so He can reclaim everything the enemy has stolen from you: your children, your marriage, your finances, your livelihood, your relationships, your health, your dreams and so much more.

I have developed meaningful relationships with my older son and some of my siblings and unexpectedly, one year before this book was published I was able to acquire a photograph of my biological father, Stanley whom I never had the chance to meet. I called my birth mother, Nettie to wish her a Happy Birthday when she turned 80 and to reassure her that I had forgiven her for the decision she made to give me up for adoption. It was a very emotional conversation for both of us, but it helped me to recognize how necessary it is to be able **to forgive.** It is one of the key elements in the renewing of one's mind and to become grounded emotionally and spiritually. Let's start practicing that habit right now. It is your choice: it is your passport to freedom.

Until we meet again, Shalom.

Scripture References on Adoption.

Romans 8 vs. 15 NIV

The spirit you received does not make you slaves so that you live in fear again rather the spirit you received brought about your adoption to Sonship and by him we say, "Abba, Father."

Deuteronomy 10 vs. 18 NIV

He defends the cause of the fatherless and the widow and loves the foreigner residing among you giving them food and clothing.

Isaiah 40 vs.31 NIV

But those who hope in the Lord will renew their strength. They will soar on wings like eagles, they will run and not grow weary, they will walk and not be faint.

Jeremiah 29 vs.11 NIV

For I know the plans I have for you declares the Lord, plans to prosper you and not to harm you, plans to give you hope and a future.

Matthew 25 vs. 40 NIV

The king will reply, truly I tell you whatever you did for one of the least of these brothers and sisters of mine, you did for me.

Psalms 146 vs. 9 NIV

The Lord watches over the foreigner and sustains the fatherless and the widow, but He frustrates the ways of the wicked.

John 1vs 12-13 NIV

Yet to all who did receive him, to those who believed in His name, He gave the right to become children of God. Children born not of natural descent, nor of human decision or a husband's will, but born to God

Galatians 4 vs. 4-5 NIV

But when the set time had fully come, God sent His son, born of a woman, born under the law. To redeem those under the law, that we might receive adoption to Sonship.

Psalms 10 vs. 17,18 NIV

You Lord hear the desire of the afflicted, you encourage them and you listen to their cry. Defending the fatherless and the oppressed, so that mere earthly mortals will never again strike terror.

Ephesians 1 vs.5 NIV

He predestined us for adoption as sons through Jesus Christ, according to the purpose of His will.

Psalm 27 vs. 10 NIV

For my father and mother have forsaken me, but the Lord will take me in.

John 14 vs. 18 NIV

I will not leave you as orphans, I will come to you

Significant words

The Lord says to come away with Him to His hiding place and sit. Commitment cannot be negotiated ...Gen. 22 vs 7-8

Ulit

Russell and Venetia

Stanley

Antoinette (Nette)

Venetia

Biography of the author

Monica Blackman was raised in Jamaica, migrating to North America as a teenager and resided there for several years. She eventually settled in the Caribbean island of Barbados where she raised her family and established her career in the tourism industry. Forever pushing boundaries and finding solutions to problems, she co-founded the non-profit organization called "Pillow Talk Prayer Time" to meet the felt-needs of the underprivileged and to establish a safe place for women to pray and be ministered to. She created "Suddenly by Monique", a hair product for individuals having challenges with hair breakage and growth. She designed prayer pillows, some of which were donated to the Pink Ribbon organization in Barbados. Now in this new decade to add to her many accomplishments and legacy, she has become an author, showcasing the journey to becoming a mother, entrepreneur, and a Christian woman of God who believes for a better quality life, one family at a time.

She successfully completed her education by gaining her management degree from the University of the West Indies, Cave Hill campus.

9 781728 344065